The
Reference Shelf®

Representative American Speeches

2007–2008

Edited by Brian Boucher

The Reference Shelf
Volume 80 • Number 6
The H.W. Wilson Company
New York • Dublin
2008

The Reference Shelf

The books in this series contain reprints of articles, excerpts from books, addresses on current issues, and studies of social trends in the United States and other countries. There are six separately bound numbers in each volume, all of which are usually published in the same calendar year. Numbers one through five are each devoted to a single subject, providing background information and discussion from various points of view and concluding with a subject index and comprehensive bibliography that lists books, pamphlets, and abstracts of additional articles on the subject. The final number of each volume is a collection of recent speeches, and it contains a cumulative speaker index. Books in the series may be purchased individually or on subscription.

Library of Congress has cataloged this serial title as follows:

Representative American speeches. 1937 / 38–
  New York, H. W. Wilson Co.™
    v. 21 cm.—The Reference Shelf
Annual
Indexes:
  Author index: 1937/38–1959/60, with 1959/60; 1960/61–1969/70, with 1969/70;
1970/71–1979/80, with 1979/80; 1980/81–1989/90, 1990.
Editors: 1937/38–1958/59, A. C. Baird.—1959/60–1969/70, L. Thonssen.—1970/ 71–1979/80, W. W. Braden.—1980/81–1994/95, O. Peterson.—1995/96–1998/99, C. M. Logue and J. DeHart.—1999/2000–2002/2003, C. M. Logue and L. M. Messina.—2003/2004–2005/2006, C. M. Logue, L. M. Messina, and J. DeHart.—2006/ 2007– , J. Currie, P. McCaffrey, L. M. Messina.—2007/ 2008–, B. Boucher.
  ISSN 0197-6923 Representative American speeches.
    1. Speeches, addresses, etc., American. 2. Speeches, addresses, etc.
     I. Baird, Albert Craig, 1883–1979 ed. II. Thonssen, Lester, 1904–III. Braden, Waldo
     Warder, 1911–1991 ed. IV. Peterson, Owen, 1924– ed. V. Logue, Calvin McLeod,
     1935– , Messina, Lynn M., and DeHart, Jean, eds. VI. Series.
PS668.B3   815.5082   38-27962
                                                                      MARC-S
  Library of Congress [8503r85] rev4

Cover: CHICAGO - NOVEMBER 04: U.S. President elect Barack Obama gives his victory speech to supporters during an election night gathering in Grant Park on November 4, 2008 in Chicago, Illinois. Obama defeated Republican nominee Sen. John McCain (R-AZ) by a wide margin in the election to become the first African-American U.S. President elect. (Photo by Joe Raedle/Getty Images)

Visit H.W. Wilson's Web site: www.hwwilson.com

Printed in the United States of America

Contents

Preface

The years 2007 and 2008 in the United States were marked by both a historic presidential election, featuring minority and female aspirants in the top tier of candidates, and unprecedented turmoil in the financial markets, leading to massive government intervention. With Illinois Senator Barack Obama's groundbreaking campaign for the presidency and as immigration continued to be a topic of public discourse, the perennial issue of race garnered national attention. Meanwhile, as two more years passed without a major terrorist attack on American soil, other threats to the American way of life, perceived and real, came under consideration. As the housing crisis worsened and led to a freeze in vitally important credit markets, the state of the American economy was even described as a national security issue. In the cultural realm, legislators and religious thinkers debated the issue of same-sex marriage; while in the medical arena, politicians and public health professionals cautioned of an epidemic of obesity in America.

This volume begins with a collection of speeches by the contenders for president and vice president. As George W. Bush's second term drew to a close, both major political parties fronted notable fields of candidates. Continuing a meteoric rise since his speech at the 2004 Democratic National Convention, Obama accomplished what previously seemed unthinkable: he defeated Senator Hillary Clinton, part of the most powerful Democratic machine in decades and the candidate over whom there hung, in the words of countless pundits, an air of inevitability. When Obama won the Iowa Caucuses and continued to run a highly disciplined campaign that drew tens of thousands to his public appearances, the certainty of a Clinton nomination disintegrated. Obama ultimately became the first African-American nominee of a major political party for president, and from there went on to win the nation's highest office.

The Republican nominee was Senator John McCain of Arizona, a Vietnam veteran and former prisoner of war who had served for decades in Congress. After being defeated by George W. Bush in the 2000 Republican presidential primary in a divisive campaign, McCain opposed the president's positions on some issues, largely alienating the Republican base and setting himself an especially difficult task in 2008. But his choice of Governor Sarah Palin of Alaska, a relative unknown on the national political scene, generated a great deal of excitement among the Republican base, owing to Palin's conservative positions and personal magnetism. But McCain's "Country First" campaign did not succeed in swaying a majority of voters.

Obama's candidacy catalyzed a discussion about race in America, an issue that has perplexed the nation for centuries and was notably revived in the aftermath of Hurricane Katrina, which disproportionately impacted New Orleans's African American population. Obama himself addressed the subject after controversial statements by his former pastor, Reverend Jeremiah Wright, came to light. This seemed only to spur Wright to further public appearances, culminating in his speech at the National Press Club. Meanwhile, U.S. immigration policy was expected, at times during the presidential primary season, to be a central issue of the campaign; National Council of La Raza president Janet Murguía considers immigration, in this volume, in the context of the historical attempts to scapegoat ethnic groups for the nation's troubles. Amid the discussion of race, was also the question of whether reparations ought to be paid to the descendants of slaves, an issue examined in two of the speeches presented herein.

In other quarters, a major national debate ensued over gay marriage. Colorado Representative Marilyn Musgrave (R), for example, described same-sex marriage in 2006 as "the most important issue we face today," and many activists and commentators perceived same-sex marriage as a threat to the structure of families and the very definition of marriage. By contrast, supporters of marriage rights for same-sex couples cast the issue as one of civil rights and equality. In 1996, the federal Defense of Marriage Act defined marriage as a union between a man and a woman. As of May 2007, 26 states had likewise passed constitutional amendments barring recognition of same-sex marriages; at present, 19 states have statutes that define marriage as a union between opposite-sex couples. By contrast, several states have civil-union or domestic-partnership laws that extend some rights to same-sex couples. Three of the speeches in this volume were given in debates over such initiatives. One of them comes from Mildred Loving, whose legal battle over her interracial marriage led to a Supreme Court decision striking down Virginia's miscegenation statutes; in the final year of her life, she spoke out, describing same-sex marriages as equivalent to interracial bonds.

The next collection of speeches concerns the crisis resulting from the mortgage meltdown. As 2008 wore on, the economic landscape changed dramatically as banks failed, or faced possible failure, due to toxic mortgage-backed securities that had permeated the entire financial system, and the federal government committed hundreds of billions of dollars to a rescue plan. The economy proved to be one of the deciding issues, if not *the* deciding issue, in the presidential election. As political rhetoric and media commentary focused increasingly on "Wall Street" vs. "Main Street" during the fall of 2008, the plaintive words of Chicago homeowner Nettie McGee in her Senate testimony give voice to the latter: "Please help people like me, people who waited their entire lives to own a home. Please, help us keep our homes."

Finally, this volume includes several speeches regarding what medical and public-health professionals have labeled the American obesity epidemic. The crisis is a global one, and the World Health Organization (WHO) warns that obesity may soon replace more traditional public health concerns, such as malnutrition and infectious diseases, as the most significant cause of poor health. In this volume, public figures such as the mayor of Boston, the governor of New Mexico, and the Acting Surgeon General have addressed local, state, and national initiatives to encourage better fitness. In emotional testimony before a House committee, included here, fitness guru Richard Simmons points out that today's children may not live as long as their parents.

Brian Boucher
December 2008

1

Electing a President:
The 2008 Campaign

Nine Nineties in Nine[*]

Newt Gingrich

Senior fellow, American Enterprise Institute, 1999– ; born Harrisburg, PA, June 17, 1943; B.A., Emory University, 1965; M.A., Tulane University, 1968; Ph.D., Tulane, 1971; taught history at University of West Georgia, Carrollton, GA, 1970–78; U.S. Representative (R), Georgia, 1979–99; House minority whip, 1989–95; Speaker of the House, 1995–99; author, nonfiction including The Government's Role in Solving Societal Problems *(1982),* To Renew America *(1996),* Rediscovering God in America: Reflections on the Role of Faith in Our Nation's History and Future *(2006),* Real Change: From the World That Fails to the World That Works *(2008); fiction including* 1945 *(1995),* Pearl Harbor: A Novel of December 8th *(2008, with William R. Fortschen).*

Editor's introduction: Speaking at the National Press Club on August 7, 2007, former Speaker of the House Newt Gingrich described the 1858 debates between Abraham Lincoln and Stephen A. Douglas, who were competing for a seat in the U.S. Senate, as a model for the political process in times of national challenge. In his speech, he laments the current state of electoral politics and the media coverage thereof, especially in view of national challenges, in Gingrich's view, greater than any that arose in the 20th century. Gingrich suggests that to better choose our national leaders, we should stage nine one-on-one debates, of 90 minutes, over nine weeks, between presidential candidates.

Newt Gingrich's speech: Thank you very, very much. And I thank all of you. Calista and I are delighted to be here.

I want to thank Marvin Kalb, who really sparked this particular event by calling me out of the blue and saying that he had seen what Mario Cuomo and I had talked about and he was glad that we had, a mere 16 years later, picked up on his idea.

(LAUGHTER)

And really it was a wonderful and a very encouraging conversation at the time that it happened.

---

[*] Delivered on August 7, 2007, at Washington, D.C.

I also want to thank Governor Cuomo, who agreed to the 90-minute discussion at Cooper Union, which you can see if you go to AmericanSolutions.com. It is still posted there. And I want to thank Tim Russert, who agreed to come up and be the moderator that night, and who really added a lot to the event and to its impact.

But Governor Cuomo was remarkably generous. And it was totally appropriate that he would be the person to join me at Cooper Union, because it was his press secretary who got me thinking about this. Some of you may know Harold Holzer, who is a remarkable figure in his own right.

He was Bella Abzug's press secretary, then he was Mario Cuomo's press secretary—as you can tell, somebody who obviously is somebody I'd hang out with

(LAUGHTER)

He's now the vice president of the Metropolitan Museum of Art.

But he is a great Lincoln scholar. He edited, for C-SPAN, the most accurate edition of the Lincoln-Douglas debates ever published. And it is really worth your reading his introduction to understand the complexity of those debates and their importance in American history. He then wrote a book which I think is a work of genius, one of the best strategy books I've ever read, called simply "Lincoln at Cooper Union."

And he makes the case in both these works, both about the Lincoln-Douglas debates and about Cooper Union, that Abraham Lincoln understood that America was at a crossroads from which it might never recover, that he had been drawn into politics by the Supreme Court's stunningly wrong decision that slavery could be extended everywhere in the country—the Dred Scott case. And he was determined to stop the spread of slavery and to stand for freedom, even at the risk of war. And he understood that this was not a topic you discussed in a vaudeville room, that this was a topic for adults, discussed by adults in an adult setting.

HISTORICAL CONTEXT: LINCOLN-DOUGLAS DEBATES

He and Douglas had known each other for many, many years. They both served in the legislature. Illinois was not that big a state. Douglas was a very successful United States senator, and Lincoln decided to take him on and nagged him to debate. And everywhere—Douglas didn't want to debate because he was the incumbent senator. Lincoln was a well-known and very successful lawyer but nonetheless, why if you're the incumbent take the risk? And so Lincoln adopted the practice of going one day behind Douglas.

If Douglas was in Springfield, the next day, Lincoln was in Springfield. If Douglas was in Chicago, the next day, Lincoln was in Chicago. If Douglas went to Peoria, the next day, Lincoln went to Peoria. And after about three weeks of this, Douglas finally said, all right, let's just agree to the debates; I got it; I mean, I'm tired of you following me.

(LAUGHTER)

And they ultimately agreed to seven. The debates lasted three hours each. They had a timekeeper but no moderator—one of the points when we get to questions that Marv and I don't totally agree on.

I represent the political leadership model that says the two guys running for power should in fact be responsible for deciding their own topics. He legitimately represents a different interest, which believes the news media might have some role in that. But in the case of the Lincoln-Douglas debates, everything in the debates was decided by Lincoln and Douglas.

And by the way if you read them, they're much more partisan, much more narrow. But there are those brief moments of brilliance that are stunningly historic. Lincoln won the popular vote but lost the election, because the legislature picked the senator. And the way it was gerrymandered, the Democrats kept control of the legislature. However, Lincoln thought the debates were good enough. They happened to be published the following day—following year.

And they introduced Lincoln to the nation as a serious political leader based on thought.

He campaigned everywhere in 1859 that Douglas went, across Indiana, Ohio, Wisconsin, Michigan. And everywhere—they had a lot of off-year elections back then. Everywhere they both campaigned in November of 1859, the Republicans won. He was then invited the day after the election to come to New York to speak, originally at a church, but then they decided it would be too big a crowd. And they moved it to Cooper Union, which is a great workingman's college that had just been founded a few years earlier.

And this is what I want to pose for you to think about. I'm walking you through this to understand what serious leaders do when they think their country's in serious trouble. Lincoln personally spent three months at the Illinois State Library researching one speech, which he personally wrote, came East—sign of the technology of the times—he had to change trains eight times, because the track widths were different in these different states—arrives in New York City and delivers a 7,300 word, two-hour speech.

After the speech, he goes down to the major newspapers to make sure they get it edited correctly.

(LAUGHTER)

And because they're all printing the complete text. He goes on to Rhode Island, Massachusetts and New Hampshire, gives the same speech once in each state, goes home in early March. And the next speech Lincoln gives is the farewell address at Springfield on the way to being inaugurated—does not give another speech the entire year.

And when people come to him, he says, read the speech. I'm not going to give you an answer you can take out of context. Read the speech. The estimate is that one-third of the adults in the North read the speech before the election. And it's a very, very sober speech because it is at the crux of the survival of America as a country.

Now reading that—I'm encouraged by my good friend Barry Castleman, who is a wonderful populist idealist—I reached the following proposition.

CURRENT SYSTEM NOT WORKING

The current political system is not working. I had not heard the Roger Ailes story, but the truth is, Roger was right. What was not all that happy in 1988 was worse in '92, even worse in '96, stunningly bad in 2000, and in 2004 was almost unendurable. For the most powerful nation on Earth to have an election in which swiftboat veterans versus National Guard papers becomes a major theme verges on insane. I mean, it's just—and to watch those debates I found painful, for both people. They're both smarter than the debates.

But here's what's happened. We have invented a system where we replace big-city machine bosses with consultant bosses. Read the newspaper coverage. Who's your pollster? What advertising firm have you hired? Who's your consultant? Who did you hire in Iowa? Who did you hire in South Carolina? This is the new Boston.

And what's the job of the candidate in this world? The job of the candidate is to raise the money, to hire the consultants, to do the focus groups, to figure out the 30-second answers to be memorized by the candidate. This is stunningly dangerous. When your leaders shrink—I used a term there that was actually a quote from General de Gaulle. I talked about pygmies. I was referring to General de Gaulle describing the Fourth Republic. But the fact is—and I wasn't referring to Republican candidates. I was referring to a process by which candidates spend more and more time raising less and less money, and that's maniacally how we count it. Who came in first last quarter? How many consultants can they hire?

We don't say: Who has thought—it was actually captured—Tim Russert asked Governor Cuomo at one point, "Who would be your party's best candidate?" And instantly Mario turned and said, "Tim, shouldn't you ask me who I think would be the best president?" Let's think about the difference.

Then you combine this stultifying, exhausting shrinking process with the way that these auditions have occurred. These aren't debates. This is a cross between "The Bachelor," "American Idol," and "Who's Smarter Than a Fifth Grader?" (sic; "Are You Smarter Than a Fifth Grader?").

(LAUGHTER, APPLAUSE)

And on top of that, you have the challenge of the news media, which unfortunately was taught by a cross between H.L. Mencken's cynicism and Theodore White's wonderful writing but focused far too much on politics as a horse race, and on an unavoidable desire for "Gotcha!" And what does that do?

It turns the candidates into rigidity, because if a candidate says something in March of 2007, and in the course of the campaign they learn something fundamentally different, and they mature, and they change, and in August or September or October, they adopt a new position based on having grown during the year, they will promptly have flip-flopped.

And so you begin to trap people—as the campaigns get longer, you're asking a person who's going to be sworn in, in January of 2009 to tell you what they'll do in January of 2007 when they haven't got a clue, because they don't know what the world will be like. And you're suggesting they won't learn anything through the two years of campaigning.

It was John F. Kennedy, campaigning in West Virginia, being horrified by poverty, which profoundly changed him in 1960.

And so we now have a system that is overly focused on money, overly delegated to technicians, and in which candidates are held to a rigidity standard that is very dangerous, while their answers are held to a sound bite and 30-second standard, which is just frankly absurd. What's your answer on Iraq, in 30 seconds? What's your answer on health care, in 30 seconds?

Now I believe this is really, really serious. First of all, when you start getting into these 30-second processes, you end up doing what Senator Obama did the other day, which is say a very insightful thing in a very dangerous way, when he pointed out, correctly, that Pakistan is enormously dangerous, that we need to have a strategy for Pakistan, but it came out that he—came out with him saying he'd use military force. Now I don't think he would have said that in a more thoughtful setting with more preparation.

And I don't know that it's very good training to be president to see how quick people are on their feet when they're tossed a question with no preparation, because I don't frankly want to have a president who gets up and decides off the cuff what they'll do about a major public policy problem.

STRATEGY AND REALITY NOT CONNECTED

But what's more difficult is the answer was to attack Senator Obama, not to explore the underlying kernel of what he said, which is a very important kernel, which is we do not today have a strategy large enough to match the problems that we are facing in the war on terrorism. And Pakistan is a great case study of the mismatch between strategy and reality. And that's an important conversation, but it's not a 30-second answer in an audition.

Let me carry it one step further, then describe what we're trying to do, and we're trying to lay all of this out, at American Solutions, where we'll have nationwide workshops on September 27th until September 29th on the Internet. They'll be available to everybody at no charge, and all of the polling we do at American Solutions is made available to all the candidates in both parties. But our goal is try to create on the Internet a solutions lab where people can participate almost like a wikipedia, and they can be—and they can focus on solutions. And I think this country is so sick of red versus blue, and the country's so ready to go back to being red, white and blue that it is—that there's an enormous gap between the political news media system and the average American.

CHALLENGES ARE IMMENSE

I also think there's something else at stake here that I think we have to put on the table. I believe we are in a Lincoln kind of period. I believe the challenges we face as a country are larger than the Cold War, larger than the Second World War, larger than the Great Depression.

I believe if you list all the different major challenges we face, they are larger than any period in American history since the 1850s. We're going to have economic competition from China and India for which we are not prepared.

To compete in an age when we're going to have four to seven times as much new science in the next 25 years as we had in the last 25 years while competing in the world market with China and India, we have to sow fundamentally overall our learning system, which is so carefully protected today by an entrenched unionized bureaucracy that it is staggering.

The Detroit Public Schools, according to a Gates Foundation financed report, graduate 25 percent of their entering freshmen on time. They cheat three out of every four entering students. At a time when, if you're an African-American male and you drop out of high school, you face a 73 percent unemployment rate in your 20s and a 60 percent chance of going to jail.

We have a war here at home between organized crime, many of which comes through international gangs, drug dealing. More young Americans are killed in the United States every month than were killed in Iraq last year, and nobody's talking about it in a serious way. The right thinks it's not its job to talk about it, and the left doesn't want to take on its own allies, and so we stumble forward.

And we're going to compete with China under those circumstances?

New York, it is projected by a McKenzie Study, will be replaced by London as the center of world finance by the end of the decade. The answer of this Congress is to raise taxes in the financial sector. Our visa system is a nightmare.

People go—people now go from around the world to London to do business, even though it's dramatically more expensive, because they're so insulted by the American visa system, and we do nothing. The fact is that there's a real parallel between the collapse of the bridge in Minneapolis and the collapse of the levees in New Orleans—bureaucratic government does not work. It is collapsing all around you.

The federal highway system obviously didn't inspect very well and the state highway system obviously didn't as well. Maybe I'm being too radical, but I want to state a proposition.

None of us believe we grew up in an America where levees broke and bridges fell, and today we live in a country where it is a fiasco.

Furthermore, they're now talking about taking till the end of next year to replace the bridge—totally bureaucratic. I'll give you a specific example. When the Northridge earthquake shattered a bridge in California, the most heavily-traveled bridge in the world, they went to an incentivized contractor.

Sacramento, the state highway department said it would take two years and two months to fix the bridge. They offered an incentive contract, where the contractor actually could make more money by getting done quickly than he could make out of the entire contract normally—they finished the bridge in two months and two days. Now, here you have two months and two days; here you have two years and two months. And I just want to take one minute to drive this home.

There is a world that works and there's a world that fails. And you can see this as a YouTube—three and a half minutes we did called FedEx versus Federal Bureaucracy.

(LAUGHTER)

UPS AND FEDEX SUPERIOR TO FEDERAL BUREAUCRACY

And it's very straightforward. How many of you have gone online to check a package at UPS or FedEx? Just raise your hand. Look around the room. This is not—and I want to drive this home for the news media—this is not a theory, this is not Gingrich having interesting, unrealistic ideas.

It is an objective fact in the world that works that if you invest in technology, you reward competence—there are consequences for incompetence—you focus on the customer, you have market signals, you have the Toyota production system, Six Sigma, Lee Manufacturing, the writing of Drucker, Deming, Juran and Womack—it works, right?

Now, UPS tracks 15 million packages a day.

A UPS truck has more computing power than Apollo 13.

(LAUGHTER)

FedEx tracks 8 million packages a day. That's the world that works. Here's the world that failed—the federal government. The United States government today cannot find between 12 and 20 million illegal immigrants when they're sitting still.

(LIGHT LAUGHTER)

So just take those two comparisons. My answer, frankly, as a policy proposal, is that we spend a couple hundred million dollars, send a package to every illegal immigrant.

(LAUGHTER, APPLAUSE)

When they deliver it, we'll know where they are.

(LAUGHTER)

THE SCALE OF CHANGE

Let me carry you just two stages further to understand the scale of change. We are going to live longer than any generation in human history. That has clear consequences for retirement, clear consequences for health care, clear consequences for quality of life. And where's the dialogue? I mean, I helped co-chair with Bob Kerrey a quality long-term care commission. We are working on projects at the Center for Health Transformation. But this needs to be a fundamental national conversation because no society in history—and by the way, this is mostly about success. I'm now 64. I regard living longer as good. This is not a problem— you know, the crisis of aging, no. There'd be a crisis of dying. We need to think through the opportunity of aging, and we need to figure out what are we going to do realistically to make it sustainable, affordable and fair to everybody.

BRITAIN'S PHONY WAR

And finally, we have, I think, a real crisis—and I said something the other day that seemed to be confusing to people, so let me put it in context. There's a terrific new book out called *Troublesome Young Men*, which is a study of the younger Tories who spent two years trying to drive Chamberlain out of office. It was very striking in reading the book, which I did shortly after the British prime minister found it impossible to be candid about the eight people they arrested in Great Britain.

It was very—six of them, by the way, were medical doctors working for the National Health Service. It was very striking to read a book in which Chamberlain was so committed to not fighting Hitler that even after war was declared in September 3rd, 1939, they fought what was called a "phony war," and I always thought the phony war was bureaucratic passivity. It wasn't.

It was a deliberate policy of the Chamberlain government. They asked the British media not to be offensive to the Germans. They dropped leaflets rather than bombs. They moved at half speed to prepare for war.

And during the entire time they were doing nothing, the German army was preparing for the onslaught against Holland, Belgium, Luxembourg and France.

OUR PHONY WAR: THE SCALE OF THE CHALLENGE

And as I read that, I thought, I can't find a better historical parallel to what we've been through for six years. Compared to the scale of the challenge, we are engaged in a phony war—now not the young men and women in Iraq and Afghanistan, they're actually at war every morning, but the rest of the society. You pick up six people in New Jersey, two people in South Carolina yesterday, four people who wanted to blow up JFK, eight people in Great Britain; you lose Gaza to Hamas; you have Pakistan totally uncontrollable, all of Northwestern Pakistan is a sanctuary.

We're not going to win this war until we have an honest conversation, and it's going to be a frightening conversation, and it's going to be a difficult conversation.

This is going to be much harder than the Cold War, and we're not ready even to have this conversation. That cannot be captured in 30-second answers for 12 people standing in a row.

CONVERSATIONS ABOUT OUR FUTURE: BETTER DEBATES

Here's the proposal, which is exactly parallel to Marvin. I believe that every candidate should be challenged to commit that if they are their party's nominee, they will agree to meet once a week—and Sunday night would be fine—once a week with their main opponent, and the two of them would have a dialogue.

Now, Marvin, I disagree with you slightly; I'd like to have a time keeper and require that the two candidates to pick the topics and require the two candidates to have a conversation without being interrupted except for fairness on time. He'd like to have some more role for the media.

We can talk out the details. There are two core premises.

The first is that it has to be open-ended. You should give the answer the length your answer should be. And the second is, it should be focused on a series of large questions around which people would be expected to bring solutions. And I believe two things would happen. I believe, first of all, an amazing percent of the American people would watch, and in the age of the Internet, all of the dialogue would be cached and people could go back to it.

People would analyze it, people would take it apart. I believe, second, that candidates would grow and change. And I think the American people would have a very good sense—after nine 90-minute conversations in their living room, the American people would have a remarkable sense of the two personalities and which person they thought had the right ideas, the right character, the right capacity to be a leader. Now this requires the candidates to take a risk.

But I want to close with this thought. The Founding Fathers did not invent this process for the enrichment of consultants, for the cynical maneuvering of those who seek power. The Founding Fathers invented this process to enable the America people to determine who they would lend power to. And the process should start with what is the kind of campaign the American people need in order to have the kind of country the American people deserve, in order to give our children and grandchildren the kind of future that our parents and grandparents worked and fought to give us.

I think that ought to be the challenge for every candidate in both parties, and I do think committing to nine dialogues, one a week, for 90 minutes, for nine weeks, would remarkably improve the quality of the system and remarkably improve the training of the candidates.

Thank you very, very much.

(APPLAUSE)

Faith in America[*]

Mitt Romney

Candidate for 2008 Republican presidential nomination, 2006–08; born Detroit, MI, March 12, 1947; B.A., Brigham Young University, 1971; M.B.A., Harvard Business School, 1975; J.D., Harvard Law School, 1975; consultant, Boston Consulting Group, 1975–77; consultant, Bain & Co., Boston, 1977–78; vice president, Bain & Company, 1978–1984; managing partner and CEO, Bain Capital, 1984–2001; chairman and CEO, Bain & Co., 1991–2001; president and CEO, Salt Lake Organizing Committee (Winter Olympics), 1999–2002; governor (R) of Massachusetts, 2002–06.

Editor's introduction: In this address delivered at the George Bush Presidential Library on December 6, 2007, Governor Mitt Romney describes his views on religious liberty, America's tradition of religious tolerance, and how faith would inform his presidency. While not the first member of the Church of Jesus Christ of Latter-day Saints (LDS) to vie for the presidency, Romney was believed to be the strongest Mormon candidate to date. Consequently, concerns about the role his faith would play arose in certain quarters, leading Romney to address these questions head on. He asserts that the church's authority is over the church, and does not intrude on that of the state. Notably, he claims to have "[seen his] father march with Martin Luther King," though he later acknowledged that he did not mean it literally.

Mitt Romney's speech: Thank you, Mr. President, for your kind introduction.

It is an honor to be here today. This is an inspiring place because of you and the First Lady and because of the film exhibited across the way in the Presidential library. For those who have not seen it, it shows the president as a young pilot, shot down during the Second World War, being rescued from his life-raft by the crew of an American submarine. It is a moving reminder that when America has faced challenge and peril, Americans rise to the occasion, willing to risk their very lives to defend freedom and preserve our nation. We are in your debt. Thank you, Mr. President.

---

[*] Delivered on December 6, 2007, at College Station, TX. Reprinted with permission.

Mr. President, your generation rose to the occasion, first to defeat Fascism and then to vanquish the Soviet Union. You left us, your children, a free and strong America. It is why we call yours the greatest generation. It is now my generation's turn. How we respond to today's challenges will define our generation. And it will determine what kind of America we will leave our children, and theirs.

America faces a new generation of challenges. Radical violent Islam seeks to destroy us. An emerging China endeavors to surpass our economic leadership. And we are troubled at home by government overspending, overuse of foreign oil, and the breakdown of the family.

Over the last year, we have embarked on a national debate on how best to preserve American leadership. Today, I wish to address a topic which I believe is fundamental to America's greatness: our religious liberty. I will also offer perspectives on how my own faith would inform my Presidency, if I were elected.

There are some who may feel that religion is not a matter to be seriously considered in the context of the weighty threats that face us. If so, they are at odds with the nation's founders, for they, when our nation faced its greatest peril, sought the blessings of the Creator. And further, they discovered the essential connection between the survival of a free land and the protection of religious freedom. In John Adams' words: "We have no government armed with power capable of contending with human passions unbridled by morality and religion . . . Our constitution was made for a moral and religious people."

Freedom requires religion just as religion requires freedom. Freedom opens the windows of the soul so that man can discover his most profound beliefs and commune with God. Freedom and religion endure together, or perish alone.

Given our grand tradition of religious tolerance and liberty, some wonder whether there are any questions regarding an aspiring candidate's religion that are appropriate. I believe there are. And I will answer them today.

Almost 50 years ago another candidate from Massachusetts explained that he was an American running for president, not a Catholic running for president. Like him, I am an American running for president. I do not define my candidacy by my religion. A person should not be elected because of his faith nor should he be rejected because of his faith.

Let me assure you that no authorities of my church, or of any other church for that matter, will ever exert influence on presidential decisions. Their authority is theirs, within the province of church affairs, and it ends where the affairs of the nation begin.

As governor, I tried to do the right as best I knew it, serving the law and answering to the Constitution. I did not confuse the particular teachings of my church with the obligations of the office and of the Constitution—and of course, I would not do so as president. I will put no doctrine of any church above the plain duties of the office and the sovereign authority of the law.

As a young man, Lincoln described what he called America's "political religion"—the commitment to defend the rule of law and the Constitution. When I place my hand on the Bible and take the oath of office, that oath becomes my highest promise to God. If I am fortunate to become your president, I will serve no one religion, no one group, no one cause, and no one interest. A president must serve only the common cause of the people of the United States.

There are some for whom these commitments are not enough. They would prefer it if I would simply distance myself from my religion, say that it is more a tradition than my personal conviction, or disavow one or another of its precepts. That I will not do. I believe in my Mormon faith, and I endeavor to live by it. My faith is the faith of my fathers—I will be true to them and to my beliefs.

Some believe that such a confession of my faith will sink my candidacy. If they are right, so be it. But I think they underestimate the American people. Americans do not respect believers of convenience.

Americans tire of those who would jettison their beliefs, even to gain the world.

There is one fundamental question about which I often am asked: What do I believe about Jesus Christ? I believe that Jesus Christ is the Son of God and the Savior of mankind. My church's beliefs about Christ may not all be the same as those of other faiths. Each religion has its own unique doctrines and history. These are not bases for criticism but rather a test of our tolerance. Religious tolerance would be a shallow principle indeed if it were reserved only for faiths with which we agree.

There are some who would have a presidential candidate describe and explain his church's distinctive doctrines. To do so would enable the very religious test the founders prohibited in the Constitution. No candidate should become the spokesman for his faith. For if he becomes president he will need the prayers of the people of all faiths.

I believe that every faith I have encountered draws its adherents closer to God. And in every faith I have come to know, there are features I wish were in my own: I love the profound ceremony of the Catholic Mass, the approachability of God in the prayers of the Evangelicals, the tenderness of spirit among the Pentecostals, the confident independence of the Lutherans, the ancient traditions of the Jews, unchanged through the ages, and the commitment to frequent prayer of the Muslims. As I travel across the country and see our towns and cities, I am always moved by the many houses of worship with their steeples, all pointing to heaven, reminding us of the source of life's blessings.

It is important to recognize that while differences in theology exist between the churches in America, we share a common creed of moral convictions. And where the affairs of our nation are concerned, it's usually a sound rule to focus on the latter—on the great moral principles that urge us all on a common course. Whether it was the cause of abolition, or civil rights, or the right to life itself, no movement of conscience can succeed in America that cannot speak to the convictions of religious people.

We separate church and state affairs in this country, and for good reason. No religion should dictate to the state nor should the state interfere with the free practice of religion. But in recent years, the notion of the separation of church and state has been taken by some well beyond its original meaning. They seek to remove from the public domain any acknowledgment of God. Religion is seen as merely a private affair with no place in public life. It is as if they are intent on establishing a new religion in America—the religion of secularism. They are wrong.

The founders proscribed the establishment of a state religion, but they did not countenance the elimination of religion from the public square. We are a nation "Under God" and in God, we do indeed trust.

We should acknowledge the Creator as did the Founders—in ceremony and word. He should remain on our currency, in our pledge, in the teaching of our history, and during the holiday season, nativity scenes and menorahs should be welcome in our public places. Our greatness would not long endure without judges who respect the foundation of faith upon which our constitution rests. I will take care to separate the affairs of government from any religion, but I will not separate us from "the God who gave us liberty."

Nor would I separate us from our religious heritage. Perhaps the most important question to ask a person of faith who seeks a political office, is this: Does he share these American values: the equality of human kind, the obligation to serve one another, and a steadfast commitment to liberty?

They are not unique to any one denomination. They belong to the great moral inheritance we hold in common. They are the firm ground on which Americans of different faiths meet and stand as a nation, united.

We believe that every single human being is a child of God—we are all part of the human family. The conviction of the inherent and inalienable worth of every life is still the most revolutionary political proposition ever advanced. John Adams put it that we are "thrown into the world all equal and alike."

The consequence of our common humanity is our responsibility to one another, to our fellow Americans foremost, but also to every child of God. It is an obligation which is fulfilled by Americans every day, here and across the globe, without regard to creed or race or nationality.

Americans acknowledge that liberty is a gift of God, not an indulgence of government. No people in the history of the world have sacrificed as much for liberty. The lives of hundreds of thousands of America's sons and daughters were laid down during the last century to preserve freedom, for us and for freedom loving people throughout the world. America took nothing from that century's terrible wars—no land from Germany or Japan or Korea; no treasure; no oath of fealty. America's resolve in the defense of liberty has been tested time and again. It has not been found wanting, nor must it ever be. America must never falter in holding high the banner of freedom.

These American values, this great moral heritage, is shared and lived in my religion as it is in yours. I was taught in my home to honor God and love my neighbor. I saw my father march with Martin Luther King. I saw my parents provide compassionate care to others, in personal ways to people nearby, and in just as consequential ways in leading national volunteer movements. I am moved by the Lord's words: "For I was an hungered, and ye gave me meat: I was thirsty, and ye gave me drink: I was a stranger, and ye took me in: naked, and ye clothed me . . . "

My faith is grounded on these truths. You can witness them in Ann and my marriage and in our family. We are a long way from perfect and we have surely stumbled along the way, but our aspirations, our values, are the self-same as those from the other faiths that stand upon this common foundation. And these convictions will indeed inform my presidency.

Today's generations of Americans have always known religious liberty. Perhaps we forget the long and arduous path our nation's forbearers took to achieve it. They came here from England to seek freedom of religion. But upon finding it for themselves, they at first denied it to others. Because of their diverse beliefs, Ann Hutchinson was exiled from Massachusetts Bay, a banished Roger Williams founded Rhode Island, and two centuries later, Brigham Young set out for the West. Americans were unable to accommodate their commitment to their own faith with an appreciation for the convictions of others to different faiths. In this, they were very much like those of the European nations they had left.

It was in Philadelphia that our founding fathers defined a revolutionary vision of liberty, grounded on self evident truths about the equality of all, and the inalienable rights with which each is endowed by his Creator.

We cherish these sacred rights, and secure them in our Constitutional order. Foremost do we protect religious liberty, not as a matter of policy but as a matter of right. There will be no established church, and we are guaranteed the free exercise of our religion.

I'm not sure that we fully appreciate the profound implications of our tradition of religious liberty. I have visited many of the magnificent cathedrals in Europe. They are so inspired . . . so grand . . . so empty. Raised up over generations, long ago, so many of the cathedrals now stand as the postcard backdrop to societies just too busy or too "enlightened" to venture inside and kneel in prayer. The establishment of state religions in Europe did no favor to Europe's churches. And though you will find many people of strong faith there, the churches themselves seem to be withering away.

Infinitely worse is the other extreme, the creed of conversion by conquest: violent Jihad, murder as martyrdom . . . killing Christians, Jews, and Muslims with equal indifference. These radical Islamists do their preaching not by reason or example, but in the coercion of minds and the shedding of blood. We face no greater danger today than theocratic tyranny, and the boundless suffering these states and groups could inflict if given the chance.

The diversity of our cultural expression, and the vibrancy of our religious dialogue, has kept America in the forefront of civilized nations even as others regard religious freedom as something to be destroyed.

In such a world, we can be deeply thankful that we live in a land where reason and religion are friends and allies in the cause of liberty, joined against the evils and dangers of the day. And you can be certain of this: Any believer in religious freedom, any person who has knelt in prayer to the Almighty, has a friend and ally in me. And so it is for hundreds of millions of our countrymen: We do not insist on a single strain of religion—rather, we welcome our nation's symphony of faith.

Recall the early days of the First Continental Congress in Philadelphia, during the fall of 1774. With Boston occupied by British troops, there were rumors of imminent hostilities and fears of an impending war. In this time of peril, someone suggested that they pray. But there were objections. "They were too divided in religious sentiments," what with Episcopalians and Quakers, Anabaptists and Congregationalists, Presbyterians and Catholics.

Then Sam Adams rose, and said he would hear a prayer from anyone of piety and good character, as long as they were a patriot.

And so together they prayed, and together they fought, and together, by the grace of God . . . they founded this great nation.

In that spirit, let us give thanks to the divine "author of liberty." And together, let us pray that this land may always be blessed, "with freedom's holy light."

God bless the United States of America.

A Four-Year Vision for America[*]

John McCain

U.S. senator (R) from Arizona, 1987– ; born Panama Canal Zone, August 29, 1936; graduated United States Naval Academy, 1958; naval aviator, 1958–1980; shot down over Vietnam, 1967, and held as prisoner-of-war in Hanoi, 1967–73; retired from the Navy as captain, 1981; U.S. representative (R), Arizona's First District, 1983–87; elected to U.S. Senate, 1986; U.S. Senate committees: Armed Services (ranking member); Commerce, Science, and Transportation; and Indian Affairs; military honors include Bronze Star, Legion of Merit, Purple Heart, and Distinguished Flying Cross; author, Worth the Fighting For: The Education of an American Maverick, and the Heroes Who Inspired Him *(2003),* Character is Destiny: Inspiring Stories Every Young Person Should Know and Every Adult Should Remember *(2007),* Why Courage Matters: The Way to a Braver Life *(2008),* Faith of My Fathers: A Family Memoir *(2008), and* Hard Call: The Art of Great Decisions *(2008).*

Editor's introduction: Having defeated his opponents in the Republican presidential primary, Senator John McCain now turned his attention to the general election. In this speech, delivered at the Greater Columbus Convention Center, he outlines some of the goals he hoped to achieve by the end of his first term in office—an ambitious agenda ranging from an end to the Iraq War, robust economic growth, and improvements in public education to increased accessibility to health care, reductions in illegal immigration, and a surge in voluntary national service. He further pledges to stem the tide of partisanship in Washington by working with Democrats and to honor the Constitution's separation of powers.

John McCain's speech: Thank you. The hectic but repetitive routine of presidential campaigns often seems to consist entirely of back and forth charges between candidates, punctuated by photo ops, debates and the occasional policy speech, followed by another barrage of accusations and counter accusations, formulated into the soundbites preferred by cable news producers. It is a little hypocritical for candidates or reporters to criticize these deficiencies. They are our creation.

---

[*] Delivered on May 15, 2008, at Columbus, OH.

Campaigns and the media collaborated as architects of the modern presidential campaign, and we deserve equal blame for the regret we feel from time to time over its less than inspirational features.

Voters, however, even in this revolutionary communications age, with its 24-hour news cycle, can be forgiven their uncertainty about what the candidates actually hope to achieve if they have the extraordinary privilege of being elected president of the United States. We spend too little time and offer too few specifics on that most important of questions. We make promises, of course, about what kind of policies we would pursue in office. But they often are obscured, mischaracterized and forgotten in the heat and fog of political battle.

Next January, the political leadership of the United States will change significantly. It is important that the candidates who seek to lead the country after the Bush administration define their objectives and what they plan to achieve not with vague language but with clarity.

So, what I want to do today is take a little time to describe what I would hope to have achieved at the end of my first term as president. I cannot guarantee I will have achieved these things. I am presumptuous enough to think I would be a good president, but not so much that I believe I can govern by command. Should I forget that, Congress will, of course, hasten to remind me. The following are conditions I intend to achieve. And toward that end, I will focus all the powers of the office; every skill and strength I possess; and seize every opportunity to work with members of Congress who put the national interest ahead of partisanship, and any country in the world that shares our hopes for a more peaceful and prosperous world.

By January 2013, America has welcomed home most of the servicemen and women who have sacrificed terribly so that America might be secure in her freedom. The Iraq War has been won. Iraq is a functioning democracy, although still suffering from the lingering effects of decades of tyranny and centuries of sectarian tension. Violence still occurs, but it is spasmodic and much reduced. Civil war has been prevented; militias disbanded; the Iraqi Security Force is professional and competent; al Qaeda in Iraq has been defeated; and the government of Iraq is capable of imposing its authority in every province of Iraq and defending the integrity of its borders. The United States maintains a military presence there, but a much smaller one, and it does not play a direct combat role.

The threat from a resurgent Taliban in Afghanistan has been greatly reduced but not eliminated. U.S. and NATO forces remain there to help finish the job, and continue operations against the remnants of al Qaeda. The government of Pakistan has cooperated with the U.S. in successfully adapting the counterinsurgency tactics that worked so well in Iraq and Afghanistan to its lawless tribal areas where al Qaeda fighters are based. The increase in actionable intelligence that the counterinsurgency produced led to the capture or death of Osama bin Laden, and his chief lieutenants. There is no longer any place in the world al Qaeda can consider a safe haven. Increased cooperation between the United States and its allies in the concerted use of military, diplomatic, and economic power and reforms in the intelligence capabilities of the United States has disrupted terrorist networks and exposed plots around the world. There still has not been a major terrorist attack in the United States since September 11, 2001.

The United States and its allies have made great progress in advancing nuclear security. Concerted action by the great democracies of the world has persuaded a reluctant Russia and China to cooperate in pressuring Iran to abandon its nuclear ambitions, and North Korea to discontinue its own. The single greatest threat facing the West—the prospect of nuclear materials in the hands of terrorists—has been vastly diminished.

The size of the Army and Marine Corps has been significantly increased, and are now better equipped and trained to defend us. Long overdue reforms to the way we acquire weapons programs, including fixed price contracts, have created sufficient savings to pay for a larger military. A substantial increase in veterans educational benefits and improvements in their health care has aided recruitment and retention. The strain on the National Guard and reserve forces has been relieved.

After efforts to pressure the government in Sudan over Darfur failed again in the U.N. Security Council, the United States, acting in concert with a newly formed League of Democracies, applied stiff diplomatic and economic pressure that caused the government of Sudan to agree to a multinational peacekeeping force, with NATO countries providing logistical and air support, to stop the genocide that had made a mockery of the world's repeated declaration that we would "never again" tolerate such inhumanity. Encouraged by the success, the League is now occupied with using the economic power and prestige of its member states to end other gross abuses of human rights, such as the despicable crime of human trafficking.

The United States has experienced several years of robust economic growth, and Americans again have confidence in their economic future. A reduction in the corporate tax rate from the second highest in the world to one on par with our trading partners; the low rate on capital gains; allowing business to deduct in a single year investments in equipment and technology, while eliminating tax loopholes and ending corporate welfare, have spurred innovation and productivity, and encouraged companies to keep their operations and jobs in the United States. The Alternate Minimum Tax is being phased out, with relief provided first to middle income families. Doubling the size of the child exemption has put more disposable income in the hands of taxpayers, further stimulating growth.

Congress has just passed by a single up or down vote a tax reform proposal that offers Americans a choice of continuing to file under the rules of the current complicated and burdensome tax code or use a new, simpler, fairer and flatter tax, with two rates and a generous deduction. Millions of taxpayers are expected to file under the flat tax, and save billions in the cost of preparing their returns.

After exercising my veto several times in my first year in office, Congress has not sent me an appropriations bill containing earmarks for the last three years. A top to bottom review of every federal bureaucracy has yielded great reductions in government spending by identifying programs that serve no important purpose; and instigating far reaching reforms of procurement and operating policies that have for too long extravagantly wasted money for no better purpose than to increase federal payrolls.

New free trade agreements have been ratified and led to substantial increases in both exports and imports. The resulting growth in prosperity in countries from South America to Asia to Africa has greatly strengthened America's security and the global progress of our political ideals. U.S. tariffs on agricultural imports have been eliminated and unneeded farm subsidies are being phased out. The world food crisis has ended, inflation is low, and the quality of life not only in our country, but in some of the most impoverished countries around the world, is much improved.

Americans, who through no fault of their own, lost jobs in the global economy they once believed were theirs for life, are assisted by reformed unemployment insurance and worker retraining programs. Older workers who accept lower paying jobs while they acquire new skills are provided assistance to make up a good part of the income they have lost. Community colleges and technical schools all over the country have developed worker retraining programs suited to the specific economic opportunities available in their communities and are helping millions of workers who have lost a job that won't come back find a new one that won't go away.

Public education in the United States is much improved thanks to the competition provided by charter and private schools; the increase of quality teachers through incentives like merit pay and terrific programs that attract to the classroom enthusiastic and innovative teachers from many disciplines, like Teach for America and Troops to Teachers. Educational software and online teaching programs endorsed by qualified nonprofits are much more widely in use, bringing to the smallest classrooms in America some of the greatest math, English, and science teachers in the country. This revolution in teaching methods has especially benefited rural America. Test scores and graduation rates are rising everywhere in the country.

Health care has become more accessible to more Americans than at any other time in history. Reforms of the insurance market; putting the choice of health care into the hands of American families rather than exclusively with the government or employers; walk-in clinics as alternatives to emergency room care; paying for outcome in the treatment of disease rather than individual procedures; and competition in the prescription drug market have begun to wring out the runaway inflation once endemic in our health care system. More small businesses offer their employees health plans. Schools have greatly improved their emphasis on physical education and nutritional content of meals offered in school cafeterias. Obesity rates among the young and the diseases they engender are stabilized and beginning to decline. The federal government and states have cooperated in establishing backstop insurance pools that provide coverage to people hard pressed to find insurance elsewhere because of pre-existing illness.

The reduction in the growth of health care costs has begun to relieve some of the pressure on Medicare; encouraging Congress to act in a bipartisan way to extend its solvency for twenty-five years without increasing taxes and raising premiums only for upper income seniors. Their success encouraged a group of congressional leaders from both parties to work with my administration to fix Social Security as well, without reducing benefits to those near retirement. The reforms include some form of personal retirement accounts in safe and reliable index funds, such as have been available to government employees since their retirement plans were made solvent a quarter century ago.

The United States is well on the way to independence from foreign sources of oil; progress that has not only begun to alleviate the environmental threat posed from climate change, but has greatly improved our security as well. A cap and trade system has been implemented, spurring great innovation in the development of green technologies and alternative energy sources. Clean coal technology has advanced considerably with federal assistance. Construction has begun on twenty new nuclear reactors thanks to improved incentives and a streamlined regulatory process.

Scores of judges have been confirmed to the federal district and appellate courts, including the U.S. Supreme Court, who understand that they were not sent there to write our laws but to enforce them and make sure they are consistent with the Constitution. They are judges of exceptional character and quality, who enforce and do not make laws, and who respect the values of the people whose rights, laws and property they are sworn to defend.

Border state governors have certified and the American people recognize that after tremendous improvements to border security infrastructure and increases in the border patrol, and vigorous prosecution of companies that employ illegal aliens, our southern border is now secure. Illegal immigrants who broke our laws after they came here have been arrested and deported. Illegal immigration has been finally brought under control, and the American people accepted the practical necessity to institute a temporary worker program and deal humanely with the millions of immigrants who have been in this country illegally.

Voluntary national service has grown in popularity in part because of the educational benefits used as incentives, as well as frequent appeals from the bully pulpit of the White House, but mostly because the young Americans, no less than earlier generations, understand that true happiness is much greater than the pursuit of pleasure, and can only be found by serving causes greater than self-interest. Scores of accomplished private sector leaders have joined the ranks of my administration for a dollar a year and have instituted some of the most innovative reforms of government programs ever known, often in partnership with willing private sector partners. A sense of community, a kinship of ideals, has invigorated public service again.

This is the progress I want us to achieve during my presidency. These are the changes I am running for president to make. I want to leave office knowing that America is safer, freer, and wealthier than when I was elected; that more Americans have more opportunities to pursue their dreams than at any other time in our history; that the world has become less threatening to our interests and more hospitable to our values; and that America has again, as she always has, chosen not to hide from history but to make history.

I am well aware I cannot make any of these changes alone. The powers of the presidency are rightly checked by the other branches of government, and I will not attempt to acquire powers our founders saw fit to grant Congress. I will exercise my veto if I believe legislation passed by Congress is not in the nation's best interests, but I will not subvert the purpose of legislation I have signed by making statements that indicate I will enforce only the parts of it I like. I will respect the responsibilities the Constitution and the American people have granted Congress, and will, as I often have in the past, work with anyone of either party to get things done for our country.

For too long, now, Washington has been consumed by a hyper-partisanship that treats every serious challenge facing us as an opportunity to trade insults, disparage each other's motives, and fight about the next election. For all the problems we face, if you ask Americans what frustrates them most about Washington, they will tell you they don't think we're capable of serving the public interest before our personal and partisan ambitions; that we fight for ourselves and not for them. Americans are sick of it, and they have every right to be. They are sick of the politics of selfishness, stalemate and delay. They despair when every election—no matter who wins—always seems to produce four more years of unkept promises and a government that is just a battleground for the next election. Their patience is at an end for politicians who value ambition over principle, and for partisanship that is less a contest of ideas than an uncivil brawl over the spoils of power. They want to change not only the policies and institutions that have failed the American people, but the political culture that produced them. They want to move this country forward and stake our claim on this century as we did in the last. And they want their government to care more about them than preserving the privileges of the powerful.

There are serious issues at stake in this election, and serious differences between the candidates. And we will argue about them, as we should. But it should remain an argument among friends; each of us struggling to hear our conscience, and heed its demands; each of us, despite our differences, united in our great cause, and respectful of the goodness in each other. That is how most Americans treat each other. And it is how they want the people they elect to office to treat each other.

If I am elected president, I will work with anyone who sincerely wants to get this country moving again. I will listen to any idea that is offered in good faith and intended to help solve our problems, not make them worse. I will seek the counsel of members of Congress from both parties in forming government policy before I ask them to support it. I will ask Democrats to serve in my administration. My administration will set a new standard for transparency and accountability. I will hold weekly press conferences. I will regularly brief the American people on the progress our policies have made and the setbacks we have encountered. When we make errors, I will confess them readily, and explain what we intend to do to correct them. I will ask Congress to grant me the privilege of coming before both houses to take questions, and address criticism, much the same as the Prime Minister of Great Britain appears regularly before the House of Commons.

We cannot again leave our problems for another unluckier generation of Americans to fix after they have become even harder to solve. I'm not interested in partisanship that serves no other purpose than to gain a temporary advantage over our opponents. This mindless, paralyzing rancor must come to an end. We belong to different parties, not different countries. We are rivals for the same power. But we are also compatriots. We are fellow Americans, and that shared distinction means more to me than any other association. I intend to prove myself worthy of the office, of our country, and of your respect. I won't judge myself by how many elections I've won. I won't spend one hour of my presidency worrying more about my re-election than keeping my promises to the American people. There is a time to campaign, and a time to govern. If I'm elected president, the era of the permanent campaign will end. The era of problem solving will begin. I promise you, from the day I am sworn into office until the last hour of my presidency, I will work with anyone, of either party, to make this country safe, prosperous and proud. And I won't care who gets the credit.

Thank you.

Remarks in Washington, D.C.[*]

Hillary Clinton

U.S. senator (D) from New York, 2001– ; born Chicago, IL, October 26, 1947; B.A., Wellesley College, 1969; J.D., Yale University, 1973; postgraduate study on children and medicine at Yale Child Study Center, during which staff attorney at Children's Defense Fund and consultant to Carnegie Council on Children; advised House Committee on the Judiciary, 1974; joined faculty of School of Law at University of Arkansas, Fayetteville, 1974; joined Rose Law Firm 1977, became full partner 1979; First Lady of Arkansas, 1979–1981, 1983–1992; First Lady of the United States, 1993–2001; Chair, Task Force on National Health Care Reform, 1993–94; committees: Budget; Armed Services; Environment and Public Works; Health, Education, Labor and Pensions; Aging; commissioner, Commission on Security and Cooperation in Europe (since 2001); author, It Takes a Village and Other Lessons Children Teach Us *(1996),* An Invitation to the White House: At Home with History *(2000),* Living History *(2004).*

Editor's introduction: After a hard-fought primary campaign and following numerous calls to drop out of the race, Senator Hillary Clinton conceded the Democratic presidential nomination to Senator Barack Obama at the National Building Museum in Washington, D.C., on June 7, 2008. In her remarks, she asks her supporters to help elect Obama, while promising to continue her own fight to bolster the American economy and ensure access to health care for every American. Though her campaign did not manage to "shatter that highest, hardest glass ceiling this time," she tells her supporters in what has become one of the signature rhetorical flourishes of her campaign, "thanks to you, it's got about 18 million cracks in it."

Hillary Clinton's speech: Thank you so much. Thank you all.

Well, this isn't exactly the party I'd planned, but I sure like the company.

I want to start today by saying how grateful I am to all of you—to everyone who poured your hearts and your hopes into this campaign, who drove for miles

---

* Delivered on June 7, 2008, at Washington, D.C.

and lined the streets waving homemade signs, who scrimped and saved to raise money, who knocked on doors and made calls, who talked and sometimes argued with your friends and neighbors, who emailed and contributed online, who invested so much in our common enterprise, to the moms and dads who came to our events, who lifted their little girls and little boys on their shoulders and whispered in their ears, "See, you can be anything you want to be."

To the young people like 13-year-old Ann Riddle from Mayfield, Ohio, who had been saving for two years to go to Disney World, and decided to use her savings instead to travel to Pennsylvania with her Mom and volunteer there as well. To the veterans and the childhood friends, to New Yorkers and Arkansans who traveled across the country, telling anyone who would listen why you supported me.

To all those women in their 80s and their 90s born before women could vote who cast their votes for our campaign. I've told you before about Florence Steen of South Dakota, who was 88 years old, and insisted that her daughter bring an absentee ballot to her hospice bedside. Her daughter and a friend put an American flag behind her bed and helped her fill out the ballot. She passed away soon after, and under state law, her ballot didn't count. But her daughter later told a reporter, "My dad's an ornery old cowboy, and he didn't like it when he heard mom's vote wouldn't be counted. I don't think he had voted in 20 years. But he voted in place of my mom."

To all those who voted for me, and to whom I pledged my utmost, my commitment to you and to the progress we seek is unyielding. You have inspired and touched me with the stories of the joys and sorrows that make up the fabric of our lives and you have humbled me with your commitment to our country.

Eighteen million of you from all walks of life—women and men, young and old, Latino and Asian, African-American and Caucasian, rich, poor and middle class, gay and straight—you have stood strong with me. And I will continue to stand strong with you, every time, every place, and every way that I can. The dreams we share are worth fighting for.

Remember—we fought for the single mom with a young daughter, juggling work and school, who told me, "I'm doing it all to better myself for her." We fought for the woman who grabbed my hand, and asked me, "What are you going to do to make sure I have health care?" and began to cry because even though she works three jobs, she can't afford insurance. We fought for the young man in the Marine Corps t-shirt who waited months for medical care and said, "Take care of my buddies over there and then, will you please help take care of me?" We fought for all those who've lost jobs and health care, who can't afford gas or groceries or college, who have felt invisible to their president these last seven years.

I entered this race because I have an old-fashioned conviction: that public service is about helping people solve their problems and live their dreams. I've had every opportunity and blessing in my own life—and I want the same for all Americans. Until that day comes, you will always find me on the front lines of democracy—fighting for the future.

The way to continue our fight now—to accomplish the goals for which we stand—is to take our energy, our passion, our strength and do all we can to help elect Barack Obama the next president of the United States.

Today, as I suspend my campaign, I congratulate him on the victory he has won and the extraordinary race he has run. I endorse him, and throw my full support behind him. And I ask all of you to join me in working as hard for Barack Obama as you have for me.

I have served in the Senate with him for four years. I have been in this campaign with him for 16 months. I have stood on the stage and gone toe-to-toe with him in 22 debates. I have had a front row seat to his candidacy, and I have seen his strength and determination, his grace and his grit.

In his own life, Barack Obama has lived the American Dream. As a community organizer, in the state senate, as a United States Senator—he has dedicated himself to ensuring the dream is realized. And in this campaign, he has inspired so many to become involved in the democratic process and invested in our common future.

Now when I started this race, I intended to win back the White House, and make sure we have a president who puts our country back on the path to peace, prosperity, and progress. And that's exactly what we're going to do by ensuring that Barack Obama walks through the doors of the Oval Office on January 20, 2009.

I understand that we all know this has been a tough fight. The Democratic Party is a family, and it's now time to restore the ties that bind us together and to come together around the ideals we share, the values we cherish, and the country we love.

We may have started on separate journeys—but today, our paths have merged. And we are all heading toward the same destination, united and more ready than ever to win in November and to turn our country around because so much is at stake.

We all want an economy that sustains the American Dream, the opportunity to work hard and have that work rewarded, to save for college, a home and retirement, to afford that gas and those groceries and still have a little left over at the end of the month. An economy that lifts all of our people and ensures that our prosperity is broadly distributed and shared.

We all want a health care system that is universal, high quality, and affordable so that parents no longer have to choose between care for themselves or their children or be stuck in dead end jobs simply to keep their insurance. This isn't just an issue for me—it is a passion and a cause—and it is a fight I will continue until every single American is insured—no exceptions, no excuses.

We all want an America defined by deep and meaningful equality—from civil rights to labor rights, from women's rights to gay rights, from ending discrimination to promoting unionization to providing help for the most important job there is: caring for our families.

We all want to restore America's standing in the world, to end the war in Iraq and once again lead by the power of our values, and to join with our allies to confront our shared challenges from poverty and genocide to terrorism and global warming.

You know, I've been involved in politics and public life in one way or another for four decades. During those forty years, our country has voted ten times for president. Democrats won only three of those times. And the man who won two of those elections is with us today.

We made tremendous progress during the 90s under a Democratic president, with a flourishing economy, and our leadership for peace and security respected around the world. Just think how much more progress we could have made over the past 40 years if we had a Democratic president. Think about the lost opportunities of these past seven years—on the environment and the economy, on health care and civil rights, on education, foreign policy and the Supreme Court. Imagine how far we could've come, how much we could've achieved if we had just had a Democrat in the White House.

We cannot let this moment slip away. We have come too far and accomplished too much.

Now the journey ahead will not be easy. Some will say we can't do it. That it's too hard. That we're just not up to the task. But for as long as America has existed, it has been the American way to reject "can't do" claims, and to choose instead to stretch the boundaries of the possible through hard work, determination, and a pioneering spirit.

It is this belief, this optimism, that Senator Obama and I share, and that has inspired so many millions of our supporters to make their voices heard.

So today, I am standing with Senator Obama to say: Yes, we can.

Together we will work. We'll have to work hard to get universal health care. But on the day we live in an America where no child, no man, and no woman is without health insurance, we will live in a stronger America. That's why we need to help elect Barack Obama our president.

We'll have to work hard to get back to fiscal responsibility and a strong middle class. But on the day we live in an America whose middle class is thriving and growing again, where all Americans, no matter where they live or where their ancestors came from, can earn a decent living, we will live in a stronger America and that is why we must elect Barack Obama our president.

We'll have to work hard to foster the innovation that makes us energy independent and lift the threat of global warming from our children's future. But on the day we live in an America fueled by renewable energy, we will live in a stronger America. That's why we have to help elect Barack Obama our president.

We'll have to work hard to bring our troops home from Iraq, and get them the support they've earned by their service. But on the day we live in an America that's as loyal to our troops as they have been to us, we will live in a stronger America and that is why we must help elect Barack Obama our president.

This election is a turning point election and it is critical that we all understand what our choice really is. Will we go forward together or will we stall and slip backwards. Think how much progress we have already made. When we first started, people everywhere asked the same questions:

Could a woman really serve as Commander-in-Chief? Well, I think we answered that one.

And could an African American really be our president? Senator Obama has answered that one.

Together Senator Obama and I achieved milestones essential to our progress as a nation, part of our perpetual duty to form a more perfect union.

Now, on a personal note—when I was asked what it means to be a woman running for president, I always gave the same answer: that I was proud to be running as a woman but I was running because I thought I'd be the best president. But I am a woman, and like millions of women, I know there are still barriers and biases out there, often unconscious.

I want to build an America that respects and embraces the potential of every last one of us.

I ran as a daughter who benefited from opportunities my mother never dreamed of. I ran as a mother who worries about my daughter's future and a mother who wants to lead all children to brighter tomorrows. To build that future I see, we must make sure that women and men alike understand the struggles of their grandmothers and mothers, and that women enjoy equal opportunities, equal pay, and equal respect. Let us resolve and work toward achieving some very simple propositions: There are no acceptable limits and there are no acceptable prejudices in the 21st century.

You can be so proud that, from now on, it will be unremarkable for a woman to win primary state victories, unremarkable to have a woman in a close race to be our nominee, unremarkable to think that a woman can be the president of the United States. And that is truly remarkable.

To those who are disappointed that we couldn't go all the way—especially the young people who put so much into this campaign—it would break my heart if, in falling short of my goal, I in any way discouraged any of you from pursuing yours. Always aim high, work hard, and care deeply about what you believe in. When you stumble, keep faith. When you're knocked down, get right back up. And never listen to anyone who says you can't or shouldn't go on.

As we gather here today in this historic magnificent building, the 50th woman to leave this Earth is orbiting overhead. If we can blast 50 women into space, we will someday launch a woman into the White House.

Although we weren't able to shatter that highest, hardest glass ceiling this time, thanks to you, it's got about 18 million cracks in it. And the light is shining through like never before, filling us all with the hope and the sure knowledge that the path will be a little easier next time. That has always been the history of progress in America.

Think of the suffragists who gathered at Seneca Falls in 1848 and those who kept fighting until women could cast their votes. Think of the abolitionists who struggled and died to see the end of slavery. Think of the civil rights heroes and foot-soldiers who marched, protested and risked their lives to bring about the end to segregation and Jim Crow.

Because of them, I grew up taking for granted that women could vote. Because of them, my daughter grew up taking for granted that children of all colors could go to school together. Because of them, Barack Obama and I could wage a hard fought campaign for the Democratic nomination. Because of them, and because of you, children today will grow up taking for granted that an African American or a woman can yes, become president of the United States.

When that day arrives and a woman takes the oath of office as our president, we will all stand taller, proud of the values of our nation, proud that every little girl can dream and that her dreams can come true in America. And all of you will know that because of your passion and hard work you helped pave the way for that day.

So I want to say to my supporters, when you hear people saying—or think to yourself—"if only" or "what if," I say, "please don't go there." Every moment wasted looking back keeps us from moving forward.

Life is too short, time is too precious, and the stakes are too high to dwell on what might have been. We have to work together for what still can be. And that is why I will work my heart out to make sure that Senator Obama is our next president and I hope and pray that all of you will join me in that effort.

To my supporters and colleagues in Congress, to the governors and mayors, elected officials who stood with me, in good times and in bad, thank you for your strength and leadership. To my friends in our labor unions who stood strong every step of the way—I thank you and pledge my support to you. To my friends, from every stage of my life—your love and ongoing commitments sustain me every single day. To my family—especially Bill and Chelsea and my mother, you mean the world to me and I thank you for all you have done. And to my extraordinary staff, volunteers and supporters, thank you for working those long, hard hours. Thank you for dropping everything—leaving work or school—traveling to places you'd never been, sometimes for months on end. And thanks to your families as well because your sacrifice was theirs too. All of you were there for me every step of the way. Being human, we are imperfect. That's why we need each other. To catch each other when we falter. To encourage each other when we lose heart. Some may lead; others may follow; but none of us can go it alone. The changes we're working for are changes that we can only accomplish together. Life, liberty, and the pursuit of happiness are rights that belong to each of us as individuals. But our lives, our freedom, our happiness, are best enjoyed, best protected, and best advanced when we do work together.

That is what we will do now as we join forces with Senator Obama and his campaign. We will make history together as we write the next chapter in America's story. We will stand united for the values we hold dear, for the vision of progress we share, and for the country we love. There is nothing more American than that.

And looking out at you today, I have never felt so blessed. The challenges that I have faced in this campaign are nothing compared to those that millions of Americans face every day in their own lives. So today, I'm going to count my blessings and keep on going. I'm going to keep doing what I was doing long before the cameras ever showed up and what I'll be doing long after they're gone: Working to give every American the same opportunities I had, and working to ensure that every child has the chance to grow up and achieve his or her God-given potential.

I will do it with a heart filled with gratitude, with a deep and abiding love for our country– and with nothing but optimism and confidence for the days ahead. This is now our time to do all that we can to make sure that in this election we add another Democratic president to that very small list of the last 40 years and that we take back our country and once again move with progress and commitment to the future.

Thank you all and God bless you and God bless America.

Speech to the Democratic National Convention[*]

Joe Biden

Vice president-elect, 2008– ; born Scranton, PA, November 20, 1942; B.A., University of Delaware, 1965; J.D., Syracuse University College of Law, 1968; attorney, private practice, 1968–1972; council member, New Castle County Council, 1970–72; U.S. senator (D), Delaware, 1973–2008; candidate for 1988 Democratic presidential nomination; adjunct professor, Widener University School of Law, 1991– ; candidate for 2008 Democratic presidential nomination; author, Promises to Keep: On Life and Politics *(2008).*

Editor's introduction: Though they began the 2008 presidential campaign as rivals, Senators Barack Obama and Joe Biden ended it on the same winning ticket. In his speech to the Democratic National Convention accepting the party's vice presidential nomination, Biden describes his humble upbringing and offers high praise for his running mate. While Biden had criticized Obama for his supposed inexperience during the primary, he now characterizes the Illinois senator as the right man at the right time. Using the refrain, "John McCain was wrong. Barack Obama was right," Biden lists a number of issues where he believes the latter's judgment had proven wiser than the former's, despite McCain's impressive resume and decades of government service.

Joe Biden's speech: Beau, I love you. I am so proud of you. Proud of the son you are. Proud of the father you've become. And I'm so proud of my son Hunter, my daughter Ashley, and my wife Jill, the only one who leaves me breathless and speechless at the same time.

It is an honor to share this stage tonight with President Clinton. And last night, it was moving to watch Hillary, one of the great leaders of our party, a woman who has made history and will continue to make history: my colleague and my friend, Senator Hillary Clinton.

And I am honored to represent our first state—my state—Delaware.

* Delivered on August, 27, 2008, at Denver, CO.

Since I've never been called a man of few words, let me say this as simply as I can: Yes. Yes, I accept your nomination to run and serve alongside our next President of the United States of America, Barack Obama.

Let me make this pledge to you right here and now. For every American who is trying to do the right thing, for all those people in government who are honoring their pledge to uphold the law and respect our Constitution, no longer will the eight most dreaded words in the English language be: "The vice president's office is on the phone."

Barack Obama and I took very different journeys to this destination, but we share a common story. Mine began in Scranton, Pennsylvania, and then Wilmington, Delaware. With a dad who fell on hard economic times, but who always told me: "Champ, when you get knocked down, get up. Get up."

I wish that my dad was here tonight, but I am so grateful that my mom, Catherine Eugenia Finnegan Biden, is here. You know, she taught her children—all the children who flocked to our house—that you are defined by your sense of honor, and you are redeemed by your loyalty. She believes bravery lives in every heart and her expectation is that it will be summoned.

Failure at some point in everyone's life is inevitable, but giving up is unforgivable. As a child I stuttered, and she lovingly told me it was because I was so bright I couldn't get the thoughts out quickly enough. When I was not as well dressed as others, she told me how handsome she thought I was. When I got knocked down by guys bigger than me, she sent me back out and demanded that I bloody their nose so I could walk down that street the next day.

After the accident, she told me, "Joey, God sends no cross you cannot bear." And when I triumphed, she was quick to remind me it was because of others.

My mother's creed is the American creed: No one is better than you. You are everyone's equal, and everyone is equal to you.

My parents taught us to live our faith, and treasure our family. We learned the dignity of work, and we were told that anyone can make it if they try.

That was America's promise. For those of us who grew up in middle-class neighborhoods like Scranton and Wilmington, that was the American dream and we knew it.

But today that American dream feels as if it's slowly slipping away. I don't need to tell you that. You feel it every single day in your own lives.

I've never seen a time when Washington has watched so many people get knocked down without doing anything to help them get back up. Almost every night, I take the train home to Wilmington, sometimes very late. As I look out the window at the homes we pass, I can almost hear what they're talking about at the kitchen table after they put the kids to bed.

Like millions of Americans, they're asking questions as profound as they are ordinary. Questions they never thought they would have to ask:

- Should mom move in with us now that dad is gone?
- Fifty, sixty, seventy dollars to fill up the car?
- Winter's coming. How we gonna pay the heating bills?

- Another year and no raise?
- Did you hear the company may be cutting our health care?
- Now, we owe more on the house than it's worth. How are we going to send the kids to college?
- How are we gonna be able to retire?

That's the America that George Bush has left us, and that's the future John McCain will give us. These are not isolated discussions among families down on their luck. These are common stories among middle-class people who worked hard and played by the rules on the promise that their tomorrows would be better than their yesterdays.

That promise is the bedrock of America. It defines who we are as a people. And now it's in jeopardy. I know it. You know it. But John McCain doesn't get it.

Barack Obama gets it. Like many of us, Barack worked his way up. His is a great American story.

You know, I believe the measure of a man isn't just the road he's traveled; it's the choices he's made along the way. Barack Obama could have done anything after he graduated from college. With all his talent and promise, he could have written his ticket to Wall Street. But that's not what he chose to do. He chose to go to Chicago. The South Side. There he met men and women who had lost their jobs. Their neighborhood was devastated when the local steel plant closed. Their dreams deferred. Their dignity shattered. Their self-esteem gone.

And he made their lives the work of his life. That's what you do when you've been raised by a single mom, who worked, went to school and raised two kids on her own. That's how you come to believe, to the very core of your being, that work is more than a paycheck. It's dignity. It's respect. It's about whether you can look your children in the eye and say: we're going to be ok.

Because Barack made that choice, 150,000 more children and parents have health care in Illinois. He fought to make that happen. And because Barack made that choice, working families in Illinois pay less taxes and more people have moved from welfare to the dignity of work. He got it done.

And when he came to Washington, I watched him hit the ground running, leading the fight to pass the most sweeping ethics reform in a generation. He reached across party lines to pass a law that helps keep nuclear weapons out of the hands of terrorists. And he moved Congress and the president to give our wounded veterans the care and dignity they deserve.

You can learn an awful lot about a man campaigning with him, debating him and seeing how he reacts under pressure. You learn about the strength of his mind, but even more importantly, you learn about the quality of his heart.

I watched how he touched people, how he inspired them, and I realized he has tapped into the oldest American belief of all: We don't have to accept a situation we cannot bear.

We have the power to change it. That's Barack Obama, and that's what he will do for this country. He'll change it.

John McCain is my friend. We've known each other for three decades. We've traveled the world together. It's a friendship that goes beyond politics. And the personal courage and heroism John demonstrated still amaze me.

But I profoundly disagree with the direction that John wants to take the country. For example, John thinks that during the Bush years "we've made great progress economically." I think it's been abysmal.

And in the Senate, John sided with President Bush 95 percent of the time. Give me a break. When John McCain proposes $200 billion in new tax breaks for corporate America, $1 billion alone for just eight of the largest companies, but no relief for 100 million American families, that's not change; that's more of the same.

Even today, as oil companies post the biggest profits in history—a half trillion dollars in the last five years—he wants to give them another $4 billion in tax breaks. But he voted time and again against incentives for renewable energy: solar, wind, biofuels. That's not change; that's more of the same.

Millions of jobs have left our shores, yet John continues to support tax breaks for corporations that send them there. That's not change; that's more of the same.

He voted 19 times against raising the minimum wage. For people who are struggling just to get to the next day, that's not change; that's more of the same.

And when he says he will continue to spend $10 billion a month in Iraq when Iraq is sitting on a surplus of nearly $80 billion, that's not change; that's more of the same.

The choice in this election is clear. These times require more than a good soldier; they require a wise leader, a leader who can deliver change—the change everybody knows we need.

Barack Obama will deliver that change. Barack Obama will reform our tax code. He'll cut taxes for 95 percent of the American people who draw a paycheck. That's the change we need.

Barack Obama will transform our economy by making alternative energy a genuine national priority, creating 5 million new jobs and finally freeing us from the grip of foreign oil. That's the change we need.

Barack Obama knows that any country that out teaches us today will out-compete us tomorrow. He'll invest in the next generation of teachers. He'll make college more affordable. That's the change we need.

Barack Obama will bring down health care costs by $2,500 for the typical family, and, at long last, deliver affordable, accessible health care for all Americans. That's the change we need.

Barack Obama will put more cops on the streets, put the "security" back in Social Security and never give up until we achieve equal pay for women. That's the change we need.

As we gather here tonight, our country is less secure and more isolated than at any time in recent history. The Bush-McCain foreign policy has dug us into a very deep hole with very few friends to help us climb out. For the last seven years, this administration has failed to face the biggest forces shaping this century: the emergence of Russia, China and India as great powers; the spread of lethal weapons; the shortage of secure supplies of energy, food and water; the challenge of climate change; and the resurgence of fundamentalism in Afghanistan and Pakistan, the real central front against terrorism.

In recent days, we've once again seen the consequences of this neglect with Russia's challenge to the free and democratic country of Georgia. Barack Obama and I will end this neglect. We will hold Russia accountable for its actions, and we'll help the people of Georgia rebuild.

I've been on the ground in Georgia, Iraq, Pakistan and Afghanistan, and I can tell you in no uncertain terms: this Administration's policy has been an abject failure. America cannot afford four more years of this.

Now, despite being complicit in this catastrophic foreign policy, John McCain says Barack Obama isn't ready to protect our national security. Now, let me ask you: whose judgment should we trust? Should we trust John McCain's judgment when he said only three years ago, "Afghanistan—we don't read about it anymore because it's succeeded"? Or should we trust Barack Obama, who more than a year ago called for sending two additional combat brigades to Afghanistan?

The fact is, al-Qaida and the Taliban—the people who actually attacked us on 9/11—have regrouped in those mountains between Afghanistan and Pakistan and are plotting new attacks. And the Chairman of the Joint Chiefs of Staff echoed Barack's call for more troops.

John McCain was wrong. Barack Obama was right.

Should we trust John McCain's judgment when he rejected talking with Iran and then asked: What is there to talk about? Or Barack Obama, who said we must talk and make it clear to Iran that its conduct must change.

Now, after seven years of denial, even the Bush administration recognizes that we should talk to Iran, because that's the best way to advance our security.

Again, John McCain was wrong. Barack Obama was right.

Should we trust John McCain's judgment when he says there can be no timelines to draw down our troops from Iraq—that we must stay indefinitely? Or should we listen to Barack Obama, who says shift responsibility to the Iraqis and set a time to bring our combat troops home?

Now, after six long years, the Bush administration and the Iraqi government are on the verge of setting a date to bring our troops home.

John McCain was wrong. Barack Obama was right.

Again and again, on the most important national security issues of our time, John McCain was wrong, and Barack Obama was proven right.

Folks, remember when the world used to trust us? When they looked to us for leadership? With Barack Obama as our president, they'll look to us again, they'll trust us again, and we'll be able to lead again.

Jill and I are truly honored to join Barack and Michelle on this journey. When I look at their young children—and when I look at my grandchildren—I realize why I'm here. I'm here for their future.

And I am here for everyone I grew up with in Scranton and Wilmington. I am here for the cops and firefighters, the teachers and assembly line workers—the folks whose lives are the very measure of whether the American dream endures.

Our greatest presidents—from Abraham Lincoln to Franklin Roosevelt to John Kennedy—they all challenged us to embrace change. Now, it's our responsibility to meet that challenge.

Millions of Americans have been knocked down. And this is the time as Americans, together, we get back up. Our people are too good, our debt to our parents and grandparents too great, our obligation to our children is too sacred.

These are extraordinary times. This is an extraordinary election. The American people are ready. I'm ready. Barack Obama is ready. This is his time. This is our time. This is America's time.

May God bless America and protect our troops.

Welcome to the Rally for the Republic and the Revolution[*]

Ron Paul

U.S. representative (R), Texas, 1997– ; born Pittsburgh, PA, August 20, 1935; B.S., Gettysburg College, 1957; captain, United States Air Force, 1963–65; flight surgeon, Air National Guard, 1965–68; M.D., Duke University, 1967; obstetrician-gynecologist, 1968–1996; candidate for U.S. House of Representatives, 1974; U.S. representative (R), Texas, 1976–77; U.S. representative (R), Texas, 1979–1985; ran for the U.S. Senate, 1984; 1988 Libertarian presidential nominee; candidate for 2008 Republican presidential nomination; congressional committees: House Financial Services, Foreign Affairs, Joint Economic; author, The Case for Gold: A Minority Report of the U.S. Gold Commission *(1982);* Abortion and Liberty *(1983);* Freedom Under Siege: The U.S. Constitution After 200 Years *(1987);* Challenge to Liberty: Coming to Grips with the Abortion Issue *(1990);* A Foreign Policy of Freedom*, (2007);* The Revolution: A Manifesto *(2008).*

Editor's introduction: While John McCain wore the maverick label throughout the 2008 presidential race, Congressman Ron Paul of Texas was at least his equal in bucking the status quo, leading an energetic long-shot bid for the Republican presidential nomination. Decrying what he considered American adventurism abroad and espousing a truly hands-off approach on the part of government toward the economy, Paul won a host of admirers and became the cult sensation of the 2008 campaign. Though he remained a Republican, Paul held his own "Rally for the Republic" convention at the Blaine National Sports Center in Blaine, Minnesota, in an attempt to upstage the Republican gathering in nearby St. Paul and draw attention to his concerns. In his speech, calling for a "revolution to save the Republic," Paul describes his governing philosophy and enumerates the dangers he sees threatening the country.

Ron Paul's speech: It's not much of an overstatement to say that everyone attending this Rally for the Republic knows that the American Republic hangs by a thread, and a thin one at that.

---

[*] Delivered on September 1, 2008, at Blaine, MN.

Every day the financial, political and foreign policy news verifies the crisis we face. The financial system teeters on collapse, our personal liberties continue to melt away, and the constant threat from foreign adversaries escalates daily. Yet, there's something exciting in the air. A revolutionary spirit has erupted and it will not be suppressed. We are indeed involved in an historic event.

It's been nearly two years since the presidential exploratory committee was formed, yet despite my strong reservations at the time, much has been accomplished. The Revolution to save the Republic has been ignited. It was a revolution in waiting. The campaign became the catalyst that excited millions who, in their own quiet way, were already working diligently to save our Constitution, preserve our liberties, and reject outright the notion of an American world empire.

Not only was I surprised at the reception for the ideas of liberty, the establishment was shocked because of the millions who were responding. The response from those who feared a challenge to the status quo, controlled by the special interests, was silence, ridicule, and marginalization. But that treatment was only met with energized determination to spread the message using the internet, radio, short-wave, letter writing, campaigning, and by word of mouth and through music. I've always been convinced that any movement of significance would have two things: the involvement of young people and creative music. And we have both.

Though the revolutionary spirit was much stronger than I ever dreamed, the growth that continues is truly inspiring. It is clear to me that people are hurting financially; they are deeply concerned about their freedom; and they are sick and tired of paying for a failed foreign policy. They indeed are demanding change and it's a change that only we can provide. When others offer change, it's only a political reaction to a demand that they cannot ignore.

The future of the Republic is bleak. As conditions deteriorate those in charge use the problems they created to solidify their power with more spending, taxes, rules, inflation, and militarism. This must be reversed or tyranny will triumph and the grand experiment of the American Republic will end.

During the past two years, a lot of us have been excited to find so many other like-minded individuals who have been just waiting to join an organized effort to challenge the corrupt power structure that is controlling our country. Not only that, but tens of thousands of young people have excitedly joined the effort after realizing that what they're getting handed to them is not a system of opportunity, but a broken system plagued with a debt that they'll be expected to pay.

No one knows the exact number of people involved, but it's huge and growing. The Republic can be saved. It will be difficult, but it can't be saved without an army of enthusiastic revolutionaries who know and understand exactly what this struggle is all about. There's every reason to be more optimistic today than two years ago. The support is out there and it is ready to be tapped.

I want to acknowledge my deep appreciation for the confidence you placed in me in helping to spread this message. Without your encouragement, financial support, and hard work, there would not have been a campaign of note. The revolution would still have come, but I'm pleased to have been part of speeding up the process. The task before us is continuing and building on this momentum.

We can expect many obstacles to be placed in our way. Though we preach non-violence, our opponents who feel threatened, will not hesitate to use force against us. Since the opposition is the state, using the armed might of government to stifle our effort should not surprise us. Recent changes in the law voiding protection of our civil liberties since 9/11, make it quite convenient for hostile government agents to undermine our right to speak out and protest.

Although this struggle is difficult, we know that ultimately ideas are superior to brute force and can penetrate where armies and police are unable to go. For that reason we should remain optimistic and continue our effort, since doing nothing is unacceptable and guarantees failure.

Responsibility falls on each and every one of us — much more so on those who come to know the truth and can convince others of the moral correctness and benefits of Liberty.

To get us out of this mess, we must first understand how we got ourselves into it and then proceed to correct the problems.

HOW AND WHY WE LOST THE REPUBLIC

The simplest explanation comes from the early warning that the survival of freedom requires a moral people. Absent this, the Constitution has no meaning, no matter how well written. But the immorality of a political system hinges on those who seek power or largess and are supported by a false ideology justifying the forced wealth transfer known as "legal plunder." Along with a negligent or complicit electorate, this sets the stage for the undermining of the Republic.

Although those who hunger for power are small in numbers, it's easy to entice the masses into believing that government can provide for everyone's needs and safety. Yet the others who continue to produce are misled into believing that they must accept the system or be labeled selfish and lacking compassion. To do this, they accept the idea that a person's needs, desires or demands equate to rights. Thus we hear from those who say they object to the welfare/socialist state that they nevertheless accept the fact that the few truly in need deserve help from the government. They claim it's only the abuse of the system that must be stopped. This concedes the intellectual and moral argument that a need is equal to a right and now is referred to as an "entitlement." No one should be entitled or have a right to someone else's labor. This idea opens the door to the special interests to manipulate the system to their advantage at the expense of all others. Without this understanding liberty cannot survive.

Even though the Constitution was written to keep power from being placed in the hands of the few, the apathy of the people and the belief that they may benefit from such a system allows the centralization of power to continue.

It has been said that power for some is an aphrodisiac and it feeds on itself, even after those in charge have adequately stolen enough to be comfortable for the rest of their lives. There are some who are quite content to use government to increase their wealth without directly wielding power. Well-connected lobbyists seek influence to enhance their economic well-being without running for office or becoming a figurehead with authority.

Ignorance of how the economy works significantly contributes to central economic planning by the politicians, bureaucrats and central bankers. The major reason for this is that government schools do not teach free-market economics.

These same schools teach that it's an outdated notion to strictly adhere to the Constitution. They claim the Constitution must be a living, breathing document, capable of adapting to modern times. They assume that there are no long-lasting truths, such as might be found in the Bill of Rights. It should surprise no one that constitutional restraint on the federal government is nonexistent. It no longer is seen as an instrument to restrain the government, but instead is constantly distorted to justify restraining the people in all their activities and travels.

Distortion of history influences the thinking of almost everyone with a government education. War presidents are always portrayed as the greatest presidents—Lincoln, Wilson, Roosevelt. The economic ideas that are taught are always Keynesian or socialist. Ideas on banking always support central banking and never commodity money, as mandated by the Constitution. This problem only gets worse as every aspect of public schools is more controlled by the Congress, federal bureaucrats, the Department of Education and the federal courts. The Republic cannot be saved without addressing this issue of education.

The idea is well-entrenched that if one supports free markets, private property, commodity money, no Federal Reserve, no income tax, no welfare and no foreign militarism, one cannot be a humanitarian concerned about the well-being of all citizens. The truth is exactly the opposite. Although the socialist/welfare state may be supported by some who are truly concerned about their fellow man, there is no evidence that any system can provide more prosperity for the greatest number than a system based on individual liberty.

The idea of patriotism has been grossly distorted. Too often, if one does not support unconstitutional aggression it is said that he is unpatriotic, un-American, and doesn't support the troops. It is assumed today that a patriot is one who is blindly obedient to the government—right or wrong. But the people and the government are not the same. Support for freedom and the Constitution compels the patriot to challenge the government when it goes wrong. That means today a true patriot must challenge our government at every step of the way. The original American patriots were hardly the ones that were steadfastly loyal to the King—despite his abuse of the rights of the American colonists.

We are expected to believe that freedom is old-fashioned and must be rejected. It's claimed that modern times require a centralized government with power placed in the hands of the few. This is completely false. Freedom, as protected by our Constitution, is a new idea in the historical sense. It's been tried and found to be amazingly successful in producing great abundance, yet the notion that it's outdated permeates our society. What is old is the idea of tyranny. We must never be willing to give up the principles of individual liberty; instead we must convince people that progress depends on advancing even further this concept rather than succumbing to the ancient idea of political power residing in the hands of a few.

Personal freedom and economic freedom cannot remain separate. If we have a right to our lives, we have a right to live our lives as we chose and to keep the fruits of our labor. These two rights are the same.

We must forever eliminate the notion that a tax reduction is a cost to government. That notion is based on the assumption that everything we earn belongs to the government and the government decides what portion we're allowed to keep. This is why today our lives, the fruits of our labor, and all our property are controlled by the state and we must get permission for everything we do.

This is equivalent to prior restraint. This would not sit well with a journalist in reporting and writing opinions and should not sit well with any of us who are tired of being constantly spied on and monitored in every transaction we make and needing to get permission for our every move.

One of the most dangerous ideas that has undermined the Republic, and one which a majority of the American people have come to accept, is that of preventive war. This is another name for aggression and allowing wars for perceived or imagined dangers. Tragically the Congress is complicit, failing to take responsibility to declare or reject war and instead obediently funding the wars the President starts out of fear of being called unpatriotic. We are bogged down in Iraq and Afghanistan and we're about to spread our military commitment to taking on Iran and maybe even getting involved in the Russian/Georgia dispute, in spite of the fact that no Arab or Muslim nation has posed a threat to us. We're fighting third-world nations, 6,000 miles from our shore, who have no military force of note. Iran spends 1% of what we spend on our military operation, and they can't even refine their own gasoline. Yet our government tells us that they are equivalent to Nazi Germany pre-World War II.

Too many American believe that war is good for the economy, which is a completely false assumption, and many believe our presence in the Middle East is required to protect "our" oil. The truth is "war is the health of the state" and the profiteers. War always hurts the economy. General Smedley Butler correctly said that "war is a racket," serving American business interests.

Our carelessness with the Constitution and wit hallowing our elected leaders to sell us a bill of goods has allowed the special interests to take over the government for their benefit. This is not inherent in free-market capitalism but a predictable outcome of interventionist economic and foreign policy. It's not capitalism; it's corporatism drifting toward fascism. This system permits those inclined to abuse power for their own selfish purposes and egos to undermine the whole notion of individual freedom. Without an understanding of these flaws a reversal of current trends is impossible.

We must never forget that the internal threats to liberties have always been of greater danger to us than the external threats. The internal threats obviously come from abuse of government power.

National sovereignty is not a great concern for most Americans. Our drift toward internationalism has diminished our interest in maintaining our borders and this has diminished the importance of our Constitution as a protector of our liberties. International courts, the UN, the IMF, the World Bank, the WTO, and NAFTA and CAFTA and regional governments like NAU and the European Union are generally accepted by a majority of Americans with little concern. A republic does not thrive under these conditions; instead liberty is always compromised.

THE CONSEQUENCES

The Republic was not lost precipitously. It's been gradual and insidious, thus making it more palatable and less noticeable. Although the Republic has been destroyed, prosperity has persisted due to our ability to borrow and inflate, based on our past laurels. The superficial prosperity has conditioned many to care little for their lost liberties and the disappearance of the Republic.

But the serious consequences are less evident. We're in a mess. Debt at all levels is growing exponentially. Inflation is rearing its ugly head, reducing the standard of living of most Americans.

The foreign policy of empire building has given us perpetual war while undermining our own national security. We have more enemies and fewer allies than ever. Our troops are spread across the world, and dissent is increasing here at home. The foreign policy and economic failures are a cause for concern here at home—an attitude that perpetuates violence and competition for the control of a government which becomes more aggressive against its citizens daily. The failure of government at all levels has become more obvious, precipitating the demand for change.

Osama bin Laden is pleased with our response to 9/11 and desperately wants us to stay in Iraq and Afghanistan. It verifies all his assertions about America's intentions and serves his recruiting efforts.

Some claim that all our problems stem from radical Islamists who want to kill us because of their religious beliefs. That's a cop-out. A few might like to, but to enlist a suicide bomber there has to be a strong incentive-like occupation by a foreign power.

The religious conflict that motivates al Qaeda is between the radicals and secular Muslims. The fundamentalists highly resent our support for secular puppets in countries like Saudi Arabia to secure access to oil. They see we're setting up the same type of government in Iraq and Afghanistan with plans to do the same in Iran.

This is the issue—it's not the clash of civilization as we've been told. It's not the Muslims against the Christians and Jews. Suicide terrorists have been radicalized by our occupation of their countries that they view as holy land.

These reactions are logical once one understands what causes the hatred to boil over. Without this understanding don't expect our presence in the Middle East to ever bring peace and tranquility to the region. Nor will the oil ever be secure for the West.

The war on drugs has been a total failure and has wasted hundreds of billions of dollars. It has been used as an excuse to undermine our liberties while wasting time and money arresting and incarcerating tens of thousands of individuals who have never committed a violent crime. It has motivated Congress to pass laws forcing mandatory minimum sentences, cluttering our courts and prisons with non-violent individuals while violent criminals get off on technicalities. We live in a country where the federal government can't even resist regulating the consumption of raw milk.

Although we generally still recognize that citizens here have a right to decide what to put into their minds and souls the assumption is that only government can tell us what we can ingest or smoke. Government has assumed the role of parent in the runaway nanny state.

We need to talk more of our alliance with those whose main issue is the environment. Property rights, the market economy and the Constitution are friends of the environment. In a free society, no one has the right to pollute or damage a neighbor's land, water, or air. Collusion between the government and corporations has allowed pollution that would not be permissible in a society with strict protection of property rights. Government, over the years, since the Industrial Revolution, has been complicit in many of the problems we have today. This is one reason that I don't place a lot of confidence in the regulatory approach to protecting the environment. Special interests get special treatment. Also consider the Pentagon's contribution to pollution through unnecessary wars and huge consumption of hydro carbon energy.

PRACTICAL ANSWERS

Our answers are not complex, although they are considered radical by those who want to maintain power. But how can they get away with labeling common sense as extreme or kooky, as they so often do. When government needs money, they print some. That sounds kooky to me, as does huge deficits, and totally ignoring the Constitution. No income tax makes a lot of sense to many Americans. Protecting privacy is an American tradition. Respecting the Rule of Law and the Constitution should never be ridiculed as being silly and regressive, as so many do.

Local government is far superior to strong federal controls. Local and private schools have always proven to be superior to government run schools especially when they are run by the federal government.

There's no reason we can't restore the tradition of American neutrality in the affairs of the world. It makes no sense for us to be involved in the internal affairs of other nations. Nor is there a need for us to be the politician of the world. Our presence in the Middle East to guarantee a steady flow of oil from that region is a miscalculation of monumental proportions, since we get the opposite results. Private property, sound money, respect for all voluntary economic and social contracts, and rejecting the notion of wealth transfer through legislative fiat needed to restore our liberties and prosperity.

PHILOSOPHIC ANSWERS

Since the problems we face are a result of rejecting the principles of liberty and our Constitution, the answers should be apparent to everyone. Restore and improve on the freedom revolution started by the Founders of this country.

We do need change—lots of it. But it has to be the right kind of change or it will only make things worse.

The mess we're in guarantees that we will have change eventually. The status quo cannot be maintained. Tyranny is on its way unless we use this opportunity to reenergize the freedom movement and reinstate the Rule of Law that guarantees our liberties in a Constitutional Republic.

The Constitution must once again be used as an instrument to restrain the government, not the people. Creative energy must be allowed to thrive without the heavy hand of government monitoring every move.

Some say man's problems result from a persistent class struggle; others say ours is a cultural war. The conflicts that seem to be permanent and unavoidable are nothing more than a consequence of government abuse of power. When outsiders were less involved in the Middle East and the local people determined relationships, Jews, Christians, and Muslims were more capable of living peaceably side by side. Not today. Iraq is also an example of how outside interference makes problems worse.

Let there be no doubt that freedom brings people together, authoritarianism divides us and generates class, religious, gender, generational, social, cultural, and racial conflicts. If we continue to try to solve all human conflicts by more rules, regulations, threats and taxes, our divisions will only grow. Freedom provides the answers.

Truth and the love of liberty are far superior to the illicit use of government power.

Ideas, peaceful persuasion, the principle of the right of self determination are better tools in both domestic and foreign affairs. Armies of individuals with correct ideas can reach places that conventional armies cannot. Ideas and revolutions whose time has come cannot be stopped by governments or the status quo.

We must never forget that freedom is the catalyst of all creative energy.

Our competitors are now intellectually and financially bankrupt which should make our job easier every day.

Some worry that our numbers are small compared to the majority that remains complacent about the current system of welfarism, corporatism, and militarism. But revolutions are never driven by a solid majority. Instead they are led by a small number of dedicated individuals working in unity for a cause. We benefit because our cause is freedom. It brings people from all walks of life together. This means there are no victims. We work together to achieve the right to run our own lives as we see fit and assume responsibility for ourselves and be permitted to keep and spend the fruits of our labor.

Knowing that these ideas guarantee a greater chance for peace and prosperity than any other system of government certainly generates the enthusiasm for the Revolution.

With this enthusiasm, and unity we can influence the majority to eventually join—or at least not obstruct—the Revolution. The failure of the current system will prompt many to look to us for answers to problems we face.

There are many parts in the world that provide a fertile field for this message as well. The campaign message, to my complete surprise and pleasure actually reached many around the world—thanks to modern technology. A tremendous opportunity has arrived for spreading of the message of liberty far and wide.

The question of civil disobedience is of great importance. I personally don't want to participate in any acts of violence or set the stage where violence will easily break out. But we're nearing the point where all of us who are struggling to bring about change will have to make a decision regarding civil disobedience.

A gradual transition through elections and persuasion should be our goal. Realistically, that is not likely to bring satisfactory results quickly. An economic crisis and political chaos are a more likely scenario. That is when we are most likely to participate in a rebuilding and remaking of the American Republic.

Already many Americans practice civil disobedience. Some are outwardly at risk and have suffered for it. Protesters of our monetary and tax system on constitutional grounds are legitimate yet we do know that the state will use armed might to arrest and imprison those who make any headway in revealing the truth.

When the military draft is in effect—something which is still a possibility—many will have to make the decision to resist or not. Many have suffered over the years resisting a draft and today many have resisted our unconstitutional war in Iraq and now face imprisonment.

I can conceive of the day when the decision regarding civil disobedience will be of paramount importance. It will always be an individual choice, but history has shown that peaceful resistance to government injustice is a powerful weapon. Gandhi and Martin Luther King showed that this process can bring about a lot of positive changes.

Revolutions are not equivalent to reforming a political party. A successful revolution will reform all parties, possibly with one leading the way.

Ideas are pervasive and spread spontaneously and, when acceptable, influence everyone. There's nothing wrong working within the Republican Party and I endorse and encourage this. It's hard to ignore the fact that I've been elected 10 times to Congress as a Republican. But there should not be hostility toward those who seek opportunities in any party. The goal is to spread the message in every way possible. As a matter of fact, if the ideas didn't invade all political factions, it would not be a true revolution. Economic planning, inflationism, Keynesianism, foreign interventionism, empire building, legislating morality, all have been endorsed by mainstream politicians in both parties for decades. That's why the power brokers are not threatened by either candidate in our presidential elections of recent decades. What needs to be done is to replace the principle of illicit use of government force with the principles of individual liberty.

Ironically, people with evil motives, whose goals are to perpetuate dangerous government power, have been quite successful in appealing to the idealism of good people. They are experts in deception. There's no reason why we can't appeal to these good people, without deception, with a program of peace, prosperity and freedom.

Over the years I have argued that the two weakest arguments to be used on the House floor are moral and constitutional. The strongest is to list the special interests who support a particular piece of legislation. The Revolution must change this attitude.

Over the course of my study of politics and economics, I found that one of the greatest evils that has been perpetrated by our presidents was the use of war to promote their personal political agenda. The willingness to use war to enhance their political position has led to the death of many innocent people and many of those have been American soldiers. There have also been presidents who have been quite willing to violate civil liberties while claiming to make us safe and free, an attitude that has been catastrophically dangerous to us since 9/11.

JFK was said to have feared being labeled a dove by the Republicans in the election of 1964 and escalated the Vietnam War to prove otherwise. He said then after he won the election he would de-escalate and bring our troops home because he really did not support the war. This was an atrocious act.

Leading up to the 1968 election, LBJ massively escalated the war in order to "win," believing it would be impossible to win the election without a military victory. He didn't want to be the first president to lose a war—the necessity or moral justification for the war was irrelevant. Deliberate efforts by both Wilson and Roosevelt to manipulate us into war have been well documented.

And now we have an administration that uses "total victory" as a political ploy to play on the patriotism of the people. Wanting to play the ancient role of the great warrior, today's politicians pump up the need for war in Iraq, Afghanistan, and Iran and now hints of escalation of our presence and interference in Georgia—just looking for another fight.

The current administration should disavow any plan to escalate the conflict in the Middle East or Central Asia with an October surprise designed to benefit John McCain and sway the election to the more radical neo conservatives.

The most disturbing reaction in the Campaign was the hostility some evangelical Christians showed toward our strong opposition to preemptive war—which is essentially a war of aggression.

How it's possible to profess to follow the Prince of Peace, and at the same time support preventive war, is totally baffling to me. However, I received strong support from many evangelicals who support home schooling. They respect the Constitution and oppose preventive wars like me and are strong supporters of home schooling. I stand fast in opposition to abortion, and I found it disappointing that some evangelicals would rather support a candidate weak on the abortion issue and home schooling as long as the candidate supports war over diplomacy. When it comes to the Middle East, Israel was a key factor in their decision making.

The current civil war breaking out in Georgia and dragging in the Russians is closely related to our policy of foreign military interventionism. Our money and troops have trained the Georgian army to provoke the Russians. We're there to protect a vital pipeline running from the Caspian Sea to Turkey and we prod NATO to join in our empire building by bringing Georgia into NATO. Our obsession with putting anti-ballistic missiles in Eastern Europe has nothing to do with defending America. It has more to do with resurrecting the Cold War. Our insistence on doing so and having troops in countries like Georgia is doing nothing more than provoking a fight with Russia—exactly what would delight the war mongering neo-cons. Fighting in Georgia is not worth one American life.

Only a total overhaul of our foreign policy can prevent us from getting ourselves into so much trouble and neither of the two major candidates offers us a solution.

Ultimately, it is the use of force that determines the advancement of civilization. Brute force and the survival of the fittest are the least civilized. Using force only as a defense against those who initiate force shows society is advancing. If government is granted a monopoly over the use of force, even if given to stop the evil doers, it nevertheless sets the stage for the destruction of civilization. When force is restrained by individuals and government, society becomes more productive as was the case in our early history.

The world is threatened once again by those who use government force to undermine the benefits of civilization while serving the powerful elites. They always claim they are only trying to help the poor.

Insecure politicians cling to the notion that only the warrior can stabilize a country by killing, robbing and enslaving their enemy, and they demand war and militarism to solve all the world's problems. Today, instead of depending upon the market to produce the energy we need, we send our armies to protect "our" oil in the Middle East and the Caspian Sea, all in the name of serving mankind.

Advancing civilization depends on this understanding of the use of force. If current attitudes of the political leaders of our country are not changed in this regard, the future looks bleak. It need not be. Freedom provides the answer.

SEND A MESSAGE

We're here today to send a message, not just to the Republican Party, not just to the politicians in power, but to the whole country, and possibly the entire world.

The power brokers are convinced they can maintain control with no serious challenge. They have it wrong. We will challenge them on all fronts—in every state and at all levels of government. First of all, the philosophic revolution will propel the political revolution. The educational effort will spread the message of the Freedom Philosophy. Individual liberty must be our goal. Prosperity and peace will follow. Without liberty, peace and prosperity are unachievable.

Without liberty, all we have are the leeches and looters fighting over the spoils that the victims are required to produce. This rotten system of redistribution must end. And it will, because victims of authoritarian rule eventually quit being victimized. War and domestic violence always complicate matters once the moral defense of individual rights is rejected.

Endless war and economic pain never pacifies the people. We must prevail, for once the people demand change, there will be lots of counterfeit offers for change—all of which will make conditions worse.

Change for the sake of change but not doing the right thing is pure folly. Our Revolution for the Republic must prevail. And it will!

Speech at the Republican National Convention[*]

Sarah Palin

Governor (R) of Alaska, 2006– ; born Sand Point, ID, February 11, 1964; winner, Miss Wasilla, AK, pageant, 1984; first runner up, Miss Alaska pageant, 1984; B.S., University of Idaho, communications-journalism, 1987; sports reporter, KTUU-TV, KTVA-TV, Anchorage, AK, 1988; member, Wasilla, city council, 1992–96; mayor, Wasilla, 1996–2002; chairwoman, Alaska Oil and Gas Conservation Commission, 2003–04.

Editor's introduction: Largely unknown outside of Alaska, Governor Sarah Palin became a national figure overnight in August 2008, when Senator John McCain of Arizona chose her as his running mate in his campaign for the presidency. Palin was kept relatively secluded from the press in the days that followed the initial announcement, allowing rumor and innuendo to flourish. When she finally took the dais at the Republican National Convention at the XCel Energy Center to accept the vice presidential nomination, few knew what to anticipate. Interrupted repeatedly by boisterous applause, Palin offered a rousing endorsement of McCain's candidacy and a pointed rebuke to the Democratic aspirant, Senator Barack Obama, taking aim at his professional background, eloquence, and supposed elitism. Mixing a folksy delivery with a razor-sharp wit, she describes the contest between McCain and Obama as a choice between "a gifted speaker [who] can inspire with his words," and "a man [who] has inspired with his deeds." While many blamed Palin in part for McCain's eventual loss in the 2008 election, her speech rallied the party's base, which up until that point had failed to embrace McCain's candidacy, and helped propel the Republican ticket to a short-lived lead in the polls.

Sarah Palin's speech: Mr. Chairman, delegates, and fellow citizens, I will be honored to accept your nomination for vice president of the United States.

    (APPLAUSE)

---

[*] Delivered on September 3, 2008, at St. Paul, MN.

I accept the call to help our nominee for president to serve and defend America. And I accept the challenge of a tough fight in this election against confident opponents at a crucial hour for our country.

And I accept the privilege of serving with a man who has come through much harder missions, and met far graver challenges, and knows how tough fights are won, the next president of the United States, John S. McCain.

(APPLAUSE)

It was just a year ago when all the experts in Washington counted out our nominee because he refused to hedge his commitment to the security of the country he loves.

With their usual certitude, they told us that all was lost, there was no hope for this candidate, who said that he would rather lose an election than see his country lose a war. But the pollsters . . .

The pollsters and the pundits, they overlooked just one thing when they wrote him off. They overlooked the caliber of the man himself, the determination, and resolve, and the sheer guts of Senator John McCain.

The voters knew better, and maybe that's because they realized there's a time for politics and a time for leadership, a time to campaign and a time to put our country first.

Our nominee for president is a true profile in courage, and people like that are hard to come by. He's a man who wore the uniform of his country for 22 years and refused to break faith with those troops in Iraq who now have brought victory within sight.

(APPLAUSE)

And as the mother of one of those troops, that is exactly the kind of man I want as commander in chief.

I'm just one of many moms who will say an extra prayer each night for our sons and daughters going into harm's way. Our son, Track, is 19. And one week from tomorrow, September 11th, he'll deploy to Iraq with the Army infantry in the service of his country.

My nephew, Casey (ph), also enlisted and serves on a carrier in the Persian Gulf.

My family is so proud of both of them and of all the fine men and women serving the country in uniform.

(APPLAUSE)

(AUDIENCE: USA! USA! USA! USA! USA!)

So Track is the eldest of our five children. In our family, it's two boys and three girls in between, my strong and kind-hearted daughters, Bristol, and Willow, and Piper.

(APPLAUSE)

And we were so blessed in April. Todd and I welcomed our littlest one into the world, a perfectly beautiful baby boy named Trig.

You know, from the inside, no family ever seems typical, and that's how it is with us. Our family has the same ups and downs as any other, the same challenges and the same joys.

Sometimes even the greatest joys bring challenge. And children with special needs inspire a very, very special love. To the families of special-needs . . .

(APPLAUSE)

To the families of special-needs children all across this country, I have a message for you: For years, you've sought to make America a more welcoming place for your sons and daughters. And I pledge to you that, if we're elected, you will have a friend and advocate in the White House.

(APPLAUSE)

And Todd is a story all by himself. He's a lifelong commercial fisherman and a production operator in the oil fields of Alaska's North Slope, and a proud member of the United Steelworkers union. And Todd is a world champion snow machine racer.

(APPLAUSE)

Throw in his Yup'ik Eskimo ancestry, and it all makes for quite a package. And we met in high school. And two decades and five children later, he's still my guy.

(APPLAUSE)

My mom and dad both worked at the elementary school in our small town. And among the many things I owe them is a simple lesson that I've learned, that this is America, and every woman can walk through every door of opportunity.

And my parents are here tonight.

(APPLAUSE)

I am so proud to be the daughter of Chuck and Sally Heath (ph).

(APPLAUSE)

Long ago, a young farmer and a haberdasher from Missouri, he followed an unlikely path—he followed an unlikely path to the vice presidency. And a writer observed, "We grow good people in our small towns, with honesty and sincerity and dignity," and I know just the kind of people that writer had in mind when he praised Harry Truman.

I grew up with those people. They're the ones who do some of the hardest work in America, who grow our food, and run our factories, and fight our wars. They love their country in good times and bad, and they're always proud of America.

(APPLAUSE)

I had the privilege of living most of my life in a small town. I was just your average hockey mom and signed up for the PTA.

(APPLAUSE)

I love those hockey moms. You know, they say the difference between a hockey mom and a pit bull? Lipstick.

(APPLAUSE)

So I signed up for the PTA because I wanted to make my kids' public education even better. And when I ran for city council, I didn't need focus groups and voter profiles because I knew those voters, and I knew their families, too.

Before I became governor of the great state of Alaska . . .

(APPLAUSE)

. . . I was mayor of my hometown. And since our opponents in this presidential election seem to look down on that experience, let me explain to them what the job involved.

(APPLAUSE)

I guess—I guess a small-town mayor is sort of like a community organizer, except that you have actual responsibilities.

(APPLAUSE)

I might add that, in small towns, we don't quite know what to make of a candidate who lavishes praise on working people when they're listening and then talks about how bitterly they cling to their religion and guns when those people aren't listening.

(APPLAUSE)

No, we tend to prefer candidates who don't talk about us one way in Scranton and another way in San Francisco.

(APPLAUSE)

As for my running mate, you can be certain that wherever he goes and whoever is listening, John McCain is the same man.

(APPLAUSE)

Well, I'm not a member of the permanent political establishment. And . . .

(APPLAUSE)

. . . I've learned quickly these last few days that, if you're not a member in good standing of the Washington elite, then some in the media consider a candidate unqualified for that reason alone.

(AUDIENCE BOOS)

But—now, here's a little newsflash. Here's a little newsflash for those reporters and commentators: I'm not going to Washington to seek their good opinion. I'm going to Washington to serve the people of this great country.

(APPLAUSE)

Americans expect us to go to Washington for the right reason and not just to mingle with the right people. Politics isn't just a game of clashing parties and competing interests. The right reason is to challenge the status quo, to serve the common good, and to leave this nation better than we found it.

(APPLAUSE)

No one expects us all to agree on everything, but we are expected to govern with integrity, and goodwill, and clear convictions, and a servant's heart.

And I pledge to all Americans that I will carry myself in this spirit as vice president of the United States.

(APPLAUSE)

This was the spirit that brought me to the governor's office when I took on the old politics as usual in Juneau, when I stood up to the special interests, and the lobbyists, and the Big Oil companies, and the good old boys.

Suddenly, I realized that sudden and relentless reform never sits well with entrenched interests and power-brokers. That's why true reform is so hard to achieve.

But with the support of the citizens of Alaska, we shook things up. And in short order, we put the government of our state back on the side of the people.

(APPLAUSE)

I came to office promising major ethics reform to end the culture of self-dealing. And today, that ethics reform is a law.

While I was at it, I got rid of a few things in the governor's office that I didn't believe our citizens should have to pay for. That luxury jet was over-the-top.

(APPLAUSE)

I put it on eBay.

(APPLAUSE)

I love to drive myself to work. And I thought we could muddle through without the governor's personal chef, although I got to admit that sometimes my kids sure miss her.

(APPLAUSE)

I came to office promising to control spending, by request if possible, but by veto, if necessary.

(APPLAUSE)

Senator McCain also—he promises to use the power of veto in defense of the public interest. And as a chief executive, I can assure you it works.

(APPLAUSE)

Our state budget is under control. We have a surplus. And I have protected the taxpayers by vetoing wasteful spending, nearly $500 million in vetoes.

(APPLAUSE)

We suspended the state fuel tax and championed reform to end the abuses of earmark spending by Congress. I told the Congress, "Thanks, but no thanks," on that Bridge to Nowhere.

(APPLAUSE)

If our state wanted to build a bridge, we were going to build it ourselves.

(APPLAUSE)

When oil and gas prices went up dramatically and filled up the state treasury, I sent a large share of that revenue back where it belonged: directly to the people of Alaska.

(APPLAUSE)

And despite fierce opposition from oil company lobbyists, who kind of liked things the way that they were, we broke their monopoly on power and resources. As governor, I insisted on competition and basic fairness to end their control of our state and return it to the people.

(APPLAUSE)

I fought to bring about the largest private-sector infrastructure project in North American history. And when that deal was struck, we began a nearly $40 billion natural gas pipeline to help lead America to energy independence.

(APPLAUSE)

That pipeline, when the last section is laid and its valves are open, will lead America one step farther away from dependence on dangerous foreign powers that do not have our interests at heart.

The stakes for our nation could not be higher. When a hurricane strikes in the Gulf of Mexico, this country should not be so dependent on imported oil that we're forced to draw from our Strategic Petroleum Reserve. And families cannot throw away more and more of their paychecks on gas and heating oil.

With Russia wanting to control a vital pipeline in the Caucasus and to divide and intimidate our European allies by using energy as a weapon, we cannot leave ourselves at the mercy of foreign suppliers.

(APPLAUSE)

To confront the threat that Iran might seek to cut off nearly a fifth of the world's energy supplies, or that terrorists might strike again at the Abqaiq facility in Saudi Arabia, or that Venezuela might shut off its oil discoveries and its deliveries of that source, Americans, we need to produce more of our own oil and gas. And . . .

(APPLAUSE)

And take it from a gal who knows the North Slope of Alaska: We've got lots of both.

(APPLAUSE)

Our opponents say again and again that drilling will not solve all of America's energy problems, as if we didn't know that already.

(LAUGHTER)

But the fact that drilling, though, won't solve every problem is no excuse to do nothing at all.

(APPLAUSE)

Starting in January, in a McCain-Palin administration, we're going to lay more pipelines, and build more nuclear plants, and create jobs with clean coal, and move forward on solar, wind, geothermal, and other alternative sources. We need . . .

(APPLAUSE)

We need American sources of resources. We need American energy brought to you by American ingenuity and produced by American workers.

(APPLAUSE)

And now, I've noticed a pattern with our opponent, and maybe you have, too. We've all heard his dramatic speeches before devoted followers, and there is much to like and admire about our opponent.

But listening to him speak, it's easy to forget that this is a man who has authored two memoirs but not a single major law or even a reform, not even in the State Senate.

(APPLAUSE)

This is a man who can give an entire speech about the wars America is fighting and never use the word "victory," except when he's talking about his own campaign.

(APPLAUSE)

But when the cloud of rhetoric has passed, when the roar of the crowd fades away, when the stadium lights go out, and those Styrofoam Greek columns are hauled back to some studio lot . . .

(APPLAUSE)

. . . when that happens, what exactly is our opponent's plan? What does he actually seek to accomplish after he's done turning back the waters and healing the planet?

(APPLAUSE)

The answer—the answer is to make government bigger, and take more of your money, and give you more orders from Washington, and to reduce the strength of America in a dangerous world.

(AUDIENCE BOOS)

America needs more energy; our opponent is against producing it. Victory in Iraq is finally in sight, and he wants to forfeit. Terrorist states are seeking nuclear weapons without delay; he wants to meet them without preconditions.

Al Qaida terrorists still plot to inflict catastrophic harm on America, and he's worried that someone won't read them their rights.

(APPLAUSE)

Government is too big; he wants to grow it. Congress spends too much money; he promises more. Taxes are too high, and he wants to raise them. His tax increases are the fine print in his economic plan.

And let me be specific: The Democratic nominee for president supports plans to raise income taxes, and raise payroll taxes, and raise investment income taxes, and raise the death tax, and raise business taxes, and increase the tax burden on the American people by hundreds of billions of dollars.

(AUDIENCE BOOS)

My sister, Heather, and her husband, they just built a service station that's now open for business, like millions of others who run small businesses. How are they . . .

(APPLAUSE)

How are they going to be better off if taxes go up? Or maybe you are trying to keep your job at a plant in Michigan or in Ohio . . .

(APPLAUSE)

. . . or you're trying—you're trying to create jobs from clean coal, from Pennsylvania or West Virginia.

(APPLAUSE)

You're trying to keep a small farm in the family right here in Minnesota.

(APPLAUSE)

How are you—how are you going to be better off if our opponent adds a massive tax burden to the American economy?

Here's how I look at the choice Americans face in this election: In politics, there are some candidates who use change to promote their careers, and then there are those, like John McCain, who use their careers to promote change.

(APPLAUSE)

They are the ones whose names appear on laws and landmark reforms, not just on buttons and banners or on self-designed presidential seals.

(APPLAUSE)

Among politicians, there is the idealism of high-flown speech-making, in which crowds are stirringly summoned to support great things, and then there is the idealism of those leaders, like John McCain, who actually do great things.

(APPLAUSE)

They're the ones who are good for more than talk, the ones that we've always been able to count on to serve and to defend America.

Senator McCain's record of actual achievements and reform helps explain why so many special interests, and lobbyists, and comfortable committee chairmen in Congress have fought the prospect of a McCain presidency from the primary election of 2000 to this very day.

Our nominee doesn't run with the Washington herd. He's a man who's there to serve his country and not just his party, a leader who's not looking for a fight, but sure isn't afraid of one, either.

(APPLAUSE)

Harry Reid, the majority leader of the current do-nothing Senate . . .

(AUDIENCE BOOS)

. . . he not long ago summed up his feelings about our nominee. He said, quote, "I can't stand John McCain."

Ladies and gentlemen, perhaps no accolade we hear this week is better proof that we've chosen the right man.

(APPLAUSE)

Clearly, what the majority leader was driving at is that he can't stand up to John McCain and that is only . . .

(APPLAUSE)

. . . that's only one more reason to take the maverick out of the Senate, put him in the White House.

(APPLAUSE)

My fellow citizens, the American presidency is not supposed to be a journey of personal discovery.

(LAUGHTER)

(APPLAUSE)

This world of threats and dangers, it's not just a community and it doesn't just need an organizer. And though both Senator Obama and Senator Biden have been going on lately about how they're always, quote, "fighting for you," let us face the matter squarely: There is only one man in this election who has ever really fought for you.

(APPLAUSE)

There is only one man in this election who has ever really fought for you in places where winning means survival and defeat means death. And that man is John McCain.

(APPLAUSE)

You know, in our day, politicians have readily shared much lesser tales of adversity than the nightmare world, the nightmare world in which this man and others equally brave served and suffered for their country.

And it's a long way from the fear, and pain, and squalor of a six-by-four cell in Hanoi to the Oval Office.

(APPLAUSE)

But if Senator McCain is elected president, that is the journey he will have made. It's the journey of an upright and honorable man, the kind of fellow whose name you will find on war memorials in small towns across this great country, only he was among those who came home.

To the most powerful office on Earth, he would bring the compassion that comes from having once been powerless, the wisdom that comes even to the captives by the grace of God, the special confidence of those who have seen evil and have seen how evil is overcome. A fellow . . .

(APPLAUSE)

A fellow prisoner of war, a man named Tom Moe of Lancaster, Ohio . . .

(APPLAUSE)

. . . Tom Moe recalls looking through a pinhole in his cell door as Lieutenant Commander John McCain was led down the hallway by the guards, day after day.

And the story is told, when McCain shuffled back from torturous interrogations, he would turn towards Moe's door, and he'd flash a grin and a thumbs up, as if to say, "We're going to pull through this."

My fellow Americans, that is the kind of man America needs to see us through the next four years.

(APPLAUSE)

For a season, a gifted speaker can inspire with his words. But for a lifetime, John McCain has inspired with his deeds.

(APPLAUSE)

If character is the measure in this election, and hope the theme, and change the goal we share, then I ask you to join our cause. Join our cause and help America elect a great man as the next president of the United States.

Thank you, and God bless America. Thank you.

This Is Your Victory[*]

Barack Obama

President-elect of the United States, 2008– ; born Honolulu, HI, August 4, 1961; early education in Jakarta, Indonesia, and Honolulu; B.A., Columbia University, 1983; J.D., Harvard Law School, 1992; first African-American president of the Harvard Law Review; *community organizer and civil rights lawyer in Chicago; senior lecturer, University of Chicago Law School, specializing in constitutional law; state senator, representing the South Side of Chicago, Illinois State Senate, 1997–2004; elected to U.S. Senate, 2004; U.S. senator (D), Illinois, 2005–08; U.S. Senate committees: Environment and Public Works, Foreign Relations, and Veterans' Affairs; organizations: Center for Neighborhood and Technology, Chicago Annebery Challenge, Cook County Bar, Community Law Project, Joyce Foundation, Lawyers' Committee for Civil Rights Under the Law, Leadership for Quality Education, Trinity United Church of Christ; award, 40 Under 40,* Crains Chicago Business, *1993; author,* Dreams from My Father: A Story of Race and Inheritance *(1995, reprinted 2004);* The Audacity of Hope: Thoughts on Reclaiming the American Dream *(2006).*

Editor's Introduction: After a prolonged and at times divisive primary and general election campaign, Senator Barack Obama defeated Senator John McCain to become the first African American president of the United States. His convincing and unprecedented victory saw him expand the electoral map, winning such states as Virginia and North Carolina, which no Democratic presidential candidate had carried in a generation. In so doing, he achieved the most impressive presidential win for a Democrat since Lyndon Johnson's 1964 landslide. In his victory speech, delivered in Chicago's Grant Park, Obama displays the eloquence that had become his hallmark, He highlights the historic nature of his accomplishment and thanks those who supported him while vowing to win over those who didn't. He also evokes the life of 106-year-old Ann Nixon Cooper, who was born before women could vote and before African Americans had fully secured their suffrage. Describing the progress that Cooper witnessed in her long life, Obama asks, "If our children should live to see the next century; if my daughters should be so lucky to

---

* Delivered on November 5, 2008, at Chicago, IL.

live as long as Ann Nixon Cooper, what change will they see? What progress will we have made?"

Barack Obama's speech: If there is anyone out there who still doubts that America is a place where all things are possible; who still wonders if the dream of our founders is alive in our time; who still questions the power of our democracy, tonight is your answer.

It's the answer told by lines that stretched around schools and churches in numbers this nation has never seen; by people who waited three hours and four hours, many for the very first time in their lives, because they believed that this time must be different; that their voice could be that difference.

It's the answer spoken by young and old, rich and poor, Democrat and Republican, black, white, Hispanic, Asian, Native American, gay, straight, disabled and not disabled—Americans who sent a message to the world that we have never been a collection of Red States and Blue States: we are, and always will be, the United States of America.

It's the answer that led those who have been told for so long by so many to be cynical, and fearful, and doubtful of what we can achieve to put their hands on the arc of history and bend it once more toward the hope of a better day.

It's been a long time coming, but tonight, because of what we did on this day, in this election, at this defining moment, change has come to America.

I just received a very gracious call from Senator McCain. He fought long and hard in this campaign, and he's fought even longer and harder for the country he loves. He has endured sacrifices for America that most of us cannot begin to imagine, and we are better off for the service rendered by this brave and selfless leader. I congratulate him and Governor Palin for all they have achieved, and I look forward to working with them to renew this nation's promise in the months ahead.

I want to thank my partner in this journey, a man who campaigned from his heart and spoke for the men and women he grew up with on the streets of Scranton and rode with on that train home to Delaware, the Vice President-elect of the United States, Joe Biden.

I would not be standing here tonight without the unyielding support of my best friend for the last sixteen years, the rock of our family and the love of my life, our nation's next First Lady, Michelle Obama. Sasha and Malia, I love you both so much, and you have earned the new puppy that's coming with us to the White House. And while she's no longer with us, I know my grandmother is watching, along with the family that made me who I am. I miss them tonight, and know that my debt to them is beyond measure.

To my campaign manager David Plouffe, my chief strategist David Axelrod, and the best campaign team ever assembled in the history of politics—you made this happen, and I am forever grateful for what you've sacrificed to get it done.

But above all, I will never forget who this victory truly belongs to—it belongs to you.

I was never the likeliest candidate for this office. We didn't start with much money or many endorsements. Our campaign was not hatched in the halls of Washington—it began in the backyards of Des Moines and the living rooms of Concord and the front porches of Charleston.

It was built by working men and women who dug into what little savings they had to give five dollars and ten dollars and twenty dollars to this cause. It grew strength from the young people who rejected the myth of their generation's apathy; who left their homes and their families for jobs that offered little pay and less sleep; from the not-so-young people who braved the bitter cold and scorching heat to knock on the doors of perfect strangers; from the millions of Americans who volunteered, and organized, and proved that more than two centuries later, a government of the people, by the people and for the people has not perished from this Earth. This is your victory.

I know you didn't do this just to win an election and I know you didn't do it for me. You did it because you understand the enormity of the task that lies ahead. For even as we celebrate tonight, we know the challenges that tomorrow will bring are the greatest of our lifetime—two wars, a planet in peril, the worst financial crisis in a century. Even as we stand here tonight, we know there are brave Americans waking up in the deserts of Iraq and the mountains of Afghanistan to risk their lives for us. There are mothers and fathers who will lie awake after their children fall asleep and wonder how they'll make the mortgage, or pay their doctor's bills, or save enough for college. There is new energy to harness and new jobs to be created; new schools to build and threats to meet and alliances to repair.

The road ahead will be long. Our climb will be steep. We may not get there in one year or even one term, but America—I have never been more hopeful than I am tonight that we will get there. I promise you—we as a people will get there.

There will be setbacks and false starts. There are many who won't agree with every decision or policy I make as President, and we know that government can't solve every problem. But I will always be honest with you about the challenges we face. I will listen to you, especially when we disagree. And above all, I will ask you join in the work of remaking this nation the only way it's been done in America for two-hundred and twenty-one years—block by block, brick by brick, calloused hand by calloused hand.

What began twenty-one months ago in the depths of winter must not end on this autumn night. This victory alone is not the change we seek—it is only the chance for us to make that change. And that cannot happen if we go back to the way things were. It cannot happen without you.

So let us summon a new spirit of patriotism; of service and responsibility where each of us resolves to pitch in and work harder and look after not only ourselves, but each other. Let us remember that if this financial crisis taught us anything, it's that we cannot have a thriving Wall Street while Main Street suffers—in this country, we rise or fall as one nation; as one people.

Let us resist the temptation to fall back on the same partisanship and pettiness and immaturity that has poisoned our politics for so long. Let us remember that it was a man from this state who first carried the banner of the Republican Party to the White House—a party founded on the values of self-reliance, individual liberty, and national unity. Those are values we all share, and while the Democratic Party has won a great victory tonight, we do so with a measure of humility and determination to heal the divides that have held back our progress. As Lincoln said to a nation far more divided than ours, "We are not enemies, but friends . . . though passion may have strained it must not break our bonds of affection." And to those Americans whose support I have yet to earn—I may not have won your vote, but I hear your voices, I need your help, and I will be your President too.

And to all those watching tonight from beyond our shores, from parliaments and palaces to those who are huddled around radios in the forgotten corners of our world—our stories are singular, but our destiny is shared, and a new dawn of American leadership is at hand. To those who would tear this world down—we will defeat you. To those who seek peace and security—we support you. And to all those who have wondered if America's beacon still burns as bright—tonight we proved once more that the true strength of our nation comes not from our the might of our arms or the scale of our wealth, but from the enduring power of our ideals: democracy, liberty, opportunity, and unyielding hope.

For that is the true genius of America—that America can change. Our union can be perfected. And what we have already achieved gives us hope for what we can and must achieve tomorrow.

This election had many firsts and many stories that will be told for generations. But one that's on my mind tonight is about a woman who cast her ballot in Atlanta. She's a lot like the millions of others who stood in line to make their voice heard in this election except for one thing—Ann Nixon Cooper is 106 years old.

She was born just a generation past slavery; a time when there were no cars on the road or planes in the sky; when someone like her couldn't vote for two reasons—because she was a woman and because of the color of her skin.

And tonight, I think about all that she's seen throughout her century in America—the heartache and the hope; the struggle and the progress; the times we were told that we can't, and the people who pressed on with that American creed: Yes we can.

At a time when women's voices were silenced and their hopes dismissed, she lived to see them stand up and speak out and reach for the ballot. Yes we can.

When there was despair in the dust bowl and depression across the land, she saw a nation conquer fear itself with a New Deal, new jobs and a new sense of common purpose. Yes we can.

When the bombs fell on our harbor and tyranny threatened the world, she was there to witness a generation rise to greatness and a democracy was saved. Yes we can.

She was there for the buses in Montgomery, the hoses in Birmingham, a bridge in Selma, and a preacher from Atlanta who told a people that "We Shall Overcome." Yes we can.

A man touched down on the moon, a wall came down in Berlin, a world was connected by our own science and imagination. And this year, in this election, she touched her finger to a screen, and cast her vote, because after 106 years in America, through the best of times and the darkest of hours, she knows how America can change. Yes we can.

America, we have come so far. We have seen so much. But there is so much more to do. So tonight, let us ask ourselves—if our children should live to see the next century; if my daughters should be so lucky to live as long as Ann Nixon Cooper, what change will they see? What progress will we have made?

This is our chance to answer that call. This is our moment. This is our time—to put our people back to work and open doors of opportunity for our kids; to restore prosperity and promote the cause of peace; to reclaim the American Dream and reaffirm that fundamental truth—that out of many, we are one; that while we breathe, we hope, and where we are met with cynicism, and doubt, and those who tell us that we can't, we will respond with that timeless creed that sums up the spirit of a people:

Yes We Can. Thank you, God bless you, and may God bless the United States of America.

2

Race in America

Statement to the House Subcommittee on the Constitution, Civil Rights, and Civil Liberties[*]

Eric J. Miller

Associate professor, Saint Louis University School of Law, 2008– ; born Glasgow, Scotland, 1969; bachelor of laws, University of Edinburgh, 1991; master of laws, Harvard Law School; doctor of philosophy (candidate), Oxford University, Brasenose College, 1993–96; litigation associate, Quinn Emanuel Urquhart Oliver & Hedges, LLP, 1997–98; litigation committee member, Reparations Coordinating Committee, 2001– ; assistant professor, Western New England College School of Law, 2003–05; assistant professor, Saint Louis University School of Law, 2005–08; litigation team member, Chicago Slavery Ordinance Litigation Team, 2006.

Editor's introduction: Appearing before the House Judiciary Committee Subcommittee on the Constitution, Civil Rights, and Civil Liberties, Eric J. Miller urges lawmakers to consider H.R. 40, the "Commission to Study Reparation Proposals for African Americans Act." In making his case for the bill—a controversial measure that would create a panel charged with investigating the lasting effects of slavery and determining whether the U.S. government should somehow compensate African Americans—Miller argues that the term "reparations" doesn't necessarily refer to monetary payment. He insists that reparations should have three phases: acknowledging past wrongs, examining the nature of the injustices, and determining how best to "make whole the people harmed." "Reparations as a moral argument makes it impossible for citizens to ignore the contribution of slavery and of *de jure* segregation to the current character of our society," Miller says.

Eric J. Miller's speech: Mr. Chairman, Members of the Committee:

I am honored by the Committee's request that I testify at this very important hearing on the Legacy of the Trans-Atlantic Slave Trade. Chairman Conyer's efforts to raise awareness of this issue, and to promote the study of this issue through H.R. 40, are rightly celebrated. Thanks in large part to his efforts, state

---

[*] Delivered on December 18, 2008, at Washington, D.C.

legislatures in Virginia, North Carolina, Maryland, and Alabama, have engaged in an investigation of, and apology for their sponsorship of the Slave Trade. These important developments have stimulated a national discussion of the role of slavery in American history and pose the difficult question of how to acknowledge and account for it in America's present. That discussion is one that H.R. 40 seeks to sponsor, and one that this legislature should support.

Despite being almost a century-and-a-half removed from slavery, and fifty years from *de jure* segregation, we are not very good at talking about race in America. In part, that is because we, as a public, are not very knowledgeable about that history. Even relatively recent incidents from the Jim Crow era have been deliberately hidden or forgotten.[1] Yet there are still living the survivors of the race riots that swept the South and Midwest designed to rid or coerce them into submission whole communities of African Americans.[2] Their voices are still discounted or outright silenced.

One reason our civic discussion of race and racism is so stunted is that finding the means to talk about the history and legacy of slavery and segregation for America has hardly begun. It cannot properly start until we have some shared understanding of the still-hidden aspects of slavery and segregation upon which our community is based.

Public institutions are at the forefront of recent initiatives to promote an informed and inclusive discussion of race and history in America. State legislatures, like those in Rosewood, Florida, Tulsa, Oklahoma, and Greenwood, North Carolina, have convened commissions to investigate and report upon community-sponsored killings of African Americans.[3] These innovative inquiries, explicitly modeled on the Civil Liberties Act of 1988[4] and H.R. 40,[5] have sought to publicize and provide redress or closure for the citizens or descendants of state-sponsored racial violence. Various universities have sponsored studies to determine their own involvement with slavery and educate a state and national audience about their shared responsibilities.[6] That research has led some of these institutions, including the University of Alabama, the University of North Carolina, and the Episcopal Church have actually apologized for their ties to slavery.[7]

Many of these initiatives have been formulated around or influenced by the concept of "reparations."[8] Too often, however, reparations for African Americans are characterized by a posture of confrontation pitting the descendants of African American slaves against majority of whites who claimed to have received no benefit from slavery. The confrontational model of reparations tends to focus on the establishing and seeking financial redress for some duty owed by whites to blacks for the wrong of slavery. Such theories are generally premised upon addressing the rights and duties implicated in reparations claims through the standard, bilateral model of individual or group rights, in which the rights of one individual or group are pitted against another. On this model, whosoever has the stronger right—to compensation or to be let alone—in a given instance, wins.[9]

Part of the problem presented by the confrontational reparations claim is that it is over-inclusive and so fails to provide a satisfactory theory of compensation.

The familiar argument is that it identifies too many white people as owing a duty to repay and too many African Americans as having suffered the harm.[10] But whites also play the confrontation card, arguing they have no such duty to their fellow citizens either because there is something about African Americans—usually their culture—that is peculiarly to blame for the ills besetting that community; or because the duty to compensate which once may have existed has been exhausted, perhaps simply due to the passage of time, or perhaps because African Americans who adopt a "victim" status have already received all the benefits due them.[11]

Neither of these versions accurately states the issues. The confrontational model is too narrow to capture both the harm inflicted and the strategies necessary to remedy that harm. On both sides of the debate, confrontation takes for granted that reparations proponents seek financial redress for wrongs inflicted in the past on the basis of some more-or-less moral theory of entitlement to redress. Yet the current discussion of what reparations is, and what types of reparations are appropriate, does and must depend upon a broader notion of the harm inflicted and must reflect the particular wrongs that need to be "repaired." What the various state and university sponsored public commissions have demonstrated is that the harm inflicted and the benefits accrued are not singular but plural, affecting a range of communities at different times and in different ways.

Reparations is much more than, and on occasion unconcerned with, monetary restitution. When not phrased in purely monetary terms, reparations offers an opportunity to explore our shared history to determine our mutual investment in each other. It seeks to trace and account for past behavior, and resists specifying in advance what sorts of restitution are appropriate, and from whom. At bottom, reparations seeks to develop a more accurate understanding of the story of race in America. It adopts an open-minded approach to the American past as well as the American present, while questioning which accounts of that past and present are open to challenge and reconfiguration.

Put this way, reparations encompasses three distinct stages: acknowledgment; accounting; and redemption. The first stage, acknowledgment, requires us to recognize that a harm or harms have occurred. The second stage, accounting, requires us to investigate and identify the nature of the harm, the wrongdoers and the people harmed. The third stage, redemption, requires us to disseminate the information discovered through research, and encourage, where appropriate, any wrongdoers to apologize to the people harmed for the harms done or make whole the people harmed. Given the lapse of time since slavery and segregation, such making whole may take many forms. It may stop at education or apology, or may require more direct restitution (where, for example, there are living survivors of Jim-Crow era state-sponsored violence).

The simple fact is that reparations is now in the mainstream of American discourse about race. Most Americans have accepted the first stage: acknowledgment. That is, it is now uncontroversial that slavery and segregation were wrong. What is disturbing is a subsequent history that has sought to minimize, hide, and silence broad-ranging studies of the history of slavery and segregation, and publication of the results.[12] States are taking the initiative in the second stage, accounting for the history of slavery and segregation in America. And some states, along with some of our corporations and internationally renowned centers of education are even proceeding to the redemption stage.

This mainstream version of reparations is best characterized as a conversation in which we can chart our investment in a variety of geographic, social, and political communities, and in which we can publicly accept or decline responsibility for past, present, and future. It rejects discussion of race in America as a zero-sum game, where there is only one right answer or way of doing things, discovering and taking responsibility is a dynamic process of creating and recreating the basis of our society.

This conversational model of reparations invites a process questioning the basis of our shared community. Reparations is thus part of a dynamic process in which one seeks to determine how we got where we are, and what the consequences of that should be. The claims made through reparations are useful, in part, by ruling out certain arguments from the get-go as having the weight others wish to put on them. Thus, if reparations succeeds in tracing the underdevelopment of African Americans by whites, certain notions of desert and failure, responsibility and innocence, are ruled out of the debate on race, discrimination, and their consequences for American society. Here, the question becomes one of community: whether we can find a common set of valuations that enable us to understand the present significance of our acts, given our shared and divided past.

Reparations argues that we need to account for the ways in which the federal, state, and local governments that have profited off or promoted slavery and segregation. In part, it seeks to chart the ways in which national, state, and local communities have consolidated their civic identities in response to acts of racial violence both during and after the era of slavery. At a minimum, it seeks to explore the effects that slavery and segregation played in establishing the relative social inequality of African Americans as compared to other racial or ethnic groups. Reparations as a moral argument makes it impossible for citizens to ignore the contribution of slavery and of de jure segregation to the current character of our society.

The stakes of the reparations discussion are high. To fail to acknowledge and account for America's history is to ignore and reject the past and continuing experiences of a huge segment of the population. It is to perpetuate the treatment of African Americans as somehow less worthy or interesting than other citizens.

CONCLUSION

Justice Kennedy recently suggested that "an injury stemming from racial prejudice can hurt as much when the demeaning treatment based on race identity stems from bias masked deep within the social order as when it is imposed by law. The distinction between government and private action, furthermore, can be amorphous both as a historical matter and as a matter of present-day finding of fact. Laws arise from a culture and vice versa. Neither can assign to the other all responsibility for persisting injustices."[13] It is all the more pressing, then, to engage with an open mind in the process of accounting and reckoning to make more concrete and less amorphous the source of and solution for such injuries. Investigating slavery and segregation is not an impediment to a discussion of race and justice in America, but its necessary first step.

FOOTNOTES

1 *See, e.g.,* OKLA. COMM'N TO STUDY THE TULSA RACE RIOT OF 1921, TULSA RACE RIOT (Comm. Print 2001); OKLA. STAT. ANN. tit. 74, § 8000.1 (West 2002) (making legislative findings that Oklahoma state officials engaged in "conspiracy of silence" to cover up Tulsa Race Riot of 1921).

2 *See, e.g.* JAMES W. LOEWEN, SUNDOWN TOWNS: A HIDDEN DIMENSION OF AMERICAN RACISM 90-115 (2005) (describing manner in which private and municipal actors forced African Americans out of various municipalities).

3 *See, e.g.,* OKLA. STAT. ANN. tit. 74, § 8201 (West 2002) (creating commission to study events of Tulsa Race Riot of 1921).

4 CIVIL LIBERTIES ACT OF 1988, 50 U.S.C. app. §§ 1989-1989b-9 (2000).

5 ommission to Study Reparations for African Americans Act, H.R. 40, 108th Cong. (2003). *Compare e.g.,* Act of May 4, 1994, 1994 Fla. Sess. Law Serv. ch. 94-359 (West) (relating to Rosewood, Florida) (codified in part at FLA. STAT. ch. 1004.60, 1009.55 (2003)).

6 *See, e.g.,* SLAVERY AND JUSTICE: REPORT OF THE BROWN STEERING COMMITTEE ON SLAVERY AND JUSTICE (2006).

7 Wendy Koch, *Va. 1st State to Express "Regret" Over Slavery,* USA TODAY, Feb. 25, 2007.

8 *See, e.g.,* Charles J. Ogletree, Jr., *Chapter 17 Addressing The Racial Divide: Reparations,* 20 HARV. BLACKLETTER L.J. 115 (2004).

9 Discussions of moral or legal conflict can be phrased in terms of "balancing."
T. Alexander Aleinikoff, *Constitutional Law in the Age of Balancing,* 96 YALE L.J. 943, 962 (1987); see also Patrick M. McFadden, *The Balancing Test,* 29 B.C. L. REV. 585, 596 (1988) (identifying three steps to any balancing test: "announcing the factors to be balanced, weighing those factors, and announcing the victor").

10 *See, e.g.,* David Horowitz, *Ten Reasons Why Reparations for Blacks is a Bad Idea for Blacks - and Racist, Too!* ¶¶ 3-4 (Mar. 12, 2001) (controversial anti-reparations advertisement), at http://www.adversity.net/reparations/anti_ repations_ad.htm.

11 *See, e.g.,* John McWhorter, *Blood Money; Analysis Of Slavery Reparations,* AM. ENTERPRISE, July 1, 2001, at 18 (discussing reparations as example of African American "victimology").

12 OKLA. STAT. ANN. tit. 74, § 8000.1 (West 2002) (discussing state-sponsored attempts to cover up the Tulsa Race Riot of 1921).

13 Parents Involved in Community Schools v. Seattle School Dist. No. 1, 127 S. Ct. 2738, 2795 (2007).

Testimony to the House Subcommittee on the Constitution, Civil Rights, and Civil Liberties[*]

Roger Clegg

President and general counsel, Center for Equal Opportunity, 2006– ; B.A., Rice University, 1977; J.D., Yale University Law School, 1981; attorney-advisor, Office of Legal Policy, U.S. Department of Justice, 1982; special assistant to the attorney general, U.S. Department of Justice, 1982–83; acting assistant attorney general, Office of Legal Policy, U.S. Department of Justice, 1984; associate deputy attorney general, U.S. Department of Justice, 1984–85; special litigation counsel, appellate section, civil division, U.S. Department of Justice, 1985; assistant to the solicitor general, U.S. Department of Justice, 1985–87; deputy assistant attorney general, Civil Rights Division, U.S. Department of Justice, 1987–1991; deputy assistant attorney general, Environment and Natural Resources Division, U.S. Department of Justice, 1991–93; vice president, general counsel, assistant treasurer, National Legal Center for the Public Interest, 1993–97; vice president and general counsel, Center for Equal Opportunity, 1997–2005.

Editor's introduction: In 2007 the U.S. House of Representatives took up H.R. 40, the "Commission to Study Reparation Proposals for African-Americans Act." The bill would create a panel charged with examining whether present-day hardships suffered by African Americans are due to trans-Atlantic slavery. Should the panel find a link, it might then suggest that the U.S. government issue a formal apology for slavery and compensate those who continue to feel its effects. Appearing before the House Judiciary Committee Subcommittee on the Constitution, Civil Rights, and Civil Liberties, Roger Clegg argues against the bill, insisting that modern problems are not easily traced back to historical injustices. He further claims that even if it were possible to tie slavery to problems plaguing the black community, reparations would be unconstitutional, difficult to distribute fairly, and detrimental to race relations.

Roger Clegg's speech: Thank you very much, Mr. Chairman, for the opportunity to testify today. My name is Roger Clegg, and I am president and general counsel of the Center for Equal Opportunity, a nonprofit research and educa-

---

[*] Delivered on December 18, 2008, at Washington, D.C.

tional organization that is based in Falls Church, Virginia. Our chairman is Linda Chavez, and our focus is on public policy issues that involve race and ethnicity, such as civil rights, bilingual education, and immigration and assimilation. I should also note that I was a deputy in the U.S. Department of Justice's Civil Rights Division for four years, from 1987 to 1991.

OVERVIEW

The discussion today of the legacy of the trans-Atlantic slave trade is intended, I presume, to help lay the groundwork for favorable consideration of H.R. 40, the "Commission to Study Reparation Proposals for African-Americans Act." And the enterprise that H.R. 40 would have us embark on, in turn, is as follows: First, a commission would determine what effects slavery and post-slavery discrimination had on African Americans and what "lingering negative effects" it continues to have on them; and then, second, it would suggest possible remedies for those effects. The two remedies that are explicitly mentioned are an apology and some form of compensation.

There are any number of problems with this enterprise, and I would like briefly to discuss some of them in my testimony today. (Some of the points I will make are also expressed, often in more detail, in a dialogue I have written on this topic, a version of which was published in *Engage* magazine, and which I have included as an appendix to my testimony; I've also included an op-ed I wrote on a recent Chicago ordinance requiring city contractors to document any slavery-related business in the antebellum era.)

THIS IS AN UNNECESSARY AND HOPELESS TASK FOR
SUCH A GOVERNMENT COMMISSION

First, this research project is ill-suited for a government commission. H.R. 40 says that "sufficient inquiry has not been made into the effects of the institution of slavery on living African-Americans and society in the United States." I am not sure what that statement is based on, and I am not a professional historian. But as a lay reader and a civil rights lawyer, it seems to me that there is no shortage of books and articles about slavery, and discrimination, and the problems facing the African American community today, and the way all these intersect. I am not declaring that there has been "sufficient inquiry"; just that there has been a great deal and that it continues—and that, given the intrinsic interest of these topics, especially among those in the academy, it will likely continue for the foreseeable future.

What I would declare, moreover, is that this inquiry will never end, and it will be a long time before anyone would presume to call the inquiry "sufficient." Few historical inquiries ever are: There is always some new angle to explore. Further, the conclusions that historians will draw will always be incomplete, imperfect, and challenged by contemporary and future historians. That is the nature of historical scholarship, especially for issues as complex as this one.

H.R. 40 suggests, on the other hand, that something like a definitive answer will be possible if the government takes $8 million, hires seven "especially qualified" people, and gives them a year to figure it all out. This is, of course, absurd.

No one will dispute that slavery and Jim Crow were horrible and inhumane; no one will dispute that discrimination still exists, though only a delusional person would deny that America has made radical, dramatic, inspiring progress in the last 40 years—that its society has truly been transformed in an astonishingly short period of time. But it is impossible to say how much of the present is the result of one particular kind of event in the past. Only someone very arrogant or very foolish would make such a pronouncement.

Let me give just one example. The principal hurdle facing the African American community today is the fact that 7 out of 10 African Americans are born out of wedlock. Just about any social problem you can name—crime, drugs, dropping out of school, doing poorly in school, and so forth—has a strong correlation with growing up in a home without a father. And it is very hard to argue that this problem is traceable to slavery or Jim Crow, since illegitimacy rates started to skyrocket in the African American community just at the time that Jim Crow was starting to crumble.

Given that, how can anyone say with any confidence that such-and-such amount of such-and-such a social problem facing African Americans must be due to slavery? It cannot be done.

RACE-BASED COMPENSATION WOULD BE BOTH
ILLOGICAL AND UNCONSTITUTIONAL

But let's suppose that, nonetheless, the commission decides that it can be done. Let's suppose that this commission says, "Forty-six percent of the poverty in the African American community today can be traced to slavery and discrimination, forty-five percent is caused by illegitimacy, and the remaining nine percent is just bad luck," or some such silly thing. Or let's suppose that it says something less silly, but so obvious that it does not take a government commission to figure it out--something like, "To some significant extent, the disproportionate amount of poverty facing the African American community today can be traced to slavery and the discrimination its members faced."

Would it follow that some sort of "compensation" —one of the two remedies H.R. 40 explicitly asks the commission to consider—ought to be paid to African Americans? No. It certainly wouldn't make sense to pay compensation to African Americans who are not living in poverty. It wouldn't make sense to pay compensation to African Americans who are living in poverty if that poverty was not caused by slavery and Jim Crow—to give an obvious example, to African Americans who just immigrated here. Yet requiring a particular person to prove his slave ancestry leads to many problems; presuming slave ancestry because of a person's appearance raises many problems, too; and there are problems with simply taking people at their word as well.

Also, why should an African American who could trace his poverty to slavery be entitled to compensation over, say, a poor American Indian who could not but could trace it to some other historical wrong (in this case, say, a broken treaty)? Or a poor Latino or a poor Asian or even a poor white? Any of them might be able to trace his poverty to *some* historical wrong.

But most fundamentally, why does it matter whether the poverty is traceable to a historical wrong? Suppose you have two children. One could show somehow that the reason he was poor was because of the discrimination his family suffered. The other child is poor for no reason except his mother and father just immigrated to this country from a poverty-stricken homeland. Is the government supposed to say, "We view the first child's poverty as a problem of federal concern, but not the second child's"?

Of course not. There is no reason why eligibility for a social program ought to hinge on whether a citizen can trace his need for the program to this or that historical cause.

If we design social programs to help disadvantaged people, and if disadvantaged people are disproportionately African American because of the discrimination that they have disproportionately suffered, then African Americans disproportionately will be eligible for those programs. And, indeed, that is the case today. More than that makes no sense. And if the commission simply recommends more social programs that are not race-based, then it is even harder to see why its historical focus should be on one particular subset of one particular racial group.

If, finally, we were to make a social program available to those of one race and not to others, there would be serious constitutional problems. Presumably the justification for the program would be remedial, but the Supreme Court has—quite rightly—rejected general claims of societal discrimination as not sufficiently compelling to justify racial classifications.

AN APOLOGY WOULD MAKE NO SENSE EITHER

As for an apology, the second possible remedy listed by H.R. 40: The bill asks "Whether the Government of the United States should offer a formal apology on behalf of the people of the United States for the perpetuation of gross human rights violations on African slaves and their descendants."

This is, at best, an odd apology. What would really be appropriate, of course, is for the slave-traders and the slave-masters to apologize to the slaves—but all these folks have long since passed on to their just rewards.

So instead we have the U.S. government (which actually ended slavery, at the cost of much blood and treasure) apologizing on behalf of today's American people (none of whom ever owned slaves, and most of whom never had ancestors who did, either) to . . . whom? The bill does not say. Maybe the idea is just to apologize to ourselves, but that seems rather strange. Presumably the idea is to apologize to living African Americans. But these African Americans are not slaves; many are descended from slaves, but many are not; many of the former—maybe most now—are descended from both slaves and slave-owners.

Mr. Chairman, I cannot resist pointing out that, if there is anyone in the United States today from whom an apology for slavery and Jim Crow would be appropriate, it would be, not the U.S. government, and certainly not the American people—but the Democratic Party. It, after all, was historically the party of slavery, secession, and segregation.

But let's be honest: Inevitably, such apologies are intended and interpreted as whites apologizing to blacks for slavery. (I wonder what Asians and Latinos, as well as American Indians, think of this theater?) But no white today is or ever was a slaveholder; no black today is or ever was a slave. What's the point of one apologizing to the other?

Everyone has an ancestor who was wronged by someone else's ancestor; there is no point in trying to find a thread for each present-day misfortune in an individual's life that can be followed back through the decades to a particular misdeed; and anyone's poverty today likely has many causes—some old, some recent, some other people's fault, some one's own. Nobody nowadays thinks slavery was anything but an abomination; nobody learns anything from this charade.

We are told that these apologies will help to bring closure, help enable us to move on. Nonsense—and that is not their intent, at least for many people. The idea is to reopen wounds, to keep grievance alive, to keep white people on the hook. An obsession with past wrongs, to the extent that present opportunity and future promise are ignored or slighted, is a bad thing.

A great strength of Americans is that we are forward looking. The trouble with slavery apologies is that they are designed to make whites feel guilty and to urge blacks to think of themselves as victims. Neither emotion is valid in these closing days of the year 2007; both are bad for race relations. In particular, the last thing an African American needs in 2007 is an excuse to fail. As individual white people will go about their business—and Latinos and Asians and Arab Americans and American Indians—individual black people will be left with the same choice they've had for years: embrace self-reliance and responsibility, or fail and blame it on others.

CONCLUSION

All of this is true not just for the apology issue but also for the entire enterprise that H.R. 40 would embark on: That is, it would accomplish nothing and would cost much. And I don't mean monetary costs, but social costs: Specifically, the poisonous effect it would have a racial relations, and the pernicious message it would send, in particular, to those in the African American community, that their focus should be on what was done to them in the past, rather than the opportunities they have now.

Thank you again, Mr. Chairman, for the opportunity to testify today. I would be happy to try to answer any questions the Subcommittee may have for me.

A More Perfect Union[*]

Barack Obama

Editor's introduction: Barack Obama was driven to address the topic of race in America after controversial sermons by his pastor, Reverend Jeremiah Wright, drew extensive media coverage and left many questioning Obama's judgment in choosing to associate with Wright. In these sermons, none of which Obama attended, the pastor described the terrorist attacks of September 11, 2001 as America's chickens coming home to roost, and proclaimed, "God damn America." In this speech, given at Philadelphia's Constitution Center on March 18, 2008, Obama rejects Wright's views but defends the church and his experiences there. He goes on to describe the bitter legacy of racial injustice in the form of unequal education and opportunity and details the resentment that simmers on both sides of the black-white divide. But unless we reaffirm the golden rule and the belief that our union can be improved, he argues, we will forever be caught in a politics of division.

Barack Obama's speech: "We the people, in order to form a more perfect union."

Two hundred and twenty one years ago, in a hall that still stands across the street, a group of men gathered and, with these simple words, launched America's improbable experiment in democracy. Farmers and scholars; statesmen and patriots who had traveled across an ocean to escape tyranny and persecution finally made real their declaration of independence at a Philadelphia convention that lasted through the spring of 1787.

The document they produced was eventually signed but ultimately unfinished. It was stained by this nation's original sin of slavery, a question that divided the colonies and brought the convention to a stalemate until the founders chose to allow the slave trade to continue for at least 20 more years, and to leave any final resolution to future generations.

Of course, the answer to the slavery question was already embedded within our Constitution—a Constitution that had at its very core the ideal of equal citizen-

* Delivered on March 18, 2008, at Philadelphia, PA.

ship under the law; a Constitution that promised its people liberty, and justice, and a union that could be and should be perfected over time.

And yet words on a parchment would not be enough to deliver slaves from bondage, or provide men and women of every color and creed their full rights and obligations as citizens of the United States. What would be needed were Americans in successive generations who were willing to do their part—through protests and struggle, on the streets and in the courts, through a civil war and civil disobedience and always at great risk—to narrow that gap between the promise of our ideals and the reality of their time.

This was one of the tasks we set forth at the beginning of this campaign—to continue the long march of those who came before us, a march for a more just, more equal, more free, more caring and more prosperous America. I chose to run for the presidency at this moment in history because I believe deeply that we cannot solve the challenges of our time unless we solve them together—unless we perfect our union by understanding that we may have different stories, but we hold common hopes; that we may not look the same and we may not have come from the same place, but we all want to move in the same direction—towards a better future for our children and our grandchildren.

This belief comes from my unyielding faith in the decency and generosity of the American people. But it also comes from my own American story.

I am the son of a black man from Kenya and a white woman from Kansas. I was raised with the help of a white grandfather who survived a Depression to serve in Patton's Army during World War II and a white grandmother who worked on a bomber assembly line at Fort Leavenworth while he was overseas. I've gone to some of the best schools in America and lived in one of the world's poorest nations. I am married to a black American who carries within her the blood of slaves and slaveowners—an inheritance we pass on to our two precious daughters. I have brothers, sisters, nieces, nephews, uncles and cousins, of every race and every hue, scattered across three continents, and for as long as I live, I will never forget that in no other country on Earth is my story even possible.

It's a story that hasn't made me the most conventional candidate. But it is a story that has seared into my genetic makeup the idea that this nation is more than the sum of its parts—that out of many, we are truly one.

Throughout the first year of this campaign, against all predictions to the contrary, we saw how hungry the American people were for this message of unity. Despite the temptation to view my candidacy through a purely racial lens, we won commanding victories in states with some of the whitest populations in the country. In South Carolina, where the Confederate Flag still flies, we built a powerful coalition of African Americans and white Americans.

This is not to say that race has not been an issue in the campaign. At various stages in the campaign, some commentators have deemed me either "too black" or "not black enough." We saw racial tensions bubble to the surface during the week before the South Carolina primary. The press has scoured every exit poll for the latest evidence of racial polarization, not just in terms of white and black, but black and brown as well.

And yet, it has only been in the last couple of weeks that the discussion of race in this campaign has taken a particularly divisive turn.

On one end of the spectrum, we've heard the implication that my candidacy is somehow an exercise in affirmative action; that it's based solely on the desire of wide-eyed liberals to purchase racial reconciliation on the cheap. On the other end, we've heard my former pastor, Reverend Jeremiah Wright, use incendiary language to express views that have the potential not only to widen the racial divide, but views that denigrate both the greatness and the goodness of our nation; that rightly offend white and black alike.

I have already condemned, in unequivocal terms, the statements of Reverend Wright that have caused such controversy. For some, nagging questions remain. Did I know him to be an occasionally fierce critic of American domestic and foreign policy? Of course. Did I ever hear him make remarks that could be considered controversial while I sat in church? Yes. Did I strongly disagree with many of his political views? Absolutely—just as I'm sure many of you have heard remarks from your pastors, priests, or rabbis with which you strongly disagreed.

But the remarks that have caused this recent firestorm weren't simply controversial. They weren't simply a religious leader's effort to speak out against perceived injustice. Instead, they expressed a profoundly distorted view of this country—a view that sees white racism as endemic, and that elevates what is wrong with America above all that we know is right with America; a view that sees the conflicts in the Middle East as rooted primarily in the actions of stalwart allies like Israel, instead of emanating from the perverse and hateful ideologies of radical Islam.

As such, Reverend Wright's comments were not only wrong but divisive, divisive at a time when we need unity; racially charged at a time when we need to come together to solve a set of monumental problems—two wars, a terrorist threat, a falling economy, a chronic health care crisis and potentially devastating climate change; problems that are neither black or white or Latino or Asian, but rather problems that confront us all.

Given my background, my politics, and my professed values and ideals, there will no doubt be those for whom my statements of condemnation are not enough. Why associate myself with Reverend Wright in the first place, they may ask? Why not join another church? And I confess that if all that I knew of Reverend Wright were the snippets of those sermons that have run in an endless loop on the television and YouTube, or if Trinity United Church of Christ conformed to the caricatures being peddled by some commentators, there is no doubt that I would react in much the same way

But the truth is, that isn't all that I know of the man. The man I met more than twenty years ago is a man who helped introduce me to my Christian faith, a man who spoke to me about our obligations to love one another; to care for the sick and lift up the poor. He is a man who served his country as a U.S. Marine; who has studied and lectured at some of the finest universities and seminaries in the country, and who for over thirty years led a church that serves the community by doing God's work here on Earth—by housing the homeless, ministering to the needy, providing day care services and scholarships and prison ministries, and reaching out to those suffering from HIV/AIDS.

In my first book, *Dreams From My Father*, I described the experience of my first service at Trinity:

> "People began to shout, to rise from their seats and clap and cry out, a forceful wind carrying the reverend's voice up into the rafters. . . . And in that single note—hope!—I heard something else; at the foot of that cross, inside the thousands of churches across the city, I imagined the stories of ordinary black people merging with the stories of David and Goliath, Moses and Pharaoh, the Christians in the lion's den, Ezekiel's field of dry bones. Those stories—of survival, and freedom, and hope—became our story, my story; the blood that had spilled was our blood, the tears our tears; until this black church, on this bright day, seemed once more a vessel carrying the story of a people into future generations and into a larger world. Our trials and triumphs became at once unique and universal, black and more than black; in chronicling our journey, the stories and songs gave us a means to reclaim memories that we didn't need to feel shame about . . . memories that all people might study and cherish—and with which we could start to rebuild."

That has been my experience at Trinity. Like other predominantly black churches across the country, Trinity embodies the black community in its entirety—the doctor and the welfare mom, the model student and the former gang-banger. Like other black churches, Trinity's services are full of raucous laughter and sometimes bawdy humor. They are full of dancing, clapping, screaming and shouting that may seem jarring to the untrained ear. The church contains in full the kindness and cruelty, the fierce intelligence and the shocking ignorance, the struggles and successes, the love and yes, the bitterness and bias that make up the black experience in America.

And this helps explain, perhaps, my relationship with Reverend Wright. As imperfect as he may be, he has been like family to me. He strengthened my faith, officiated my wedding, and baptized my children. Not once in my conversations with him have I heard him talk about any ethnic group in derogatory terms, or treat whites with whom he interacted with anything but courtesy and respect. He contains within him the contradictions—the good and the bad—of the community that he has served diligently for so many years.

I can no more disown him than I can disown the black community. I can no more disown him than I can my white grandmother—a woman who helped raise me, a woman who sacrificed again and again for me, a woman who loves me as much as she loves anything in this world, but a woman who once confessed her fear of black men who passed by her on the street, and who on more than one occasion has uttered racial or ethnic stereotypes that made me cringe.

These people are a part of me. And they are a part of America, this country that I love.

Some will see this as an attempt to justify or excuse comments that are simply inexcusable. I can assure you it is not. I suppose the politically safe thing would be to move on from this episode and just hope that it fades into the woodwork. We can dismiss Reverend Wright as a crank or a demagogue, just as some have dismissed Geraldine Ferraro, in the aftermath of her recent statements, as harboring some deep-seated racial bias.

But race is an issue that I believe this nation cannot afford to ignore right now. We would be making the same mistake that Reverend Wright made in his offending sermons about America—to simplify and stereotype and amplify the negative to the point that it distorts reality.

The fact is that the comments that have been made and the issues that have surfaced over the last few weeks reflect the complexities of race in this country that we've never really worked through—a part of our union that we have yet to perfect. And if we walk away now, if we simply retreat into our respective corners, we will never be able to come together and solve challenges like health care, or education, or the need to find good jobs for every American.

Understanding this reality requires a reminder of how we arrived at this point. As William Faulkner once wrote, "The past isn't dead and buried. In fact, it isn't even past." We do not need to recite here the history of racial injustice in this country. But we do need to remind ourselves that so many of the disparities that exist in the African-American community today can be directly traced to inequalities passed on from an earlier generation that suffered under the brutal legacy of slavery and Jim Crow.

Segregated schools were, and are, inferior schools; we still haven't fixed them, fifty years after *Brown v. Board of Education*, and the inferior education they provided, then and now, helps explain the pervasive achievement gap between today's black and white students.

Legalized discrimination—where blacks were prevented, often through violence, from owning property, or loans were not granted to African-American business owners, or black homeowners could not access FHA mortgages, or blacks were excluded from unions, or the police force, or fire departments—meant that black families could not amass any meaningful wealth to bequeath to future generations. That history helps explain the wealth and income gap between black and white, and the concentrated pockets of poverty that persist in so many of today's urban and rural communities.

A lack of economic opportunity among black men, and the shame and frustration that came from not being able to provide for one's family, contributed to the erosion of black families—a problem that welfare policies for many years may have worsened. And the lack of basic services in so many urban black neighborhoods—parks for kids to play in, police walking the beat, regular garbage pick-up and building code enforcement—all helped create a cycle of violence, blight and neglect that continues to haunt us.

This is the reality in which Reverend Wright and other African Americans of his generation grew up. They came of age in the late '50s and early '60, a time when segregation was still the law of the land and opportunity was systematically constricted. What's remarkable is not how many failed in the face of discrimination, but rather how many men and women overcame the odds; how many were able to make a way out of no way for those like me who would come after them.

But for all those who scratched and clawed their way to get a piece of the American Dream, there were many who didn't make it—those who were ultimately defeated, in one way or another, by discrimination. That legacy of defeat was passed on to future generations—those young men and increasingly young women who we see standing on street corners or languishing in our prisons, without hope or prospects for the future. Even for those blacks who did make it, questions of race, and racism, continue to define their worldview in fundamental ways. For the men and women of Reverend Wright's generation, the memories of humiliation and doubt and fear have not gone away; nor has the anger and the bitterness of those years. That anger may not get expressed in public, in front of white co-workers or white friends. But it does find voice in the barbershop or around the kitchen table. At times, that anger is exploited by politicians, to gin up votes along racial lines, or to make up for a politician's own failings.

And occasionally it finds voice in the church on Sunday morning, in the pulpit and in the pews. The fact that so many people are surprised to hear that anger in some of Reverend Wright's sermons simply reminds us of the old truism that the most segregated hour in American life occurs on Sunday morning. That anger is not always productive; indeed, all too often it distracts attention from solving real problems; it keeps us from squarely facing our own complicity in our condition, and prevents the African-American community from forging the alliances it needs to bring about real change. But the anger is real; it is powerful; and to simply wish it away, to condemn it without understanding its roots, only serves to widen the chasm of misunderstanding that exists between the races.

In fact, a similar anger exists within segments of the white community. Most working- and middle-class white Americans don't feel that they have been particularly privileged by their race. Their experience is the immigrant experience—as far as they're concerned, no one's handed them anything, they've built it from scratch. They've worked hard all their lives, many times only to see their jobs shipped overseas or their pension dumped after a lifetime of labor. They are anxious about their futures, and feel their dreams slipping away; in an era of stagnant wages and global competition, opportunity comes to be seen as a zero sum game, in which your dreams come at my expense. So when they are told to bus their children to a school across town; when they hear that an African American is getting an advantage in landing a good job or a spot in a good college because of an injustice that they themselves never committed; when they're told that their fears about crime in urban neighborhoods are somehow prejudiced, resentment builds over time.

Like the anger within the black community, these resentments aren't always expressed in polite company. But they have helped shape the political landscape for at least a generation. Anger over welfare and affirmative action helped forge the Reagan Coalition. Politicians routinely exploited fears of crime for their own electoral ends. Talk show hosts and conservative commentators built entire careers unmasking bogus claims of racism while dismissing legitimate discussions of racial injustice and inequality as mere political correctness or reverse racism.

Just as black anger often proved counterproductive, so have these white resentments distracted attention from the real culprits of the middle-class squeeze—a corporate culture rife with inside dealing, questionable accounting practices, and short-term greed; a Washington dominated by lobbyists and special interests; economic policies that favor the few over the many. And yet, to wish away the resentments of white Americans, to label them as misguided or even racist, without recognizing they are grounded in legitimate concerns—this too widens the racial divide, and blocks the path to understanding.

This is where we are right now. It's a racial stalemate we've been stuck in for years. Contrary to the claims of some of my critics, black and white, I have never been so naïve as to believe that we can get beyond our racial divisions in a single election cycle, or with a single candidacy—particularly a candidacy as imperfect as my own.

But I have asserted a firm conviction—a conviction rooted in my faith in God and my faith in the American people—that working together we can move beyond some of our old racial wounds, and that in fact we have no choice if we are to continue on the path of a more perfect union.

For the African-American community, that path means embracing the burdens of our past without becoming victims of our past. It means continuing to insist on a full measure of justice in every aspect of American life. But it also means binding our particular grievances—for better health care, and better schools, and better jobs—to the larger aspirations of all Americans—the white woman struggling to break the glass ceiling, the white man whose been laid off, the immigrant trying to feed his family. And it means taking full responsibility for our own lives—by demanding more from our fathers, and spending more time with our children, and reading to them, and teaching them that while they may face challenges and discrimination in their own lives, they must never succumb to despair or cynicism; they must always believe that they can write their own destiny.

Ironically, this quintessentially American—and yes, conservative—notion of self-help found frequent expression in Reverend Wright's sermons. But what my former pastor too often failed to understand is that embarking on a program of self-help also requires a belief that society can change.

The profound mistake of Reverend Wright's sermons is not that he spoke about racism in our society. It's that he spoke as if our society was static; as if no progress has been made; as if this country—a country that has made it possible for one of his own members to run for the highest office in the land and build a coalition of white and black, Latino and Asian, rich and poor, young and old—is still irrevocably bound to a tragic past. But what we know—what we have seen—is that America can change. That is the true genius of this nation. What we have already achieved gives us hope—the audacity to hope—for what we can and must achieve tomorrow.

In the white community, the path to a more perfect union means acknowledging that what ails the African-American community does not just exist in the minds of black people; that the legacy of discrimination—and current incidents of discrimination, while less overt than in the past—are real and must be addressed. Not just with words, but with deeds—by investing in our schools and our communities; by enforcing our civil rights laws and ensuring fairness in our criminal justice system; by providing this generation with ladders of opportunity that were unavailable for previous generations. It requires all Americans to realize that your dreams do not have to come at the expense of my dreams; that investing in the health, welfare, and education of black and brown and white children will ultimately help all of America prosper.

In the end, then, what is called for is nothing more, and nothing less, than what all the world's great religions demand—that we do unto others as we would have them do unto us. Let us be our brother's keeper, Scripture tells us. Let us be our sister's keeper. Let us find that common stake we all have in one another, and let our politics reflect that spirit as well.

For we have a choice in this country. We can accept a politics that breeds division, and conflict, and cynicism. We can tackle race only as spectacle—as we did in the OJ trial—or in the wake of tragedy, as we did in the aftermath of Katrina—or as fodder for the nightly news. We can play Reverend Wright's sermons on every channel, every day and talk about them from now until the election, and make the only question in this campaign whether or not the American people think that I somehow believe or sympathize with his most offensive words. We can pounce on some gaffe by a Hillary supporter as evidence that she's playing the race card, or we can speculate on whether white men will all flock to John McCain in the general election regardless of his policies.

We can do that.

But if we do, I can tell you that in the next election, we'll be talking about some other distraction. And then another one. And then another one. And nothing will change.

That is one option. Or, at this moment, in this election, we can come together and say, "Not this time." This time we want to talk about the crumbling schools that are stealing the future of black children and white children and Asian children and Hispanic children and Native American children. This time we want to reject the cynicism that tells us that these kids can't learn; that those kids who don't look like us are somebody else's problem. The children of America are not those kids, they are our kids, and we will not let them fall behind in a 21st-century economy. Not this time.

This time we want to talk about how the lines in the emergency room are filled with whites and blacks and Hispanics who do not have health care; who don't have the power on their own to overcome the special interests in Washington, but who can take them on if we do it together.

This time we want to talk about the shuttered mills that once provided a decent life for men and women of every race, and the homes for sale that once belonged to Americans from every religion, every region, every walk of life. This time we want to talk about the fact that the real problem is not that someone who doesn't look like you might take your job; it's that the corporation you work for will ship it overseas for nothing more than a profit.

This time we want to talk about the men and women of every color and creed who serve together, and fight together, and bleed together under the same proud flag. We want to talk about how to bring them home from a war that never should've been authorized and never should've been waged, and we want to talk about how we'll show our patriotism by caring for them, and their families, and giving them the benefits they have earned.

I would not be running for president if I didn't believe with all my heart that this is what the vast majority of Americans want for this country. This union may never be perfect, but generation after generation has shown that it can always be perfected. And today, whenever I find myself feeling doubtful or cynical about this possibility, what gives me the most hope is the next generation—the young people whose attitudes and beliefs and openness to change have already made history in this election.

There is one story in particular that I'd like to leave you with today—a story I told when I had the great honor of speaking on Dr. King's birthday at his home church, Ebenezer Baptist, in Atlanta.

There is a young, 23-year-old white woman named Ashley Baia who organized for our campaign in Florence, South Carolina. She had been working to organize a mostly African-American community since the beginning of this campaign, and one day she was at a roundtable discussion where everyone went around telling their story and why they were there.

And Ashley said that when she was nine years old, her mother got cancer. And because she had to miss days of work, she was let go and lost her health care. They had to file for bankruptcy, and that's when Ashley decided that she had to do something to help her mom.

She knew that food was one of their most expensive costs, and so Ashley convinced her mother that what she really liked and really wanted to eat more than anything else was mustard and relish sandwiches. Because that was the cheapest way to eat.

She did this for a year until her mom got better, and she told everyone at the roundtable that the reason she joined our campaign was so that she could help the millions of other children in the country who want and need to help their parents too.

Now Ashley might have made a different choice. Perhaps somebody told her along the way that the source of her mother's problems were blacks who were on welfare and too lazy to work, or Hispanics who were coming into the country illegally. But she didn't. She sought out allies in her fight against injustice.

Anyway, Ashley finishes her story and then goes around the room and asks everyone else why they're supporting the campaign. They all have different stories and reasons. Many bring up a specific issue. And finally they come to this elderly black man who's been sitting there quietly the entire time. And Ashley asks him why he's there. And he does not bring up a specific issue. He does not say health care or the economy. He does not say education or the war. He does not say that he was there because of Barack Obama. He simply says to everyone in the room, "I am here because of Ashley."

"I'm here because of Ashley." By itself, that single moment of recognition between that young white girl and that old black man is not enough. It is not enough to give health care to the sick, or jobs to the jobless, or education to our children.

But it is where we start. It is where our union grows stronger. And as so many generations have come to realize over the course of the 221 years since a band of patriots signed that document in Philadelphia, that is where the perfection begins.

Conventional Wisdom[*]

Janet Murguía

President and Chief Executive Officer, National Council of La Raza, 2005– ; born Kansas City, KS, September 6, 1960; B.S., journalism, 1982, B.A., Spanish, 1982, J.D., 1985, University of Kansas; legislative counsel to former Kansas Congressman Jim Slattery, 1987– 1994; worked at White House, holding positions including deputy assistant to President Clinton and deputy director of legislative affairs, 1994–2000; deputy campaign manager and director of constituency outreach, Gore/Lieberman presidential campaign, 2000; executive vice chancellor for university relations, University of Kansas, 2001–05.

Editor's introduction: Addressing the National Press Club, in Washington, D.C., on April 16, 2008, National Council of La Raza President Janet Murguía discusses the "conventional wisdom" that, after the defeat of comprehensive immigration reform in 2007, immigration would be the wedge issue of the 2008 presidential election. In her remarks she describes what she perceives as the demagoguery of anti-immigration activists—and the public's complacency—as shameful to the nation, and details the media's complicity. She calls attention to her organization's efforts to educate the public and change the discourse on race and immigration away from scapegoating, towards a more sober and realistic view.

Janet Murguía's speech: NCLR is the largest national Hispanic civil rights and advocacy organization in the United States. We were founded in 1968 and are now celebrating our 40th anniversary. We are proud to be an American institution whose mission is to create opportunities for the 45 million Hispanics in the United States. Together with our nearly 300 local affiliates across the country, NCLR works to improve the lives of Hispanics in five key areas—asset building, civil rights, education, employment and health.

The Nonprofit Times has named us among the top 50 leaders shaping the non-profit world and we have been singled out in the recent new book focusing on high-impact non-profits called Forces for Good. Our work has been honored by the U.S. Surgeon General and our former CEO and our current Board Chair have

---

[*] Delivered on April 16, 2008, at Washington, D.C.

both earned the prestigious Hubert H. Humphrey Civil Rights Award by the Leadership Conference on Civil Rights.

Ordinarily, I would take the honor of speaking before the National Press Club as an opportunity to talk about our work helping 23,000 low-income Hispanic families purchase their first homes. I would talk about how we are keeping them in those homes despite the unfolding housing and foreclosure crisis.

Perhaps I would talk about NCLR's recent efforts to build a network of charter schools that serve some 25,000 students or a system of health care clinics that serve another 85,000 families. Maybe, I'd talk about our role in public policy achievements like expanding the Earned Income Tax Credit or creating the Refundable Child Tax Credit that together lift more than two million Hispanic families out of poverty every year.

These days, however, only one of our issues seems to capture the attention of the media. Only one of our issues resonates with elected officials. Only one of our issues seems to matter to the general public. I am speaking, of course, about immigration.

Since the defeat of comprehensive immigration reform last year, conventional wisdom has touted immigration as the wedge issue of the 2008 election. It overwhelmed the presidential primary debates and has been the focal point for many of the subsequent off-year and special elections. And, despite the repeated repudiation of candidates at the national level who espouse the harshest rhetoric, conventional wisdom continues to lead candidates to demagogue this issue "down ticket" in congressional, state and local races.

I come here today out of concern. I believe that, as a nation, we are fast approaching a turning point. What started out as a public policy debate last spring is on the verge of becoming one of the largest civil rights issues of our generation. The demonizing rhetoric that surrounds this issue, the hate groups and vigilantes who promote it, the politicians and media who embrace it and the passivity of those listening, who should stop it, shame our great country. It should shame all of us.

Last week, an editorial in *Investor's Business Daily* made the absurd claim that, "There's a real movement out there that feels our Southwest is really occupied Mexico." It went on to make the ridiculous assertion that NCLR is a key player in this alleged movement. The night before, CBS and Katie Couric did an expose titled "Illegal Immigrant Births—At Your Expense," and showed a member of Congress challenging the 14th Amendment. No opposing point of view. No second opinion. This kind of lopsided viewpoint sinks to the level of demagoguery on cable television news and talk radio. But, *Investor's Business Daily?* CBS? Katie Couric? Is no one above exploiting this issue?

As a nation of immigrants, we have struggled with the demonization of others in our past. The choices we have made have not always lived up to the ideals that make this country great. We have not always listened to the "better angels of our nature." Every major civil rights abuse in our nation's history has been preceded by the vilification and scapegoating of a single group. Ask the native peoples who occupied this continent; ask the Africans who were brought here in chains; ask the Chinese immigrants who built our railroads; ask the Irish immigrants who "needed not apply"; ask the Japanese Americans who were put into internment camps; ask the German, the Italian and the Jewish immigrants who repeatedly suffered discrimination at the turn of the last century from people who called themselves patriots.

We struggled with immigration then and we are struggling now. Voices better left on the fringe of political discourse have moved front and center to define the debate. Their harsh rhetoric has filled the immigration debate with code words that demonize and dehumanize—not just immigrants—but Latinos as a threat to the American way of life. They depict us as "an army of invaders." They call us "a swarm" and "a massive horde." They say that we bring disease and crime to our country.

But, worse yet, they have had a helping hand from the media. A cursory review of network listings shows that spokespeople from hate groups and vigilantes—such as FAIR and the Minutemen—have appeared at least 120 times on cable network news programming over the last three years. That doesn't count print. That doesn't count local television. That doesn't count radio. Rarely is their background explored or challenged. Rarely do they appear with an opposing point of view. And, if that wasn't damning enough, many of the media's talk show hosts and commentators parrot their hate speech on air.

As an organization, NCLR has tried to draw back the curtain to expose those hate groups and extremists pulling the levers and turning the wheels. With the launch of our campaign and website, WeCanStoptheHate.org, we have challenged the cable television networks for putting hate groups and vigilantes on the air as immigration "experts." That's like having David Duke on television as an expert on affirmative action.

We are using this campaign to educate the public about hate groups, hate speech and its consequences—because we know that words have consequences . . . and hateful words have hateful consequences.

Log onto YouTube or Google or any major newspaper or television website and type in the word "immigration." The posts following any video or article are often so ugly they will turn your stomach.

It is no surprise that hate crimes against Latinos are up 35 percent over four years. Hate groups targeting Latinos are up 48 percent since the year 2000. Two-thirds of Latinos say that the failure of the immigration bill has made life more difficult for Latinos overall and roughly half say that it has affected them personally.

But, our detractors say, "We aren't talking about immigrants. We LOVE immigrants. We are only talking about illegal immigrants."

Most Latinos aren't immigrants. But, you can't tell just by looking at us. More than 80 percent of Hispanics in this country are U.S. citizens or legal residents. But, the truth is, Hispanics understand that this issue is about all of us.

When demonstrators in Arizona put on surgical masks whenever a Latino walks by, because they think we carry tuberculosis . . . it's personal.

When Lou Dobbs trumps up false statistics, tying immigrants to a steep rise in leprosy . . . it's personal.

When your 10-year-old nephew, who was born in Kansas is told by a school-mate, "Mexicans are stupid, and I think you should go back to Mexico" . . . it's personal.

When friends and neighbors get pulled over and asked for immigration papers—and sometimes are detained for hours—even though their families have been in this country for generations . . . it's personal.

You don't have to be an immigrant to be horrified that 13,000 American children have been separated from a parent by immigration raids.

You don't have to be an immigrant to know that those shouting "amnesty" have left mass deportation as the only solution remaining on the table.

• How much will it cost to deport 12 million people?

• How many additional police will we need?

• How many federal judges, federal prisons, and federal courts?

• How many U.S. citizens of color—or with an accent—will be picked up in such a massive sweep?

• How many boxcars will it take to move them to our borders?

You don't have to be an immigrant to know that such solutions are really not solutions. Perhaps some of those crying loudest about amnesty really don't want a solution at all.

Which brings me back to immigration as the campaign wedge issue for 2008. Four months ago, conventional wisdom pushed Rudy Giuliani and Mitt Romney to spar on national television over who was tougher on undocumented immigrants. Three months ago, conventional wisdom led 49 Democrats to support a deportation-only bill, in fear of what Rahm Emmanuel called "the third rail of American politics." Two months ago, conventional wisdom held that immigration would [be] the winning issue in the special election being held in Illinois.

But, what do the results show?

The results show that such conventional wisdom could not have been more misguided. Anti-immigration campaigns have, for the most part, failed. Immigration, as a wedge issue, does not deliver the votes.

• Most of those running anti-immigration campaigns lost their elections in 2006 and 2007.

• The presidential candidates who adopted hard-line positions on immigration have all been pushed out of the race.

• Just recently, a safe Republican district in Illinois went to Democrat Bill Foster after his opponent, Jim Oberweis, mounted a largely anti-immigrant campaign. His loss prompted John McCain to caution his own party. "We just had a loss of Denny Hastert's seat," he said. "The Republican candidate had very strong anti-immigrant rhetoric—so I would hope that many of our Republican candidates would understand the political practicalities of this issue."

So, clearly, when it comes to immigration, conventional wisdom has gotten it wrong. Simply put, that dog won't hunt.

Why is it then that one month ago, after Senator McCain had secured the nomination, conventional wisdom prompted a group of Republican Senators to introduce a raft of punitive immigration bills in the Senate? Why is it that another group in the House has fought to resurrect the Shuler-Tancredo deportation-only legislation? Why is it that over 1,400 state and local initiatives have been introduced in the last year, compared to 1,300 in the past ten years?

The answer is, all of these actions are clearly designed to exploit the issue for the elections this fall. All of these initiatives do not account for one simple dynamic: this issue not only fails to move the general public, it galvanizes the Latino vote. It is easy to understand how this could happen. The "best political teams on television" have so few Latinos in front of the cameras—who could know how Latinos might react?

Make no mistake, the Latino vote matters. And after this election, it will matter more.

• Latinos were a deciding factor in the Florida Primary for John McCain. They helped him take the lead amongst Republicans. He won 54 percent of the Latino vote in a crowded field.

• Hispanics were the decisive factor for Hillary Clinton in New York and California and gave new life to her candidacy in the Texas Primary. She carried approximately two-thirds of the Hispanic vote in that state.

• In 1996, 4.9 million Hispanics voted. In 2008, with an energized electorate, that number could double to 10 million.

• More importantly, Hispanics constitute a large share of the electorate in four states that President Bush carried by margins of 5 percentage points or less: New Mexico, Florida, Nevada and Colorado.

We know that the Latino vote will be the deciding factor in who is elected president this November. Given the importance of this election at all levels, we have launched several major new initiatives to improve Latino participation in this year's election, including our partnerships with Democracia USA and the Ya Es Hora campaign. Just as Latinos have had a significant role in selecting the candidates for president in both parties, we hope to elect a Senate, a House and state governors and legislators who will show courage and leadership in taking hate out of the debate.

Hispanic voters have spoken loudly and clearly that we will not be demonized; we will not be scapegoated; and we will not be ignored. But we cannot, and should not, do it alone.

Poll after poll shows that Americans favor solutions that require people to come out of the shadows, require them to pay a fine for entering this country without documents and require them to learn English and pay taxes in order to become citizens. Those American voices, however, are being drowned out by a small, but extremely vocal and persistent grassroots network. In short, there is a bully in the room. And all of us need to stand up to him if we are going to live up to this country's best ideals and aspirations.

Two years ago, the Latino community held some of the largest peaceful demonstrations in U.S. history. To our community it proved that each of us is not alone. It gave us confidence to stand up to the voices of hate. It gave us hope. But this time, there is only one march that will truly empower our community. There is only one march that will demonstrate our clout. There is only one march that will speak louder than all the voices of hate that are mobilized against us.

Our next march is to the voting booth this November.

I ask all Americans to join us in that march this year to oppose the voices of hate, to reject the politics of division and to support those who are serious about finding legitimate solutions to this complex problem.

Thank you.

Speech at the National Press Club[*]

Jeremiah Wright

Pastor, Trinity United Church of Christ, Chicago, 1972–2008; born Philadelphia, PA, September 22, 1941; attended Virginia Union University, Richmond, 1959–61; B.A., 1968; M.A., English, 1969, Howard University; M.A., 1975, University of Chicago Divinity School; D.Min., black sacred music, 1990, United Theological Seminary; U.S. Marine Corps, PFC, 2nd Marine Division, 1961–63; U.S. Navy, hospital corpsman 3rd class, 1964–67; interim pastor, Zion Church, 1968–69; assistant pastor, Beth Eden Church, 1969–1971; American Association of Theological Schools, researcher, 1970–72; executive director, Chicago Center for Black Religious Studies, 1974–75; lecturer, Chicago Cluster of Theological Schools, 1975–77; professor, United Theological Seminary, 1991–97; professor, Chicago Theological Seminary, 1998; professor, Garrett Evangelical Theological Seminary, 1999; author and co-author, What Makes You So Strong?: Sermons of Joy and Strength from Jeremiah A. Wright, Jr. *(1993),* Africans Who Shaped Our Faith *(Student Guide), (1995),* Good News!: Sermons of Hope for Today's Families *(1995),* From One Brother to Another: Voices of African American Men *(1996),* Adam! Where Are You? Why Most Black Men Don't Go to Church *(1997),* When Black Men Stand Up for God: Reflections on the Million Man March *(1997),* What Can Happen When We Pray: A Daily Devotional *(2002),* From One Brother To Another, Volume 2: Voices of African American Men *(2003),* Blow the Trumpet in Zion! Global Vision and Action for the 21st Century Black Church *(2005),* Tempted to Leave the Cross: Renewing the Call to Discipleship *(2007).*

Editor's introduction: Responding to Barack Obama's "A More Perfect Union" speech in Philadelphia and the extensive press coverage of the split between him and Obama, Reverend Jeremiah Wright, former senior pastor of Trinity United Church of Christ in Chicago, of which Barack Obama was a member, spoke at the National Press Club in Washington, D.C., on April 28, 2008. After declaring recent media attention "an attack on the black church," he describes the black religious tradition in America as largely invisible in the mainstream culture and elucidated its themes of transformation and liberation, as well as Trinity's efforts

* Delivered on April 28, 2008, at Washington, D.C.

toward social justice over the decades. The talk was one of Wright's many public appearances during a hard-fought Democratic primary, leading many to denounce Wright as intentionally distracting from Obama's bid for the presidency.

Jeremiah Wright's speech: Over the next few days, prominent scholars of the African-American religious tradition from several different disciplines—theologians, church historians, ethicists, professors of the Hebrew bible, homiletics, hermeneutics, and historians of religions—those scholars will join in with sociologists, political analysts, local church pastors, and denominational officials to examine the African-American religious experience and its historical, theological and political context.

The workshops, the panel discussions, and the symposium will go into much more intricate detail about this unknown phenomenon of the black church (LAUGHTER) than I have time to go into in the few moments that we have to share together. And I would invite you to spend the next two days getting to know just a little bit about a religious tradition that is as old as and, in some instances, older than this country.

And this is a country which houses this religious tradition that we all love and a country that some of us have served. It is a tradition that is, in some ways, like Ralph Ellison's the *Invisible Man.*

It has been right here in our midst and on our shoulders since the 1600s, but it was, has been, and, in far too many instances, still is invisible to the dominant culture, in terms of its rich history, its incredible legacy, and its multiple meanings.

The black religious experience is a tradition that, at one point in American history, was actually called the "invisible institution," as it was forced underground by the Black Codes.

The Black Codes prohibited the gathering of more than two black people without a white person being present to monitor the conversation, the content, and the mood of any discourse between persons of African descent in this country.

Africans did not stop worshipping because of the Black Codes. Africans did not stop gathering for inspiration and information and for encouragement and for hope in the midst of discouraging and seemingly hopeless circumstances. They just gathered out of the eyesight and the earshot of those who defined them as less than human.

They became, in other words, invisible in and invisible to the eyes of the dominant culture. They gathered to worship in brush arbors, sometimes called hush arbors, where the slaveholders, slave patrols, and Uncle Toms couldn't hear nobody pray.

From the 1700s in North America, with the founding of the first legally recognized independent black congregations, through the end of the Civil War, and the passing of the 13th and 14th Amendments to the Constitution of the United States of America, the black religious experience was informed by, enriched by, expanded by, challenged by, shaped by, and influenced by the influx of Africans from the other two Americas and the Africans brought in to this country from the

Caribbean, plus the Africans who were called "fresh blacks" by the slave traders, those Africans who had not been through the seasoning process of the middle passage in the Caribbean colonies, those Africans on the sea coast islands off of Georgia and South Carolina, the Gullah—we say in English "Gullah," those of us in the black community say "Geechee"—those people brought into the black religious experience a flavor that other seasoned Africans could not bring.

It is those various streams of the black religious experience which will be addressed in summary form over the next two days, streams which require full courses at the university and graduate-school level, and cannot be fully addressed in a two-day symposium, and streams which tragically remain invisible in a dominant culture which knows nothing about those whom Langston Hughes calls "the darker brother and sister."

It is all of those streams that make up this multilayered and rich tapestry of the black religious experience. And I stand before you to open up this two-day symposium with the hope that this most recent attack on the black church is not an attack on Jeremiah Wright; it is an attack on the black church.

(APPLAUSE)

As the vice president told you, that applause comes from not the working press.

(LAUGHTER)

The most recent attack on the black church, it is our hope that this just might mean that the reality of the African-American church will no longer be invisible.

Maybe now, as an honest dialogue about race in this country begins, a dialogue called for by Senator Obama and a dialogue to begin in the United Church of Christ among 5,700 congregations in just a few weeks, maybe now, as that dialogue begins, the religious tradition that has kept hope alive for people struggling to survive in countless hopeless situations, maybe that religious tradition will be understood, celebrated, and even embraced by a nation that seems not to have noticed why 11 o'clock on Sunday morning has been called the most segregated hour in America.

We have known since 1787 that it is the most segregated hour. Maybe now we can begin to understand why it is the most segregated hour.

And maybe now we can begin to take steps to move the black religious tradition from the status of invisible to the status of invaluable, not just for some black people in this country, but for all the people in this country.

Maybe this dialogue on race, an honest dialogue that does not engage in denial or superficial platitudes, maybe this dialogue on race can move the people of faith in this country from various stages of alienation and marginalization to the exciting possibility of reconciliation.

That is my hope, as I open up this two-day symposium. And I open it as a pastor and a professor who comes from a long tradition of what I call the prophetic theology of the black church.

Now, in the 1960s, the term "liberation theology" began to gain currency with the writings and the teachings of preachers, pastors, priests, and professors from Latin America. Their theology was done from the underside.

Their viewpoint was not from the top down or from a set of teachings which undergirded imperialism. Their viewpoints, rather, were from the bottom up, the thoughts and understandings of God, the faith, religion and the Bible from those whose lives were ground, under, mangled and destroyed by the ruling classes or the oppressors.

Liberation theology started in and started from a different place. It started from the vantage point of the oppressed.

In the late 1960s, when Dr. James Cone's powerful books burst onto the scene, the term "black liberation theology" began to be used. I do not in any way disagree with Dr. Cone, nor do I in any way diminish the inimitable and incomparable contributions that he has made and that he continues to make to the field of theology. Jim, incidentally, is a personal friend of mine.

I call our faith tradition, however, the prophetic tradition of the black church, because I take its origins back past Jim Cone, past the sermons and songs of Africans in bondage in the transatlantic slave trade. I take it back past the problem of Western ideology and notions of white supremacy.

I take and trace the theology of the black church back to the prophets in the Hebrew Bible and to its last prophet, in my tradition, the one we call Jesus of Nazareth.

The prophetic tradition of the black church has its roots in Isaiah, the 61st chapter, where God says the prophet is to preach the gospel to the poor and to set at liberty those who are held captive. Liberating the captives also liberates who are holding them captive.

It frees the captives and it frees the captors. It frees the oppressed and it frees the oppressors.

The prophetic theology of the black church, during the days of chattel slavery, was a theology of liberation. It was preached to set free those who were held in bondage spiritually, psychologically, and sometimes physically. And it was practiced to set the slaveholders free from the notion that they could define other human beings or confine a soul set free by the power of the gospel.

The prophetic theology of the black church during the days of segregation, Jim Crow, lynching, and the separate-but-equal fantasy was a theology of liberation.

It was preached to set African Americans free from the notion of second-class citizenship, which was the law of the land. And it was practiced to set free misguided and miseducated Americans from the notion that they were actually superior to other Americans based on the color of their skin.

The prophetic theology of the black church in our day is preached to set African Americans and all other Americans free from the misconceived notion that different means deficient.

Being different does not mean one is deficient. It simply means one is different, like snowflakes, like the diversity that God loves. Black music is different from European and European-American music. It is not deficient; it is just different.

Black worship is different from European and European-American worship. It is not deficient; it is just different.

Black preaching is different from European and European-American preaching. It is not deficient; it is just different. It is not bombastic; it is not controversial; it's different.

(APPLAUSE)

Those of you who can't see on C-SPAN, we had one or two working press clap along with the non-working press.

(LAUGHTER)

Black learning styles are different from European and European-American learning styles. They are not deficient; they are just different.

This principle of "different does not mean deficient" is at the heart of the prophetic theology of the black church. It is a theology of liberation.

The prophetic theology of the black church is not only a theology of liberation; it is also a theology of transformation, which is also rooted in Isaiah 61, the text from which Jesus preached in his inaugural message, as recorded by Luke.

When you read the entire passage from either Isaiah 61 or Luke 4 and do not try to understand the passage or the content of the passage in the context of a sound bite, what you see is God's desire for a radical change in a social order that has gone sour.

God's desire is for positive, meaningful and permanent change. God does not want one people seeing themselves as superior to other people. God does not want the powerless masses, the poor, the widows, the marginalized, and those underserved by the powerful few to stay locked into sick systems which treat some in the society as being more equal than others in that same society.

God's desire is for positive change, transformation, real change, not cosmetic change, transformation, radical change or a change that makes a permanent difference, transformation. God's desire is for transformation, changed lives, changed minds, changed laws, changed social orders, and changed hearts in a changed world.

This principle of transformation is at the heart of the prophetic theology of the black church. These two foci of liberation and transformation have been at the very core of the black religious experience from the days of David Walker, Harriet Tubman, Richard Allen, Jarena Lee, Bishop Henry McNeal Turner, and Sojourner Truth, through the days of Adam Clayton Powell, Ida B. Wells, Dr. Martin Luther King, Rosa Parks, Malcolm X, Barbara Jordan, Cornell West, and Fanny Lou Hamer.

These two foci of liberation and transformation have been at the very core of the United Church of Christ since its predecessor denomination, the Congregational Church of New England, came to the moral defense and paid for the legal defense of the Mende people aboard the slave ship *Amistad*, since the days when the United Church of Christ fought against slavery, played an active role in the underground railroad, and set up over 500 schools for the Africans who were freed from slavery in 1865.

And these two foci remain at the core of the teachings of the United Church of Christ, as it has fought against apartheid in South Africa and racism in the United States of America ever since the union which formed the United Church of Christ in 1957.

These two foci of liberation and transformation have also been at the very core and the congregation of Trinity United Church of Christ since it was founded in 1961. And these foci have been the bedrock of our preaching and practice for the past 36 years.

Our congregation, as you heard in the introduction, took a stand against apartheid when the government of our country was supporting the racist regime of the African government in South Africa.

(APPLAUSE)

Our congregation stood in solidarity with the peasants in El Salvador and Nicaragua, while our government, through Ollie North and the Iran-Contra scandal, was supporting the Contras, who were killing the peasants and the Miskito Indians in those two countries.

Our congregation sent 35 men and women through accredited seminaries to earn their master of divinity degrees, with an additional 40 currently being enrolled in seminary, while building two senior citizen housing complexes and running two child care programs for the poor, the unemployed, the low-income parents on the south side of Chicago for the past 30 years.

Our congregation feeds over 5,000 homeless and needy families every year, while our government cuts food stamps and spends billions fighting in an unjust war in Iraq.

(APPLAUSE)

Our congregation has sent dozens of boys and girls to fight in the Vietnam War, the first Gulf War, and the present two wars in Afghanistan and Iraq. My goddaughter's unit just arrived in Iraq this week, while those who call me unpatriotic have used their positions of privilege to avoid military service, while sending—(APPLAUSE)—while sending over 4,000 American boys and girls of every race to die over a lie.

(APPLAUSE)

Our congregation has had an HIV-AIDS ministry for over two decades. Our congregation has awarded over $1 million to graduating high school seniors going into college and an additional $500,000 to the United Negro College Fund, and the six HBCUs related to the United Church of Christ, while advocating for health care for the uninsured, workers' rights for those forbidden to form unions, and fighting the unjust sentencing system which has sent black men and women to prison for longer terms for possession of crack cocaine than white men and women have to serve for the possession of powder cocaine.

Our congregation has had a prison ministry for 30 years, a drug and alcohol recovery ministry for 20 years, a full service program for senior citizens, and 22 different ministries for the youth of our church, from pre-school through high school, all proceeding from the starting point of liberation and transformation, a prophetic theology which presumes God's desire for changed minds, changed laws, changed social orders, changed lives, changed hearts in a changed world.

The prophetic theology of the black church is a theology of liberation; it is a theology of transformation; and it is ultimately a theology of reconciliation.

The Apostle Paul said, "Be ye reconciled one to another, even as God was in Christ reconciling the world to God's self."

God does not desire for us, as children of God, to be at war with each other, to see each other as superior or inferior, to hate each other, abuse each other, misuse each other, define each other, or put each other down.

God wants us reconciled, one to another. And that third principle in the prophetic theology of the black church is also and has always been at the heart of the black church experience in North America.

When Richard Allen and Absalom Jones were dragged out of St. George's Methodist Episcopal Church in Philadelphia, during the same year, 1787, when the Constitution was framed in Philadelphia, for daring to kneel at the altar next to white worshippers, they founded the Free African Society and they welcomed white members into their congregation to show that reconciliation was the goal, not retaliation.

Absalom Jones became the rector of the St. Thomas Anglican Church in 1781, and St. Thomas welcomed white Anglicans in the spirit of reconciliation.

Richard Allen became the founding pastor of the Bethel African Methodist Episcopal Church, and the motto of the AME Church has always been, "God our father, man our brother, and Christ our redeemer." The word "man" included men and women of all races back in 1787 and 1792, in the spirit of reconciliation.

The black church's role in the fight for equality and justice, from the 1700s up until 2008, has always had as its core the nonnegotiable doctrine of reconciliation, children of God repenting for past sins against each other.

Jim Wallis says America's sin of racism has never even been confessed, much less repented for. Repenting for past sins against each other and being reconciled to one other—Jim Wallis is white, by the way—(LAUGHTER)—being reconciled to one another, because of the love of God, who made all of us in God's image.

Reconciliation, the years have taught me, is where the hardest work is found for those of us in the Christian faith, however, because it means some critical thinking and some re-examination of faulty assumptions when using the paradigm of Dr. William Augustus Jones.

Dr. Jones, in his book, *God in the Ghetto*, argues quite accurately that one's theology, how I see God, determines one's anthropology, how I see humans, and one's anthropology then determines one's sociology, how I order my society.

Now, the implications from the outside are obvious. If I see God as male, if I see God as white male, if I see God as superior, as God over us and not Immanuel, which means "God with us," if I see God as mean, vengeful, authoritarian, sexist, or misogynist, then I see humans through that lens.

My theological lens shapes my anthropological lens. And as a result, white males are superior; all others are inferior.

And I order my society where I can worship God on Sunday morning wearing a black clergy robe and kill others on Sunday evening wearing a white Klan robe. I can have laws which favor whites over blacks in America or South Africa. I can construct a theology of apartheid in the Africana church (ph) and a theology of white supremacy in the North American or Germanic church.

The implications from the outset are obvious, but then the complicated work is left to be done, as you dig deeper into the constructs, which tradition, habit, and hermeneutics put on your plate.

To say "I am a Christian" is not enough. Why? Because the Christianity of the slaveholder is not the Christianity of the slave. The God to whom the slaveholders pray as they ride on the decks of the slave ship is not the God to whom the enslaved are praying as they ride beneath the decks on that slave ship.

How we are seeing God, our theology, is not the same. And what we both mean when we say "I am a Christian" is not the same thing. The prophetic theology of the black church has always seen and still sees all of God's children as sisters and brothers, equals who need reconciliation, who need to be reconciled as equals in order for us to walk together into the future which God has prepared for us.

Reconciliation does not mean that blacks become whites or whites become blacks and Hispanics become Asian or that Asians become Europeans.

Reconciliation means we embrace our individual rich histories, all of them. We retain who we are as persons of different cultures, while acknowledging that those of other cultures are not superior or inferior to us. They are just different from us.

We root out any teaching of superiority, inferiority, hatred, or prejudice.

And we recognize for the first time in modern history in the West that the other who stands before us with a different color of skin, a different texture of hair, different music, different preaching styles, and different dance moves, that other is one of God's children just as we are, no better, no worse, prone to error and in need of forgiveness, just as we are.

Only then will liberation, transformation, and reconciliation become realities and cease being ever elusive ideals.

Thank you for having me in your midst this morning.

3

The Mortgage Meltdown

Speech at the National Press Club's Newsmakers Lunch[*]

John M. Robbins

Chairman of the Mortgage Bankers Association (MBA) and co-head and special counsel, Vertice, a division of Wachovia Securities; previously chief executive officer of American Mortgage Network (AmNet); active in the mortgage banking industry since 1972; founded American Residential Mortgage Corp.; member of Fannie Mae's National Advisory Council and served on its Western Regional Advisory Board; chairman since 1994 of the Policy Advisory Board for the University of San Diego's Burnham-Moores Center for Real Estate; board of directors of Phoenix Footwear Group and trustee and treasurer of the University of San Diego.

Editor's introduction: John M. Robbins, Chairman of the Mortgage Bankers Association (MBA), describes himself in his speech to the National Press Club as "mad as hell." Characterizing the mortgage meltdown as the product of "a few unethical actors" and damaging to the very industry that long propped up the economy, he explains the importance of Americans owning their own homes and how subprime loans can help make homeownership a reality. He introduces a series of public service announcements by the MBA, urging homeowners unable to make mortgage payments to contact their lenders. He also discusses preventive measures against fraud, such as stricter requirements for mortgage brokers and increased customer education. A national organization representing the real-estate finance industry, MBA works to expand homeownership and increase financial literacy.

John M. Robbins's speech: I am very proud of what I do for a living.

I know the good my company, my employees and thousands of my fellow mortgage bankers have done for families, for communities, for this country.

Frankly, I'd imagined my brief tenure as Chairman of the Mortgage Bankers Association would be celebratory—one part victory lap, one part implementation of initiatives with a lasting impact on the industry I cherish.

Yet I stand before you today mad as hell. I have to be angry.

---

[*] Delivered on May 22, 2007, at Washington, D.C.

It would be too depressing to accept that a very few unethical people can give my profession, and me, a black eye. But it's worse than that.

It's not just our reputations that have been damaged. People have been hurt. The very people we take pride in helping. All because of a very few unethical actors.

And here's what their actions obscure: Millions of Americans building financial security today by owning their own homes. 2.8 million families achieved homeownership for the first time in just the past five years.

Many are families who, a generation ago, thought home ownership was beyond their reach. They are today building equity, re-paying loans without undue hardship, experiencing their American dream of owning a home. This creates stronger cities and towns.

People care more deeply, and are more involved when they have an ownership stake in their neighborhood.

What makes the current situation so frustrating is that those of us now tainted by those unethical actions were the very ones out front.

Our historical data led us to predict a loosening of underwriting standards, an increase in ARMs. It occurs after every boom, and we clearly said this boom would be no different.

For years, we have been calling for legislation to create a tough national standard to protect consumers against predatory lending; we were doing so during years of record volumes, long before the increased share of subprime loans.

Years in which our industry helped keep this economy out of a recession.

Today, when faced with heartbreaking stories of people losing their homes, there's a clamor for action. It's an easy trap to fall into—regulators can regulate, so let's have more regulations. Legislators can legislate, so let's have more laws. Problem solved.

It was Maslow who said that when all you have is a hammer, every problem looks like a nail. But before we all start hammering, I propose those most intimately involved have the chance to make necessary changes.

Our industry pioneered structured finance securitization, a system that spreads risk, increases liquidity, and offers investors and borrowers opportunities they wouldn't otherwise have.

It is a global system, the envy of other nations. We developed risk-based pricing, opening more doors. Thanks to these innovations, homeownership is no longer just for the few and powerful. It is for the masses.

Nearly 70 percent of Americans are homeowners, building wealth. And building strong communities. Let's not smash this subtle, intricate and ingenious system as we fix problems in the subprime market.

We have plenty of cleaning up to do, and that's the most important thing. Help the people in trouble. The truth is, we're good at cleaning up. We had a lot of practice after what Katrina and Rita did to the Gulf Coast. We prevented widespread foreclosures for more than 18 months by providing forbearance for many homeowners.

So let's begin by looking at what corrections have already occurred, and what's left to be done. In that way we can be sure we take the right steps rather than just the expedient ones. That we do what is truly needed today. Not something that was needed a year ago but won't do much good now.

This requires an understanding of the actual magnitude of the problem. Let's look at some hard numbers.

First, let me point out that fully 35 percent of the homeowners in this country have no mortgage. They own their homes free and clear. 35 percent. Plenty of stability there.

Now, let's look at the segment where our current troubles are.

Among homeowners, 5.1 percent of them are subprime borrowers with adjustable rate mortgages.

5.1 percent.

We are seeing a foreclosure rate of 10.8 percent annualized among subprime ARMS. So what percentage of homeowners are we talking about? Ten percent of 5.1 percent of all homeowners.

And of that half of one percent of the whole, fully half of THOSE will find some solution that avoids a foreclosure sale.

In other words, one quarter of one percent will ultimately face foreclosure.

As we can clearly see, this is not a macro-economic event. No seismic financial occurrence is about to overwhelm the U.S. economy. And we're not the only ones who think so.

Chairman Bernanke said last week in his speech, and I quote, "We do not expect significant spillovers from the subprime market to the rest of the economy or to the financial system."

I know that is cold comfort to the people who have been hurt. Their pain is real, a mountain to climb each morning. They don't care what the statistics are, they're people with problems. Those figures, even at a half percent, still add up to a lot of people.

The Center for Responsible Lending released a foreclosure forecast that cites 2.2 million as the number of subprime borrowers who—and let's pay attention here—have lost or will lose their homes to foreclosure. That's been interpreted as new foreclosures, as something about to happen.

They reached that 2.2 million figure by disingenuously totaling all the subprime foreclosures since 1998—of which there were about 1.6 million—and then of recent subprime loans to about another 600,000 in the near future. So their 2.2 million figure was cumulative over at least an 11-year period, only a portion of which is a forecast.

That's still a lot of people, but out of 75 million homeowners and 50 million mortgage holders, it's not an eyebrow-raising number, when looked at over that period of years. It's within what we as a society deem as an acceptable risk for the rewards and opportunities of homeownership.

One more thing about their forecast—it assumes that every loan that goes into foreclosure is foreclosed upon. But 50 percent of foreclosures are worked out. And that's a percentage we need to keep high.

Again, for the people represented by those numbers, any one of them, it is a tragedy.

Yet we need those figures to understand how best to help those who need help.

Knowing that the system is not in imminent danger, it's clear that our first steps are to help those in trouble.

We mean homeowners living in their own homes. We are not for rescuing real estate speculators. Blanket forbearance that bails out investors could actually drive up delinquencies. Some might view it as a way to get out of their obligations— even the talk of blanket forbearance could spur a surge in delinquencies.

Second, we must find a way to prevent future abuse without eliminating sub-prime loans. I want you all to remember that 3 million Americans used a subprime loan to purchase a house.

It is an extremely important tool for providing homeownership opportunities in this country.

Again, Chairman Bernanke said, "Regulators must walk a fine line. We must do what we can to prevent abuses or bad practices, but at the same time we do not want to curtail responsible subprime lending or close off refinancing options that would be beneficial to borrowers."

Here's why that makes sense: More than 81 percent of all holders of subprime loans are making their payments on time.

So for every dramatic and heartbreaking story, there are so many more equally dramatic and uplifting stories of people who have gained a home—and in many cases not just a home, but a legacy of financial stability to pass on to the next generation—thanks to a subprime loan.

These are people like Mr. Win of San Francisco, a Vietnamese immigrant with a sound business but no credit history. A subprime loan was the only way he could purchase a home. Once in, and with the help of his excellent mortgage payment history, he established good credit, at which point he then refinanced into a prime loan.

We as the mortgage lending community want to work with our borrowers to avoid foreclosure—and we are—our partnership with Neighborworks is just one example.

Now, I'd like it to be all success stories and not a single sad one, but I am a realist.

I'm also an American, and one of the freedoms we enjoy is the freedom to take risk, the freedom to make individual choices. Sub prime or not, people are often banking on themselves when they take a mortgage, banking on their vision of a future that's more rewarding than where they may be today. For the vast majority of people it works out fine.

For others, unfortunate things happen. But we as a society deem that an acceptable risk. We like people who bet on themselves. We are indeed a risk and reward society.

One more quote from the Fed Chairman: "We must seek to preserve the benefits of financial innovation even as we address the risks that may accompany that innovation."

Personal life events—sickness, job loss—and local economic conditions are still the main drivers of delinquencies, regardless of loan types.

The states today with the highest level of serious late payments—Michigan, Ohio, Illinois, Indiana and Kentucky—all have troubled local economies.

These states have lost 460,000 jobs since 2001.

I chose Mr. Win precisely because he is an immigrant. Immigrants are arriving at the rate of 1.3 million per year; some arrive with wealth, but the vast majority arrives with little money and with no credit history.

They're a big reason our mortgage market is projected to be two times its current $10.3 trillion size in just 15 years. Our population is growing—about 14 million new households will need homes in the next 20 years.

Just two years from now, 30 million single women will own their own homes. A Brookings study states that half the buildings in which Americans will live, play and work in the year 2030 don't even exist yet.

Clearly, for a million different reasons, there remains a real need for subprime loans. Some say there are natural limits to home ownership and we've plain exceeded them.

Well I disagree.

I believe the correct homeownership rate will be achieved when every borrower who is credit worthy throughout the entire risk spectrum has access to credit to buy a house. We must continue to make increased homeownership a priority.

Until the gap between the overall average and minority ownership is closed, any talk of having reached the peak of homeownership must be tabled. Ask our minority populations, now numbering 100 million people, how important it is to them to have equal access to these opportunities.

We don't want to revert to a time when without perfect credit you couldn't buy a home. It's ironic that for years that was the rap against this industry. We were too conservative.

Yet regulatory or legislative over-reaction could prompt a return to just that— to raise the bar.

Forcing out first time low- to moderate-income borrowers. It's not the person with a 720 FICO score who needs to worry. We were concerned about this issue long before the current subprime situation.

A working paper put out three years ago from the Joint Center for Housing Studies at Harvard poses a very interesting chicken and egg problem.

Entitled "Hitting the Wall: Credit as an Impediment to Homeownership," it reports a significant increase in credit quality among homeowners measured from

1989 to 2001. Meaning today, most people who own their own homes have relatively strong credit.

However, credit quality among renters did just the opposite over the same period—it decreased significantly. Did the renters with good credit simply buy their way out of one group and into the other? Does that account for both shifts? Or does the ability to own a home create good credit?

We already know it "creates" wealth.

According to the Federal government, the average net worth of homeowners is $184,000. The average net worth of renters is $4,000. As with most complex issues, it is likely a bit of all that, plus the fact that many renters during that time were likely new immigrants with no credit.

But whichever way you interpret the findings, the one thing they tell us is that it's critical for society to improve credit among renters—we don't want to be a land of haves and have nots.

And that means improving financial literacy, teaching sound money management in our schools, getting the point across early and often that plastic isn't cash.

We urge congress to create a financial literacy requirement for public schools; I have met with many members of Congress on this subject, and see no downside. We are the most complex credit society in the world. Isn't financial literacy a little more important than wood shop?

So what steps have already been taken, by the market, and by the players involved? Underwriting has tightened.

While standards loosened in 2005 and 2006—they always do to some degree when volume declines—today the percentage of banks reporting tighter standards is the highest in 15 years.

Investors are wary of too many subprime loans in their portfolios. If lenders can't sell them on the secondary market, they won't originate them. So they're declining as a result of supply and demand.

Many of those who most abused the system are already out of business.

Today, over 40 companies have closed for being overly aggressive in their underwriting. While the market isn't perfect, it does punish mistakes severely and is much faster to correct than either legislators or regulators.

Now many people whose loans are about to reset still have subprime credit. They need to get into some other loan. Will they be able to? Many in this category are not mere victims of unscrupulous lenders.

They're smart people who took a calculated risk to get into a home, all along planning to refinance before the big jump in their ARMs. In many states, these borrowers were hit not just by the rise in interest rates, but by dramatic run-ups in property taxes and hazard insurance, too.

We can't leave these people twisting in the wind. They were practicing financial planning and attempting to take advantage of the opportunities they saw in the future.

They were betting on themselves. To keep their refinancing options open we must avoid a credit crunch.

Even so, tight credit is having an effect on home sales—the latest projections for this year revised to around a 4 percent drop compared to last year, remembering that was a near record year.

Well that's what the market has done . . . What have we, and others been doing, and what more do we propose to do?

Our first priority should be those who need help immediately. Searching for solutions, the mortgage industry has met with GSEs, with FHA, with our largest servicers, consumer groups, and civil rights leaders. We did so both separately and as a participant in Senator Dodd's housing summit last month.

There we helped draft the principles that all agreed to, including early contact of borrowers who may be in trouble and a commitment to find the best alternatives for troubled borrowers.

We continue to work toward FHA modernization. Proof of its importance was Commissioner Montgomery's announcement that FHA plans to refi over 60,000 subprime loans in 2007.

The industry has the capacity and the tools to prevent many foreclosures . . . if given the chance. It's human nature for borrowers in trouble to avoid calling their servicer and announcing that they don't have enough money to pay their mortgage. It's just not a call anyone wants to make—indeed, it's counterintuitive.

Yet it's the smartest thing a borrower facing delinquency can do.

Even 80 percent of those already in foreclosure benefit from loss mitigation techniques, resulting in about half not losing their homes. I hope this fact is mentioned in any and all coverage of subprime loan delinquency—nobody wins in a foreclosure.

On average our industry loses 40–50,000 when that happens, but the homeowner loses a lot more: their credit rating, their equity and their home.

So working something out is truly best for everyone.

For that reason, MBA, on behalf of the entire mortgage industry, has created a series of radio and television public service announcements. They let borrowers know how important it is to contact the company they make their payment to if they are having trouble.

The sooner they call, the sooner they can work together to find a solution. It helps prevent foreclosure, and minimizes damage to the borrower's credit.

MBA has partnered with NeighborWorks America, a national nonprofit organization created by Congress to provide financial support, technical assistance and training for community revitalization efforts.

Specifically, we'll be working to promote their free counseling hotline, 888-995-HOPE, manned by the Homeownership Preservation Foundation.

This month, 650 calls are coming into the hotline each and every day and nearly half of these turn into counseling sessions. That's 19,000 calls a month.

Please pass it on: 888-995-HOPE.

We'll also be establishing foreclosure intervention programs in cities with high foreclosure rates and helping to train and certify more foreclosure counselors, all through our partnership with NeighborWorks America.

And as part of the Mortgage Bankers Association's ongoing financial literacy effort, we have re-tooled and re-launched our consumer website, the Home Loan Learning Center, offering tools and information to help consumers decide which mortgages are best for them. The resources include toll free numbers, email addresses and ways to contact their servicers. I'm pleased to report that the Spanish version of the site is now being launched as well.

Now, what about prevention?

To prevent, we need to once again identify the problem: unethical people. Who made this mess? The short-term folks. People who get a commission when the deal happens.

For them, it's the number of loans that counts. Good loan? Bad loan? Who cares? For them it's all about their commission.

You know how I define a customer for life? Someone I help buy their second home seven years after their starter home—a third home when they have kids. A downsize home when the kids leave, or a retirement or vacation home. That's how most of us define a lifetime customer—four, maybe five transactions, each made possible by the previous one.

For the people who caused this problem, there's no such thing as a lifetime customer. The closest they get is someone you refi every six months until they sink. They, not people with marginal credit, are who need to be stopped.

Frankly, it's too easy to hang a shingle and call yourself an expert in mortgages. We need licensing of brokers, with a threshold that will weed out those unwilling to be responsible, to be held accountable. Some cross the line into pure fraud, and for them we have laws. But as long as there are scam artists willing to look someone in the eye and say "I'm going to get you something for nothing," people will be hurt.

So do we just throw up our hands, or do we arm the people who can be vigilant, the people there'll always be enough of: the consumers.

Arm them with the facts. Make them savvy before it's too late. Consumers are smart. Armed with good information, they make intelligent choices. Give them easy access to tools and information that clarifies what is admittedly a way too complicated process. People should be able to know and understand what they're getting into.

I characterized the real estate finance industry as complex, intricate and the envy of the world at the beginning of this speech. But for all its accomplishments, it can be improved significantly. If it's not comprehended by the consumers it will always be subject to abuse.

Consumers can't shop what they don't understand. Let's not allow the potential for abuse deprive someone of the opportunity of building financial security, of having a home. Instead, let's simplify the process for consumers.

That's why MBA launched Project Clarity in 2006, an initiative to simplify and demystify the mortgage process. Let's face it—all those documents that are for the consumers' protection at closing don't protect consumers.

There are too many to read and they're too hard to understand. We're working on upfront documents that clearly state the pros and cons of the variety of loans available today.

You know, I don't deal directly with borrowers anymore. Those days are long gone for me. But the memories never leave me. When I hear Mr. Win's story, I see the faces of all the people I worked with who had similar stories.

When I hear about Judy in West Palm Beach, who lost her home in a divorce and incurred a lot of debt those first few years. Then, on her own, using a sub-prime loan, she rebuilt both her credit and her wealth.

Having the chance to tell you these stories, to talk about what our industry has done and is doing, has been pretty good therapy today. I'm focusing less on the bad actors who caused this, and more on the millions of people we've helped and are still helping.

And it takes me back to one of my very first originations. The realtor had left the keys to the house with me, and asked if I could drop them off to the buyers once all the paperwork was done.

Well I went to their apartment, and we were sitting around a little Formica kitchen table, I can still see it, bright red, and I handed them the keys and they both started crying. They said they never imagined they could own their own home.

That was 37 years ago. You know, it just never leaves you.

There isn't a day that goes by that I don't stop and think about that scene going on thousands of times all across this country. And that's why, despite my temporary black eye, I'm proud to be a mortgage banker.

Testimony to the Senate Committee on the Judiciary[*]

Nettie McGee

Homeowner, Chicago, IL.

Editor's introduction: A Chicago homeowner, Nettie McGee unknowingly signed an adjustable rate mortgage when she refinanced her home in 2005. When she testified before the Senate Committee on the Judiciary's hearing on "The Looming Foreclosure Crisis: How to Help Families Save Their Homes," in December 2007, she was unable to make the increased payments and appeals to the Committee to help her and those like her to keep their homes.

Nettie McGee's speech: Senator Durbin, Members of the Committee, thank you for inviting me to speak before you today. My name is Nettie McGee, and I have lived in Chicago, Illinois, for 53 years. I live in a home I waited my entire life to own. Now, the interest rate on my mortgage is going up 3 percent and my payments are $200 more each month. I am here to ask you to please help me save my home.

In 1997, I began renting my current home on South Aberdeen Street in Chicago. I rented it for two years with an option to buy. Then, I finally bought it, my first home, in 1999 for $80,000. I was 65 years old.

I made the payments for six years. I had a fixed rate mortgage and I knew what to expect each month—it was $735 every month. I was able to make my payments and pay my taxes. I could afford all my bills.

Then, in October 2005, a sheriff came to my door to tell me my backyard was going to be sold at auction for $5,000 because of unpaid taxes. I paid the taxes on my house every year. I just didn't know that I had two tax bills, one for my house and one for my backyard. The tax bill for my backyard had been sent to an address across town for years since before I moved in.

I was desperate to keep my backyard and my beautiful trees, but I had to pay the city $5,000. I had to do something fast before I lost my yard. I didn't have $5,000 in the bank. I live on Social Security and I get rent from my daughter.

---

[*] Delivered on December 5, 2007, at Washington, D.C.

Then, I saw a commercial on TV about refinancing your home. I thought if I refinanced, I could get money to pay the tax bill and keep my yard. I called the number and a broker came to visit me the next day. He wrote down my personal information. A week and a half later, he called me and asked me to come downtown and sign the papers.

After I arrived at the crowded office, I was taken into a small room, handed about 40 pages, and told where to sign. The woman in charge of the closing stood over me and turned the pages as I signed them. The whole process took about 10 minutes. I thought I was signing for a fixed rate loan. Then, with no explanation of the loan, I was sent out the door.

The mortgage company paid the taxes to the county, then to my surprise they called me a few days later to come back and get a check for about $9,000. I didn't know they had me borrowing an extra $9,000, but when I asked about it, the mortgage company said that I could use it for bills. I thought it was a good idea. So, I used the money to pay some bills and fix my plumbing problems.

I started paying the loan back; the payments were about the same as my original loan. It's been difficult at times, but I have never missed a payment.

A month and a half ago, in October of this year, I got a letter from my mortgage company. It said that on December 1st, my payments were going up to $912 a month. I called my mortgage broker, but he doesn't work for that company anymore.

I thought I signed a fixed rate mortgage. I had no idea my payments would jump almost 25 percent. My interest rate went from 7.87 percent to 10.87 percent, and it could eventually go as high as 13.87 percent. I don't know how I'll make my payments now. They are higher than my Social Security check. The only reason I can get by for now is because my daughter pays me a little rent.

Right now, my lawyers from the Legal Assistance Foundation of Chicago are trying to help me negotiate with my lender, but we don't know if the bank will agree to lower my interest rate back to where it was before. But I know I'll lose the home I waited my entire life to own if I can't get my original interest rate back.

Many people who could originally afford their mortgage payments are losing their homes because they have an adjustable rate mortgage. Please help people like me, people who waited their entire lives to own a home. Please, help us keep our homes.

Speech to the Economic Club of New York*

George W. Bush

President of the United States, 2001– ; born New Haven, CT, July 6, 1946, and raised in Midland and Houston, TX; attended Phillips Academy, Andover; MA: B.A., Yale University, 1968; M.B.A., Harvard Business School, 1975; F-102 pilot in Texas Air National Guard, 1968–1973; oil and gas business, Midland, TX, 1975–1986; senior in father George H. W. Bush's presidential campaign, 1987–88; one of the partners who purchased the Texas Rangers baseball franchise, 1989–1994; governor of Texas, 1995–2000.

Editor's introduction: Addressing the difficult economic situation in this speech, the president expresses optimism that his recent growth package would help ease the slowdown, and discusses, presciently, the effect of the housing downturn on the credit markets. In his remarks, Bush describes efforts by the Federal Reserve Bank and the Federal Housing Association to improve the situation, and makes a bid for a free trade agreement with Colombia as part of the solution. Founded in 1907, the nonprofit Economic Club of New York describes itself as a nonpartisan institution with the purpose of "promoting the study and discussion of social, economic and political questions."

George W. Bush's speech: Glenn, thanks for the kind introduction. Thanks for giving me a chance to speak to the Economic Club of New York. It seems like I showed up in a interesting moment—(LAUGHTER)—during an interesting time. I appreciate the fact that you've assembled to give me a chance to share some ideas with you. I also appreciate the fact that as leaders of the business and financial community, you've helped make this city a great place, and you've helped make our country really, in many ways, the economic envy of the world.

First of all, in a free market, there's going to be good times and bad times. That's how markets work. There will be ups and downs. And after 52 consecutive months of job growth, which is a record, our economy obviously is going through a tough time. It's going through a tough time in the housing market, and it's going through a tough time in the financial markets.

---

* Delivered on March 14, 2008, at New York, NY.

And I want to spend a little time talking about that, but I want to remind you, this is not the first time since I've been the president that we have faced economic challenges. We inherited a recession. And then there was the attacks of September the 11th, 2001, which many of you saw firsthand, and you know full well how that affected our economy. And then we had corporate scandals. And I made the difficult decisions to confront the terrorists and extremists in two major fronts, Afghanistan and Iraq. And then we had devastating natural disasters. And the interesting thing, every time, this economy has bounced back better and stronger than before.

So I'm coming to you as an optimistic fellow. I've seen what happens when America deals with difficulty. I believe that we're a resilient economy, and I believe that the ingenuity and resolve of the American people is what helps us deal with these issues. And it's going to happen again.

Our job in Washington is to foster enterprise and ingenuity, so we can ensure our economy is flexible enough to adjust to adversity, and strong enough to attract capital. And the challenge is not to do anything foolish in the meantime. In the long run, I'm confident that our economy will continue to grow, because the foundation is solid.

Unemployment is low at 4.8 percent. Wages have risen, productivity has been strong. Exports are at an all-time high, and the federal deficit as a percentage of our total economy is well below the historic average. But as Glenn mentioned, these are tough times. Growth fell to 0.6 percent in the fourth quarter of last year. It's clearly slow. The economy shed more than 80,000 jobs in two months. Prices are up at the gas pump and in the supermarket. Housing values are down. Hard-working Americans are concerned—they're concerned about their families, and they're concerned about making their bills.

Fortunately, we recognized the slowdown early and took action. And it was decisive action, in the form of policies that will spur growth. We worked with the Congress. I know that may sound incongruous to you, but I do congratulate the Speaker and Leader Reid, as well as Boehner and Mitch McConnell and Secretary Paulson, for anticipating a problem and passing a robust package quickly.

This package is temporary, and it has two key elements. First, the growth package provides incentives for businesses to make investments in new equipment this year. As more businesses take advantage, investment will pick up, and then job creation will follow. The purpose was to stimulate investment. And the signal is clear—once I signed the bill, the signal to folks in businesses large and small know that there's some certainty in the tax code for the remainder of this year.

Secondly, the package will provide tax rebates to more than 130 million households. And the purpose is to boost consumer spending. The purpose is to try to offset the loss of wealth if the value of your home has gone down. The purpose is to buoy the consumer.

The rebates haven't been put in the mail yet. In other words, this aspect of the plan hasn't taken to effect. There's a lot of Americans who've heard about the plan; a lot of them are a little skeptical about this "check's in the mail" stuff that the federal government talks about. (Laughter.) But it's coming, and those checks, the Secretary assures me, will be mailed by the second week of May.

And so what [do] the folks, the experts, guys like Hubbard, anticipate to happen? I'm not so sure he is one now, but the people that have told me that they expect this consumer spending to have an effect in the second quarter, a greater effect in the third quarter. That's what the experts say.

The Federal Reserve has taken action to bolster the economy. I respect Ben Bernanke. I think he's doing a good job under tough circumstances. The Fed has cut interest rates several times. And this week the Fed—and by the way, we also hold dear this notion of the Fed being independent from White House policy. They act independently from the politicians, and they should. It's good for our country to have that kind of independence.

This week the Fed also announced a major move to ease stress in the credit markets by adding liquidity. It was strong action by the Fed, and they did so because some financial institutions that borrowed money to buy securities in the housing industry must now repair their balance sheets before they can make further loans. The housing issue has dried up some of the sources of credit that businesses need in our economy to help it grow. That's why the Fed is reacting the way they are. We believe the actions by the Fed will help financial institutions continue to make more credit available.

This morning the Federal Reserve, with support of the Treasury Department, took additional actions to mitigate disruptions to our financial markets. Today's events are fast moving, but the Chairman of the Federal Reserve and the Secretary of the Treasury are on top of them, and will take the appropriate steps to promote stability in our markets.

Now, a root cause of the economic slowdown has been the downturn in the housing market, and I want to talk a little bit about that today. After years of steady increases, home values in some parts of the country have declined. At the same time, many homeowners with adjustable rate mortgages have seen their monthly payments increase faster than their ability to pay. As a result, a growing number of people are facing the prospect of foreclosure.

Foreclosure places a terrible burden on our families. Foreclosure disrupts communities. And so the question is, what do you do about it in a way that allows the market to work, and at the same times helps people? Before I get to that, though, I do want to tell you that we fully understand that the mounting concern over housing has shaken the broader market, that it's spread uncertainty to global financial markets, and that it has tightened the credit, which makes it harder for people to get mortgages in the first place.

The temptation is for people, in their attempt to limit the number of foreclosures, is to put bad law in place. And so I want to talk about some of that. First of all, the temptation of Washington is to say that anything short of a massive government intervention in the housing market amounts to inaction. I strongly disagree with that sentiment. I believe there ought to be action, but I'm deeply concerned about law and regulation that will make it harder for the markets to recover—and when they recover, make it harder for this economy to be robust. And so we've got to be careful and mindful that any time the government intervenes in the market, it must do so with clear purpose and great care. Government actions have far-reaching and unintended consequences.

I want to talk to you about a couple of ideas that I strongly reject. First, one bill in Congress would provide $4 billion for state and local governments to buy up abandoned and foreclosed homes. You know, I guess this sounds like a good idea to some, but if your goal is to help Americans keep their homes, it doesn't make any sense to spend billions of dollars buying up homes that are already empty. As a matter of fact, when you buy up empty homes you're only helping the lenders, or the speculators. The purpose of government ought to be to help the individuals, not those who speculated in homes. This bill sends the wrong signal to the market.

Secondly, some have suggested we change the bankruptcy courts, the bankruptcy code, to give bankruptcy judges the authority to reduce mortgage debts by judicial decree. I think that sends the wrong message. It would be unfair to millions of homeowners who have made the hard spending choices necessary to pay their mortgages on time. It would further rattle credit markets. It would actually cause interest rates to go up. If banks think that judges might step in and write down the value of home loans, they're going to charge higher interest rates to cover that risk. This idea would make it harder for responsible first-time home buyers to be able to afford a home.

There are some in Washington who say we ought to artificially prop up home prices. You know, it sounds reasonable in a speech—I guess—but it's not going to help first-time home buyers, for example. A lot of people have been priced out of the market right now because of decisions made by others. The market is in the process of correcting itself; markets must have time to correct. Delaying that correction would only prolong the problem.

And so that's why we oppose those proposals, and I want to talk about what we're for. We're obviously for sending out over $150 billion into the marketplace in the form of checks that will be reaching the mailboxes by the second week of May. We're for that. We're also for helping a targeted group of homeowners, namely those who have made responsible buying decisions, avoid foreclosure with some help.

We've taken three key steps. First, we launched a new program at the Federal Housing Administration called FHA Secure. It's a program that's given FHA greater flexibility to offer refinancing for struggling homeowners with otherwise good credit. In other words, we're saying to people, we want to help you refinance your notes. Over the past six months this program has helped about 120,000 families stay in their homes by refinancing about $17 billion of mortgages, and by the end of the year we expect this program to have reached 300,000 families.

You know the issue like I do, though. I'm old enough to remember savings and loans, and remember who my savings and loan officer was, who loaned me my first money to buy a house. And had I got in a bind, I could have walked across the street in Midland, Texas, and say, I need a little help; can you help me readjust my note so I can stay in my house? There are no such things as that type of deal anymore. As a matter of fact, the paper—you know, had this been a modern era, the paper that had—you know, my paper, my mortgage, could be owned by somebody in a foreign country, which makes it hard to renegotiate the note.

So we're dealing in a difficult environment, to get the word to people, there's help for you to refinance your homes. And so Hank Paulson put together what's called the HOPE NOW Alliance to try to bring some reality to the situation, to focus our help on helping credit-worthy people refinance—rather than pass law that will make it harder for the market to adjust. This HOPE NOW Alliance is made up of industry—is made up of investors and service managers and mortgage counselors and lenders. And they set industry-wide standards to streamline the process for refinancing and modifying certain mortgages.

Last month HOPE NOW created a new program. They take a look—they took a look at the risks, and they created a program called Project Lifeline, which offers some homeowners facing imminent foreclosure a 30-day extension. The whole purpose is to help people stay in their houses. During this time they can work with their lender. And this grace period has made a difference to a lot of folks.

An interesting statistic that has just been released: Members of the Alliance report that the number of homeowners working out their mortgages is now rising faster than the number entering foreclosure. The program is beginning to work, it's beginning to help. The problem we have is a lot of folks aren't responding to over a million letters sent out to offer them assistance and mortgage counseling. And so one of the tasks we have is to continue to urge our citizens to respond to the help; to pay attention to the notices they get describing how they can find help in refinancing their homes. We got toll-free numbers and websites and mailings, and it's just really important for our citizens to understand that this help is available for them.

We've also taken some other steps that will bring some credibility and confidence to the market. Alphonso Jackson, Secretary of HUD, is proposing a rule that requires lenders to provide a standard, easy-to-read summary statements explaining the key elements of mortgage agreements. These mortgage agreements can be pretty frightening to people; I mean, there's a lot of tiny print. And I don't know how many people understood they were buying resets, or not. But one thing is for certain: There needs to be complete transparency. And to the extent that these contracts are too complex, and people made decisions that they just weren't sure they were making, we need to do something about it. We need better confidence amongst those who are purchasing loans.

And secondly, yesterday Hank Paulson announced new recommendations to strengthen oversight of the mortgage industry, and improve the way the credit ratings are determined for securities, and ensure proper risk management at financial institutions. In other words, we've got an active plan to help us get through this rough period. We're always open for new ideas, but there are certain principles that we won't violate. And one of the principles is overreacting by federal law and federal regulation that will have long-term negative effects on our economy.

There are some further things we can do, by the way, on the housing market that I call upon Congress to do. By the way, Congress did pass a good bill that creates a three-year window for American families to refinance their homes without paying taxes on any debt forgiveness they receive. The tax code create disincentives for people to refinance their homes, and we took care of that for a three-year period. And they need to move forward with reforms on Fannie Mae and Freddie Mac. They need to continue to modernize the FHA, as well as allow state housing agencies to issue tax-free bonds to homeowners to refinance their mortgages.

Congress can also take other steps to help us during a period of uncertainty—and these are uncertain times. A major source of uncertainty is that the tax relief we passed in 2001 and 2003 is set to expire. If Congress doesn't act, 116 million American households will see their taxes rise by an average of $1,800. If Congress doesn't act, capital gains and dividends are going to be taxed at a higher rate. If Congress doesn't make the tax relief permanent they will create additional uncertainty during uncertain times.

A lot of folks are waiting to see what Congress intends to do. One thing that's certain that Congress will do is waste some of your money. So I've challenged members of Congress to cut the number of, cost of earmarks in half. I issued an executive order that directs federal agencies to ignore any future earmark that is not voted on by the Congress. In other words, Congress has got this habit of just sticking these deals into bills without a vote—no transparency, no light of day, they just put them in. And by the way, this executive order extends beyond my presidency, so the next president gets to make a decision as to whether or not that executive order stays in effect.

I sent Congress a budget that meets our priorities. There is no greater priority than to make sure our troops in harm's way have all they need to do their job. That has been a priority ever since I made the difficult commitment to put those troops in harm's way, and it should be a priority of any president and any Congress. And beyond that, we've held spending at below rates of inflation—on non-security spending, discretionary spending, we've held the line. And that's why I can tell you that we've submitted a budget that's in balance by 2012—without raising your taxes.

If the Congress truly wants to send a message that will calm people's nerves they'll adopt the budget I submitted to them and make it clear they're not going to run up the taxes on the working people, and on small businesses, and on capital gains, and on dividends, and on the estate tax.

Now, one powerful force for economic growth that is under—is being questioned right now in Washington is whether or not this country is confident enough to open up markets overseas, whether or not we believe in trade. I believe strongly it's in our nation's interest to open up markets for U.S. goods and services. I believe strongly that NAFTA has been positive for the United States of America, like it's been positive for our trading partners in Mexico and Canada. I believe it is dangerous for this country to become isolationist and protectionist. I believe it shows a lack of confidence in our capacity to compete. And I know it would harm our economic future if we allow the—those who believe that walling off America from trade to have their way in Congress.

And so I made it clear that we expect for Congress to move forward on the Colombia free trade agreement. And this is an important agreement. It's important for our national security interests, and it's important for our economic interests. Most Americans don't understand that most goods and services from Colombia come into the United States duty free; most of our goods and services are taxed at about a 35-percent rate heading into Colombia. Doesn't it make sense to have our goods and services treated like those from Colombia? I think it does. I think our farmers and ranchers and small business owners must understand that with the government finding new markets for them, it will help them prosper.

But if Congress were to reject the Colombia free trade agreement, it would also send a terrible signal in our own neighborhood; it would bolster the voices of false populism. It would say to young democracies, America's word can't be trusted. It would be devastating for our national security interests if this United States Congress turns its back on Colombia and a free trade agreement with Colombia.

I intend to work the issue hard. I'm going to speak my mind on the issue because I feel strongly about it. And then once they pass the Colombia, they can pass Panama and South Korea, as well.

Let me talk about another aspect of keeping markets open. A confident nation accepts capital from overseas. We can protect our people against investments that jeopardize our national security, but it makes no sense to deny capital, including sovereign wealth funds, from access to the U.S. markets. It's our money to begin with.

(LAUGHTER)

It seems like we ought to let it back.

(APPLAUSE)

So there's some of the things that are on my mind, and I appreciate you letting me get a chance to come by to speak to you. I'm—you know, I guess the best to describe government policy is like a person trying to drive a car on a rough patch. If you ever get stuck in a situation like that, you know full well it's important not to overcorrect—because when you overcorrect you end up in the ditch. And so it's important to be steady and to keep your eyes on the horizon.

We're going to deal with the issues as we see them. We're not afraid to make decisions. This administration is not afraid to act. We saw a problem coming and we acted quickly, with the help of Democrats and Republicans in the Congress. We're not afraid to take on issues. But we will do so in a way that respects the ingenuity of the American people, that bolsters the entrepreneurial spirit, and that ensures when we make it through this rough patch, our driving is going to be more smooth.

Thank you, Glenn, for giving me a chance to come, and I'll answer some questions.

The Massachusetts Foreclosure Crisis[*]

John Kerry

U.S. senator (D) from Massachusetts, 1985– ; born Aurora, CO, December 11, 1943; B.A., Yale University, 1966; United States Navy Reserve, 1966–1970, reaching Lieutenant; J.D., Boston College, 1976; prosecutor, Office of District Attorney, Middlesex (MA) County, 1976–77; First Assistant District Attorney, 1977–79; private law practice, 1979–1982; lieutenant governor of Massachusetts, 1982–85; candidate for president of the United States, 2004.

Editor's introduction: Advocating passage of the Foreclosure Prevention Act of 2008, Senator John Kerry, in remarks on the Senate floor in April 2008, cites the effects of the mortgage crisis on his home state of Massachusetts. In his speech, Kerry lays out the causes and results of the predatory and dangerous lending that had been indulged in recent years. He also discusses provisions to aid veterans in keeping their homes.

John Kerry's speech: Earlier this month, the Federal Reserve Bank put up an estimated $400-plus billion to bail out Bear Stearns and other investment banks involved in subprime lending and its aftermath. The government showed that when there's trouble on Wall Street, they act fast.

Sure, we have to fix the troubles on Wall Street because there is the potential for a domino effect which could inflict even greater damage on the economy. But we need to show the same commitment to those Americans who are struggling every month just to pay their mortgage loans and keep their homes. As many as 8,000 foreclosures are occurring daily. Some of these loans were predatory, and some came from the very same lenders that the Fed just bailed out! I commend Majority Leader Reid for his continued efforts to bring the plight of our homeowners to the attention of Congress and the Bush Administration.

The situation in Boston has gotten so bad that Mayor Tom Menino recently opened up a "war room," where city officials can work together to fight the wave of foreclosures we've seen in recent days. Just this weekend I went to a

---

[*] Delivered on April 3, 2008, at Washington, D.C.

Homeowner Foreclosure Prevention Workshop at Madison High School in Boston. We ought to show the same sense of urgency here in Congress.

Nationwide, 2.5 million mortgages were in default by late 2007—40 percent more than just two years earlier. Communities across Massachusetts are being hit hard. Last January, foreclosures in Massachusetts alone were up 128 percent from the previous year. The foreclosure rates of five Massachusetts metro areas are in the nation's top 100.

How did we get here? The fundamental problem is that lenders lowered their standards but didn't appropriately plan for the increased risk they had incurred. They flooded the market with mortgage loans, ignoring the risks to borrowers and to their own bottom line. Since 2000 I have been concerned about predatory lending and have supported legislation to stop the excesses that these lenders have too often hoodwinked homeowners into accepting. At the same time, some borrowers inflated their incomes and misrepresented themselves in order to get a bigger home than they could actually afford.

Today we're living with the results. There's blame enough to go around, but what hasn't been shared is the help to solve the problem. Lenders are getting help, but we also need to help well-intentioned homeowners who, with a little assistance, can make their payments and avoid foreclosure and a downward spiral into bankruptcy.

Earlier this week, I went to Lawrence, Massachusetts to meet with homeowners who are facing foreclosure. Approximately 700 homes were foreclosed in Lawrence last year alone and unfortunately, this number is only expected to rise for 2008. I talked to Rosa Hernandez, who has four children and worked two jobs, one as a nursing assistant at a local nursing home, to support her family and earn enough to own her home. Rosa did everything she could to make her house a home. She fixed the roof, bought a new boiler, and updated the electrical system of her new house. After Rosa was hospitalized twice last year, she could no longer work two jobs. At the same time, her subprime mortgage interest rates went up from 4.5 percent five years ago to 7.5 percent.

Rosa told me, through a translator, that when she couldn't make the payments, her lender refused to make a loan modification that would allow her to stay in her home. She could have still made the payments on the home for the amount it was sold for. She asked the lender to work with her to stay in her home. Unfortunately, the lender refused. Now, Rosa and thousands of families just like hers are forced to start over again.

Each time a home is foreclosed upon, a family's economic dreams lie in tatters. And it's not just the family facing foreclosure that suffers—neglected buildings can bring urban blight, lower property values, increase crime rates and destroy entire neighborhoods. According to the U.S. census, by late 2007 a higher percentage of homes in the Northeast sat vacant than at any time in the last 50 years, and probably since the Great Depression.

Today, we are debating the Foreclosure Prevention Act of 2008, comprehensive legislation that will address the problems spawned by the housing crisis. This legislation reflects a bipartisan compromise. It is a good first step toward addressing the housing crisis. The Foreclosure Prevention Act of 2008 includes a provision which Senator Smith and I tried to include in the stimulus bill, to provide an additional $10 billion of tax-exempt private activity bonds to housing finance agencies.

The provision would allow the proceeds from the bonds to be used to refinance subprime loans, provide mortgages for first time homebuyers and for multifamily rental housing. This means $211 million in targeted mortgage relief to the homeowners of Massachusetts. I want to thank Chairmen Baucus and Dodd for their efforts to include this important provision in the final bill as it has enormous potential to help keep struggling families in their homes.

In 2006, state and local governments financed 120,000 new home loans with mortgage revenue bonds. With the additional $10 billion in funding, states and localities can equal that amount and finance approximately 80,000 more home loans. According to the National Association of Home Builders, every mortgage revenue bond new home loan produces almost two full-time jobs, $75,000 in additional wages and salaries and $41,000 in new federal, state and local revenues. Each new home loan results in an average of $3,700 in new spending on appliances, furnishings, and property alterations—providing an even bigger shot in the arm for our economy.

The reason this MRB proposal is so important is that too many lower-income families are having difficulty getting a mortgage or refinancing an existing mortgage. This additional funding will make it easier for families facing foreclosure and first-time homebuyers to get access to a safe, fair mortgage. The goal is simple—we want to provide assistance to those that need it most. Just think—an extra $10 billion for this program is a proven way to help homeowners like Rosa Hernandez stay in their homes.

In addition to the mortgage revenue bond provision, this legislation includes a host of other important provisions which will help with the housing crisis. The $4 billion for the Community Development Block Grant program will help local communities on the front lines in the fight to end our housing crisis. Earlier this year, Senator Kennedy and I sent a letter to Leadership underscoring the need for additional funding for CDBG because—as every Mayor in Massachusetts knows—CDBG is the best way to help local governments tackle serious housing challenges.

This legislation also specifically addresses the foreclosure concerns of our returning veterans. Those who served this country in Iraq and Afghanistan should never come home to a home in danger of foreclosure. It extends the foreclosure grace period from 90 days to nine months. It also extends the freeze on mortgage interest rates for the first year a soldier is home. Earlier this year, I introduced legislation to address these two provisions. I thank Senator Dodd for his work to include these provisions in the bill. Nobody wants to see Iraq and Afghanistan veterans joining their brothers who served in Vietnam among the ranks of homeless vets. We owe these men and women more than a polite thank you and best wishes. We owe them the security and peace of mind that this legislation offers.

We will need to continue to work on legislation to address housing issues. The cost of decent and safe, privately owned rental housing is simply out of reach for too many working families and their children. A record 37.3 million households pay more than 30 percent of their income on housing costs and more than 17 million are paying more than half their incomes on housing costs. And as we consider additional solutions to the housing crises down the road, it's important to keep in mind that we can create jobs while easing the affordable rental housing crisis through passage of the Affordable Housing Trust Fund that Senator Snowe and I have introduced. The goal of the Trust Fund is to construct, rehabilitate, and preserve 1.5 million units of housing over the next 10 years.

I urge my colleagues to support the Foreclosure Prevention Act of 2008. Until we address the housing crisis, arguably the single largest contributor to our economic slow-down, we will have failed to tackle the greatest source of economic anxiety for most Americans. We in Congress must finally take action to help hard-working families everywhere to stay in their homes.

Remarks before the FDIC's Forum on Mortgage Lending to Low and Moderate Income Households*

Henry M. Paulson, Jr.

U.S. Treasury Secretary, 2006– ; born Palm Beach, FL, March 28, 1946; B.A., Dartmouth College, 1968; M.B.A., Harvard Business School, 1970; staff assistant to Assistant Secretary of Defense, 1970–72; assistant to the Assistant to the President for Domestic Affairs, 1972–73; Goldman Sachs, 1974–2006: became partner in 1982; other positions include managing partner, Chicago office, co-head of Investment Banking, 1990–94, Chief Operating Officer, 1994–98; Chief Executive Officer, 1998–2006.

Editor's introduction: Discussing the historical importance of lending to low- and middle-income households before the Federal Deposit Insurance Corporation (FDIC) Forum on Mortgage Lending to Low and Moderate Income Households, Secretary "Hank" Paulson describes the ongoing housing correction under way in America. In his remarks, he asserts that because of regional variability in housing markets detailed statistics at times belie the unified picture suggested by national figures. He describes the Treasury's efforts to minimize unnecessary foreclosures as well as the role of Government Sponsored Entities (GSEs) Fannie Mae and Freddie Mac.

Hank Paulson's speech: Good afternoon. Thank you Chairman Bair for convening this forum, and thanks to all of you for your interest in encouraging responsible lending to low- and moderate-income households.

As we all know, this is a timely issue as the housing correction and capital markets turmoil has reduced the availability of credit for mortgages and other lending. Men and women who have worked hard and saved in order to own their own home should know that despite pressures, the mortgage market remains open to them. As the late Ned Gramlich often observed, subprime and other low- and middle-income lending has played a critical role in helping expand homeownership opportunities for these borrowers. Our responsibility is to work through

---

* Delivered on July 8, 2008, at Washington, D.C.

today's issues and do so in a way that preserves and protects responsible mortgage lending to low- and middle-income families.

U.S. HOUSING MARKET

After several years of lax lending standards and rapid home price appreciation, we are going through an inevitable housing correction. The correction began in 2006, and most forecasters expect a prolonged period of adjustment with foreclosures continuing to rise and housing prices continuing to fall. We are working through the excess new home inventory—the inventory of new single family homes is down 21 percent from its 2006 peak. Another sign that we are well into the adjustment process is that existing home sales appear to have flattened over the past several months, indicating that demand may be stabilizing.

Many of the headlines of falling national home prices are alarming. While prices are undoubtedly declining, the true picture of what homeowners are facing on the ground is varied and cannot be captured in a single national number.

We need to recognize that there is not a national housing market, but a collection of regional markets. Although home prices nationwide experienced rapid price appreciation, price increases were especially pronounced in a few regions. For example, house prices in California, Florida, Arizona and Nevada more than doubled between 2000 and 2006. Similarly, the severity of the current correction varies widely by state and region. These four states, which have 25 percent of all U.S. mortgages, accounted for 42 percent of foreclosure starts in the first quarter of this year, and almost 90 percent of the increase in foreclosure starts. When we add Indiana, Michigan and Ohio, states facing economic challenges, to the aforementioned four states, these seven states comprise 33 percent of mortgages and over 50 percent of foreclosure starts in the first quarter. Foreclosure starts in these states are up 300 percent over the past two years. Of course, that does not mean the correction isn't being felt everywhere; even in the other 43 states, foreclosure starts are up about 90 percent since early 2006. OFHEO's home price data does show, however, that in about one half of the states, home prices actually rose in the first quarter of this year.

In addition, even within a city, home price patterns can be more complex than a single number suggests. We know that foreclosure sales are making up a larger share of total sales than is typical. We also know that foreclosure sales usually occur at a discount to regular home sales. And reported average home sales price is a mix of foreclosure prices and more normal sales prices. Consequently, the prices homeowners realize when selling their home may not be as depressed as the headlines suggest. For example: data from Radar Logic show that in Los Angeles, foreclosure sales in March 2008 were 29 percent of total sales, up from 3 percent in March 2007. In fact, data from this source also show that through March of this year, foreclosure sale prices fell 11 percent in Los Angeles while prices of other homes sold fell 2 percent. This is not intended to minimize what homeowners are experiencing; rather, looking behind the statistics gives us a better understanding of what is really happening.

Beginning last summer, we have implemented a series of public and private initiatives to help struggling homeowners, while also working to minimize the impact of the housing correction, without impeding its necessary progress. The sooner we get through this correction, the sooner we will see home values stabilize, more buyers will return to the housing market and housing will again contribute to economic growth.

In the simplest of terms, the housing market is being negatively impacted by excess inventory and a reduction in the number of homebuyers. These two factors are working in tandem; we cannot reduce the inventory unless we have committed homebuyers. And the availability and price of mortgage financing will affect how many buyers come into the market and when.

There were 1.5 million foreclosures started in all of 2007, and a number of economists now estimate we will see about 2.5 million foreclosures started this year. Even with a strong economy and strong housing market, we saw 800,000 foreclosures started in 2004. Although regrettable, this is normal, and attributable to life events, such as job loss. Public policy cannot be expected to prevent these foreclosures. Many of today's unusually high number of foreclosures are not preventable. Due to the lax credit and underwriting standards of the past years, some people took out mortgages they can't possibly afford and they will lose their homes. There is little public policymakers can, or should, do to compensate for untenable financial decisions. And in the midst of rapid price appreciation, some people bought homes anticipating an immediate profit. Now that their investments have not turned out as they had hoped, these people may walk away, even though they can afford their mortgage payment. These borrowers can and should be living up to their mortgage commitment—government intervention here would be inappropriate. These two categories of foreclosures—stemming from lax underwriting standards and increased speculation—will remain elevated in the near term.

Since last summer, we have been intently focused on avoiding preventable foreclosures: where homeowners, one, want to keep their homes and two, have the financial wherewithal to do so. Here, the challenge we encountered—and it was a big one—was the impending threat of a market failure arising from the complexities and difficulties of a mortgage market that had been transformed by the wide-scale securitization of mortgage financing. Simply put, this impending market failure had the potential to result in many foreclosures that did not make economic sense because it was in the best interest of both the homeowner and the lender to modify the terms of the mortgage so the borrower could stay in the home.

This potential market failure arose from the emergence of the complex originate-to-distribute securitization model where mortgages had been sliced and diced then packaged and sold to investors around the world. The magnitude of the impending correction threatened to overwhelm the normal workout and modification processes in a way that raised a series of technical, legal and accounting issues

that likely could not be addressed in a timely fashion by individual market participants working on their own. The result would have been that many borrowers
who would otherwise get a modification or refinance would instead go into foreclosure simply because no one could respond to them in time. No responsible homeowner who has been making payments and wants to stay in their home should
go into foreclosure merely because the workout system was too busy to find them
a solution that is in both the lenders' and the homeowners' best interest.

We sought to address this potential market failure, by working with the industry to facilitate a process that approximates what would be normal behavior between a bank and a struggling borrower if the borrower were dealing with a bank
that had originated and held the mortgage. And so last summer, we encouraged
the creation of the HOPE NOW Alliance of mortgage lenders, servicers and
counselors with the urgent mission of untying the Gordian knot of complexities
surrounding the mortgage workout process. In many ways, this has been a race
against time. While there have been bumps in the road and there is still work to
do, the industry, through HOPE NOW, has made an enormous effort and great
progress toward meeting these challenges.

HOPE NOW's numerous efforts to help homeowners avoid preventable foreclosures has been successful. HOPE NOW reports that since last July, the industry has helped 1.7 million homeowners with loan workouts that allowed them to
stay in their homes. At the current pace, nearly 200,000 additional borrowers are
helped every month. This private sector effort has complemented public efforts
to avoid preventable foreclosures, including through expanded access to Federal
Housing Administration programs, which has enabled more than 250,000 borrowers to refinance into affordable FHA mortgages since last August.

In particular, there are a number of key areas where HOPE NOW is showing
substantial progress. Improved outreach strategies have dramatically increased the
response rate of troubled borrowers. Industry is more closely coordinating with
mortgage counselors, including paying for counseling. The Alliance members get
together routinely, to continuously improve efficiency and reduce the time it takes
to respond to a borrower who asks for help. Importantly, modifications as a percent of workouts have climbed from 19 percent to 41 percent for all borrowers.
For subprime borrowers, this trend has been even more pronounced, going from
17 to 50 percent. While HOPE NOW is aimed at helping all borrowers, several programs are focused specifically at subprime ARMs. In keeping with recent
trends, in the first quarter of 2008 these loans accounted for 6 percent of loans
outstanding but 37 percent of foreclosures started—that means that a subprime
ARM is four times more likely to have entered foreclosure than a prime ARM and
22 times more likely than a prime fixed-rate mortgage.

In December, HOPE NOW announced a new protocol designed to streamline
some subprime ARM borrowers into consideration for a refinancing or modification, so that resources are available for more difficult situations. The objective is
not to maximize modifications; it is to minimize foreclosures for those subprime
ARM borrowers who could afford the starter rate. From the outset of the HOPE

NOW process, I have measured success by whether a borrower who has made all the payments at the initial rate, but couldn't afford the reset and reached out for help, avoids going into foreclosure. And so far, the data on this question show an unqualified success.

Of course, lower interest rates have significantly reduced the reset problem. Still, there is no question that because [the] industry has acted to fast-track eligible borrowers, we are achieving our objective. Of the more than 700,000 subprime mortgage resets originally scheduled through May of 2008, only 1,800 loans that were current at reset have entered foreclosure. We will continue tracking that number closely to monitor progress. Entire industries do not adjust easily or quickly, even when markets are calm. The HOPE NOW Alliance is demonstrating that an industry can, through coordination, make a difference and do so without forcing American taxpayers to pay the bill.

And we are always pushing to do more. For example, second liens have proven to be an impediment to completing loan workouts as negotiations between borrowers, first lien holders, and second lien holders have been complex and time consuming. To help address this, HOPE NOW recently announced guidelines for automatic re-subordination of second liens to enable loan modifications and refinancings to execute more quickly. The American Securitization Forum (ASF) announced today that it would extend its streamlined protocol announced in December to more borrowers than just those experiencing their first rate reset, helping HOPE NOW reach more families. These and other similar efforts will help ensure that the industry as a whole moves together.

Homeowners have responsibility as well. We can't help those who aren't willing to help themselves, and we must continue to urge struggling borrowers that if they haven't already, they need to reach out for help.

AVAILABILITY OF MORTGAGE FINANCE

Essential to ending the correction is a return of homebuyers. In many parts of the country a starter home had become unaffordable, and the current correction should bring home prices back within reach for many Americans, so long as financing is available. Those of you here today will have an enormous impact on their ability to get the financing to buy a home.

Two institutions in particular—Fannie Mae and Freddie Mac—have an important role to play. They can be a constructive force in this period of stress in the housing market. I have been strongly encouraging all financial institutions to raise capital so they can continue to finance consumer and business activity that supports our economy. In particular, I am pleased that this spring both GSEs committed to raise more capital. Fannie Mae has raised $7.4 billion in capital in the last several months, and Freddie Mac has committed to raise additional capital. Fannie Mae and Freddie Mac today touch 70 percent of all new mortgages. Fresh capital will strengthen their balance sheets and allow them to provide additional mortgage capital, as they balance their responsibilities to their mission and to their shareholders during this period of housing market adjustment. The availability of mortgage finance is also supported by the Federal Housing Finance Board's decision to allow the Federal Home Loan Banks to increase their purchases of mortgage securities.

Given the very important role being played by the GSEs today, we are particularly focused on completing work to create a world-class regulator for Fannie Mae, Freddie Mac and the Federal Home Loan Banks. A strengthened regulator for Fannie and Freddie will increase investor confidence in these enterprises and will be a substantial tool to ease the housing downturn and increase the availability of affordable mortgages for Americans who want to buy a new home or refinance their current one. Creating a strong independent regulator will help ensure that the GSEs achieve their mission while operating safely and soundly.

The House and Senate have made good progress on GSE reform. As I have continually emphasized, completing this legislation is the single most powerful step Congress can take this year to help our nation get through this housing correction.

That said, working through this correction is made more challenging by the virtual disappearance of the subprime lending market. In response to excesses, that market has probably changed unalterably—as it must. Clearly, some who took out subprime mortgages never should have been approved for a mortgage in the first place. Practices, such as low or no doc loans, minimal or no down payments and other lax credit practices, are likely, as they should be, a thing of the past. At the same time, we cannot lose sight of the fact that subprime lending gave millions of responsible Americans a chance to borrow, despite a less-than-perfect credit history. We must not lose the benefits of the subprime market as we eliminate its flaws. Your discussions today will be instructive as to what products and standards can reinvigorate this important sector of the market, as we know that subprime lending is vital to bring the dream and economic good of homeownership to millions of Americans. The subprime market will evolve as markets always do, to find better ways to evaluate and manage credit risk.

Today we are also looking more broadly for ways to increase the availability and lower the cost of mortgage financing to accelerate the return of normal home-buying activity. We are working with FDIC, the Federal Reserve, the OCC and the OTS to explore the potential of covered bonds, which is one promising financing vehicle to do just that. Covered bonds provide funding to an issuer, generally a depository institution such as a commercial bank or thrift, through a secured debt instrument collateralized by a pool of residential mortgage loans that remain on the issuer's balance sheet. Interest is paid to investors from the issuer's cash flow. In the event of a default, covered bond investors' primary recourse is the pool of mortgage loans, and secondary recourse is an unsecured claim on the issuer. Covered bonds have been widely used in Europe to finance residential and commercial real estate, and municipal bonds. At the end of 2006 the European covered bond market was over 1.9 trillion Euros.

And, as Treasury seeks to encourage new sources of mortgage funding in the United States, improve underwriting standards and strengthen financial institutions' balance sheets, covered bonds have the potential to serve these purposes and reduce the costs for first-time home buyers, and for existing homeowners to refinance.

We are also strengthening efforts to improve financial literacy, so that borrowers better understand sophisticated lending products and the obligations they carry. Through the President's Advisory Council on Financial Literacy, Treasury is identifying approaches to financial education that will help potential borrowers evaluate mortgage options and avoid commitments they cannot meet.

The subprime mortgage turmoil has also revealed broader financial regulatory issues, and we are working to address these on a number of fronts, including modernizing the U.S. financial regulatory structure to better match our modern financial system. Treasury released its recommendations for reform last March, and we look forward to working with all interested parties—the Congress, regulators and market participants—to develop and put in place a better regulatory structure as we work toward an optimal one that hopefully will foster continued progress in mortgage financing while avoiding some of the problems and excesses of the past. Thank you.

Testimony to the U.S. House Committee on Government Oversight and Reform[*]

Alan Greenspan

Greenspan Associates LLC, 2006– ; born New York, NY, March 6, 1926; B.S., economics, New York University, 1948; M.A., economics, New York University, 1950; economic analyst, The Conference Board, 1948–1953; chairman and president, Townsend-Greenspan & Co., 1955–1987; chairman of the Federal Reserve, 1987–2006.

Editor's introduction: Although he had earlier, according to the *New York Times*, blamed the economic crisis of 2008 on "economic cycles and mortgage fraud," former Federal Reserve Chairman Alan Greenspan delivered the following speech to the House Committee on Government Oversight and Reform in which he explains that the crisis had become much larger than he could have anticipated. Previously opposed to regulating the exotic financial instruments known as derivatives, he acknowledges that their unrestrained use had fed the crisis. Greenspan had long been known for his view that government regulators were no better at imposing discipline than were unfettered markets; under questioning by Chairman Henry A. Waxman, Greenspan later admitted that he was "partially" wrong.

Alan Greenspan's speech: Mr. Chairman and Members of the Committee:

Thank you for this opportunity to testify before you this morning.

We are in the midst of a once-in-a-century credit tsunami. Central banks and governments are being required to take unprecedented measures. You, importantly, represent those on whose behalf economic policy is made, those who are feeling the brunt of the crisis in their workplaces and homes. I hope to address their concerns today.

This morning, I would like to provide my views on the sources of the crisis, what policies can best address the financial crisis going forward, and how I expect the economy to perform in the near and longer term. I also want discuss how my thinking has evolved and what I have learned in this past year.

---

[*] Delivered on October 23, 2008, at Washington, D.C.

In 2005, I raised concerns that the protracted period of underpricing of risk, if history was any guide, would have dire consequences. This crisis, however, has turned out to be much broader than anything I could have imagined. It has morphed from one gripped by liquidity restraints to one in which fears of insolvency are now paramount. Given the financial damage to date, I cannot see how we can avoid a significant rise in layoffs and unemployment. Fearful American households are attempting to adjust, as best they can, to a rapid contraction in credit availability, threats to retirement funds, and increased job insecurity. All of this implies a marked retrenchment of consumer spending as households try to divert an increasing part of their incomes to replenish depleted assets, not only in 401ks, but in the value of their homes as well. Indeed, a necessary condition for this crisis to end is a stabilization of home prices in the U.S. They will stabilize and clarify the level of equity in U.S. homes, the ultimate collateral support for the value of much of the world's mortgage-backed securities. At a minimum, stabilization of home prices is still many months in the future. But when it arrives, the market freeze should begin to measurably thaw and frightened investors will take tentative steps towards re-engagement with risk. Broken market ties among banks, pension, and hedge funds and all types of nonfinancial businesses will become re-established and our complex global economy will move forward. Between then and now, however, to avoid severe retrenchment, banks and other financial intermediaries will need the support that only the substitution of sovereign credit for private credit can bestow. The $700 billion Troubled Assets Relief Program is adequate to serve that need. Indeed the impact is already being felt. Yield spreads are narrowing.

As I wrote last March: those of us who have looked to the self-interest of lending institutions to protect shareholder's equity (myself especially) are in a state of shocked disbelief. Such counterparty surveillance is a central pillar of our financial markets' state of balance. If it fails, as occurred this year, market stability is undermined.

What went wrong with global economic policies that had worked so effectively for nearly four decades? The breakdown has been most apparent in the securitization of home mortgages. The evidence strongly suggests that without the excess demand from securitizers, subprime mortgage originations (undeniably the original source of crisis) would have been far smaller and defaults accordingly far fewer. But subprime mortgages pooled and sold as securities became subject to explosive demand from investors around the world. These mortgage-backed securities being "subprime" were originally offered at what appeared to be exceptionally high risk-adjusted market interest rates. But with U.S. home prices still rising, delinquency and foreclosure rates were deceptively modest. Losses were minimal. To the most sophisticated investors in the world, they were wrongly viewed as a "steal."

The consequent surge in global demand for U.S. subprime securities by banks, hedge, and pension funds supported by unrealistically positive rating designations by credit agencies was, in my judgment, the core of the problem. Demand became so aggressive that too many securitizers and lenders believed they were able to create and sell mortgage backed securities so quickly that they never put their shareholders' capital at risk and hence did not have the incentive to evaluate the credit quality of what they were selling. Pressures on lenders to supply more "paper" collapsed subprime underwriting standards from 2005 forward. Uncritical acceptance of credit ratings by purchasers of these toxic assets has led to huge losses.

It was the failure to properly price such risky assets that precipitated the crisis. In recent decades, a vast risk management and pricing system has evolved, combining the best insights of mathematicians and finance experts supported by major advances in computer and communications technology. A Nobel Prize was awarded for the discovery of the pricing model that underpins much of the advance in derivates markets. This modern risk management paradigm held sway for decades. The whole intellectual edifice, however, collapsed in the summer of last year because the data inputted into the risk management models generally covered only the past two decades, a period of euphoria. Had instead the models been fitted more appropriately to historic periods of stress, capital requirements would have been much higher and the financial world would be in far better shape today, in my judgment.

When in August 2007 markets eventually trashed the credit agencies' rosy ratings, a blanket of uncertainty descended on the investment community. Doubt was indiscriminately cast on the pricing of securities that had *any* taint of subprime backing. As much as I would prefer it otherwise, in this financial environment I see no choice but to require that all securitizers retain a meaningful part of the securities they issue. This will offset in part market deficiencies stemming from the failures of counterparty surveillance.

There are additional regulatory changes that this breakdown of the central pillar of competitive markets requires in order to return to stability, particularly in the areas of fraud, settlement, and securitization. It is important to remember, however, that whatever regulatory changes are made, they will pale in comparison to the change already evident in today's markets. Those markets for an indefinite future will be far *more* restrained than would any currently contemplated new regulatory regime.

The financial landscape that will greet the end of the crisis will be far different from the one that entered it little more than a year ago. Investors, chastened, will be exceptionally cautious. Structured investment vehicles, Alt-A mortgages, and a myriad of other exotic financial instruments are not now, and are unlikely to ever find willing investors. Regrettably, also on that list are subprime mortgages, the market for which has virtually disappeared. Home and small-business ownership are vital commitments to a community. We should seek ways to reestablish a more sustainable subprime mortgage market.

This crisis will pass, and America will reemerge with a far sounder financial system.

4

The Same-Sex Marriage Debate

Loving for All*

Mildred Loving

Homemaker; born June 22, 1939, Caroline County, VA; died Central Point, VA, May 2, 2008.

Editor's introduction: Of African and Rappahannock Native American descent, Mildred Loving married her husband Richard, who was white, in June 1958 in the District of Columbia to avoid the Racial Integrity Act, a law in their home state of Virginia, where they lived near Richmond. Upon their return, they were charged with "cohabiting as man and wife, against the peace and dignity of the Commonwealth." They pled guilty and were given a suspended sentence provided they leave Virginia. The American Civil Liberties Union (ACLU) filed a motion on their behalf in the state trial court to vacate the judgment on grounds that the statutes violated ran counter to the Fourteenth Amendment. The Supreme Court decision *Loving v. Virginia* overturned their convictions on June 12, 1967, which has been celebrated as Loving Day ever since. On the 40th anniversary of the decision, Loving delivered the following speech, in which she calls for the recognition of same-sex marriage.

Mildred Loving's speech: When my late husband, Richard, and I got married in Washington, D.C. in 1958, it wasn't to make a political statement or start a fight. We were in love and we wanted to be married.

We didn't get married in Washington because we wanted to marry there. We did it there because the government wouldn't allow us to marry back home in Virginia where we grew up, where we met, where we fell in love and where we wanted to be together and build our family. You see, I am a woman of color and Richard was white, and at that time people believed it was okay to keep us from marrying because of their ideas of who should marry whom.

When Richard and I came back to our home in Virginia, happily married, we had no intention of battling over the law. We made a commitment to each other in

---
* Delivered on June 12, 2007.

our love and lives, and now had the legal commitment, called marriage, to match. Isn't that what marriage is?

Not long after our wedding, we were awakened in the middle of the night in our own bedroom by deputy sheriffs and actually arrested for the "crime" of marrying the wrong kind of person. Our marriage certificate was hanging on the wall above the bed.

The state prosecuted Richard and me, and after we were found guilty, the judge declared:

"Almighty God created the races white, black, yellow, malay and red, and he placed them on separate continents. And but for the interference with his arrangement there would be no cause for such marriages. The fact that he separated the races shows that he did not intend for the races to mix." He sentenced us to a year in prison, but offered to suspend the sentence if we left our home in Virginia for 25 years exile.

We left and got a lawyer. Richard and I had to fight, but still were not fighting for a cause. We were fighting for our love.

Though it turned out we had to fight, happily Richard and I didn't have to fight alone. Thanks to groups like the ACLU and the NAACP Legal Defense & Education Fund, and so many good people around the country willing to speak up, we took our case for the freedom to marry all the way to the U.S. Supreme Court. And on June 12, 1967, the Supreme Court ruled unanimously that, "The freedom to marry has long been recognized as one of the vital personal rights essential to the orderly pursuit of happiness by free men," a "basic civil right."

My generation was bitterly divided over something that should have been so clear and right. The majority believed that what the judge said, that it was God's plan to keep people apart, and that government should discriminate against people in love. But I have lived long enough now to see big changes. The older generation's fears and prejudices have given way, and today's young people realize that if someone loves someone they have a right to marry. Surrounded as I am now by wonderful children and grandchildren, not a day goes by that I don't think of Richard and our love, our right to marry, and how much it meant to me to have that freedom to marry the person precious to me, even if others thought he was the "wrong kind of person" for me to marry. I believe all Americans, no matter their race, no matter their sex, no matter their sexual orientation, should have that same freedom to marry. Government has no business imposing some people's religious beliefs over others. Especially if it denies people's civil rights.

I am still not a political person, but I am proud that Richard's and my name is on a court case that can help reinforce the love, the commitment, the fairness, and the family that so many people, black or white, young or old, gay or straight seek in life. I support the freedom to marry for all.

That's what Loving, and loving, are all about.

Marriage Equality[*]

Deval Patrick

Governor (D) of Massachusetts, 2007– ; born Chicago, IL, July 31, 1956; B.A., English and American literature, Harvard College, 1978; United Nations youth training project in the Darfur region of Sudan, 1978–79; J.D., Harvard Law School, 1982; law clerk for Judge Stephen Reinhardt of U.S. Court of Appeals for the Ninth Circuit, 1982–83; attorney, NAACP Legal Defense and Educational Fund, 1983–86; private attorney, Hill and Barlow, 1986–1990, partner, 1990–94; Assistant Attorney General, Civil Rights Division, U.S. Department of Justice, 1994–97; attorney, Day, Berry and Howard, 1997–2000; executive vice president, general counsel, and corporate secretary, Coca-Cola Company, 2000–04; board-member, ACC Capital Holdings, 2004–07.

Editor's introduction: In response to a proposed amendment to the state constitution banning same-sex marriage, Governor Deval Patrick devoted his podcast of June 7, 2007 to urging his constituents to oppose it. After three years of "marriage equality" in Massachusetts, Patrick contends that no one's marriage was threatened and that in fact low divorce rates reflect the strength of marriage in the state. He describes the constitution as designed to protect rights, not to limit them, and argues that the debate is a distraction from more pressing matters. "People must be able to come before the law as equals," he concludes. The measure was defeated.

Deval Patrick's Speech: Hello, this is Governor Deval Patrick.

We continue to work hard on an ambitious agenda for the Commonwealth. We are moving forward on initiatives to keep guns and gang violence out of our communities, to create new jobs (such as with our life sciences and clean energy initiatives), to bring affordable health care to children and the uninsured, to reduce property taxes and to create the strongest system of public education (pre-K through college) in the history of our Commonwealth.

These are things that demand our focus and attention, yours and mine, now and over the next few years. None is easy. But success with each will strengthen

---

[*] Delivered on June 7, 2007.

this Commonwealth and secure the future for us and our kids. To make these initiatives succeed, we need to come together and stay together, to pull in the same direction.

But just at the moment we need to come together, another ideological issue threatens to pull us apart.

2007 marks the third year for marriage equality in Massachusetts. I know emotions run high on both sides of this issue. And while I know that some differ from me on my support for marriage equality, I think even the opponents have to acknowledge that allowing gay and lesbian couples to marry has not undermined my own or anyone else's straight marriage. The institution of marriage is as strong as ever. In fact, Massachusetts has one of the lowest divorce rates in the country.

Even though there has been no disruption to family life, and even though most of us have accepted the notion that private choices between private adults ought to be respected and legally protected, there are still those who feel we ought to decide by majority vote whether this small minority ought to have a right to private choices. So, on June 14, at a constitutional convention here in the State House, our legislators will be asked to endorse a constitutional amendment to ban marriage equality.

For several reasons, I think they should vote "no."

First, the court has not granted gay and lesbian couples any right different from anyone else. The court has affirmed the principle that people come before their government as equals, that's all, saying simply that if the government is going to give marriage licenses to anyone, it has to give them to everyone, regardless of whether the spouse you choose is of the same gender.

Second, we have never in this state used the ballot process to limit individual freedoms and personal privacy. Our constitution is designed to protect freedom and stand against discrimination. Yet with this proposal we are being asked to take freedom away from some people and to insert discrimination into our constitution. Where then does that stop? Shall we take away the freedom to worship in religions that the majority does not approve of? Of course we shouldn't.

Third, even if you don't support marriage equality, you have to realize that if this issue is placed on the ballot for a vote in 2008, for the next two years little else we need to do will get done. If we don't lay this question to rest at the constitutional convention on June 14, a toxic debate will eclipse all the other business that you and I care about and drive us apart, just when we most need to work together. Instead of advancing our agenda in Massachusetts, we will spend the next two years surrounded by advocates from all over the country trying to make Massachusetts a political circus.

A number of advocates and members of the GLBT community have asked me to help end this debate once and for all on June 14, and I will do all I can. But with due respect, it will not be just because I believe that marriage equality is right. It will be because I believe that equality is right. Because every time the court affirms basic equality for any one, it affirms basic equality for all of us. And whenever basic equality is threatened to one, all are threatened. That is as true today as it was on the great civil rights questions of the '50s and '60s.

I ask you please to stand with us. Whether you support the right of adults to make private choices about whom to marry or just feel that we have bigger challenges to face together, call your state reps and senators and tell them it's time for us all to move on. Ask them to vote to defeat the ballot initiative once and for all in the constitutional convention on June 14. Ask your friends, your family and your neighbors to reach out as well.

In our Commonwealth, all of our citizens should share the same rights and responsibilities without regard to skin color, or religion or disability. Our justice cannot be conditional. On the decision to marry or anything else, people must be able to come before the law as equals. Let's come together now and keep this item off the ballot, and, once again, let Massachusetts serve as a national model of progress.

Thank you again, and we look forward to hearing from you.

Address to the New York State Assembly[*]

Daniel J. O'Donnell

Member (D), New York State Assembly, 2003– ; born Flushing, Queens, NY, November 17, 1960; B.A., George Washington University, 1982; J.D., City University of New York School of Law, 1987; public defender, Legal Aid Society, 1987–1994; private law practice 1994–2002.

Editor's introduction: Speaking to the New York State Assembly during a debate over a bill seeking to legalize same-sex marriage, Daniel J. O'Donnell (brother of actress Rosie) appeals at times to his colleagues' sense of humor and at times to their loyalties to the gay members of their own families. In his speech, O'Donnell, the first openly gay man to win election to the State Assembly, quotes Thomas Jefferson to the effect that in America "our civil liberties have no dependence on religious opinion" and professes his wish for his partner of 26 years to have the protections of marriage. The bill arose from a lawsuit against the state that reached the court of appeals, which deferred the question to the legislature. As the *New York Times* reported, "Not everyone was convinced [by O'Donnell's speech]. Assemblyman Brian M. Kolb, a Republican from Canandaigua, said he felt personally 'threatened' by the legislation." Nevertheless, the bill passed, 85 to 61.

Daniel J. O'Donnell's speech: In November of 1960, John F. Kennedy was elected president of the United States. In that moment, the American dream moved forward. The American dream said, "You'll be judged on the merits, not on who your family is." The American dream said, "We were all created equal," and that dream came about not by people deciding, but by a revolution. America, folks, is a revolution because at the time, people thought that kings were the descendents of God on Earth and the women and men who chose to participate in that revolution said that is not the case. That is not the way our nation needs to be.

To my mother, who was a grandchild of immigrants, to see one of her own, an Irish-American man elected president, must have been a very heady experience.

---

[*] Delivered on June 19, 2007, at Albany, NY.

And, at the time, I was a week old. My mother used to sing to me. She used to sing a song "Que Sera Sera" and what does that song say? "Whatever will be, will be. The future is not ours to see." I imagine that my mother never would have foresaw that I would stand in this body and represent people the way I do, and I am more certain that my mother would never have foresaw the argument that I'm making to you tonight.

And, I also know that she could not have foresaw that within a decade she would be dead of breast cancer having left five children alone. When she died on Saint Patrick's Day 1973, I died, too.

The things that brought me joy when she was still alive were gone because all of those things no longer mattered. I had to fend for myself; I had to cook for myself; I had to clean for myself; I had to shop for myself. There was no one there in that environment to do all the things that my mother, when she held me and sang that song, was supposed to do for me. And so, I only had one choice: Learn to do it for yourself or not have it be. And so, I did those things. I graduated from high school able to cook a full Thanksgiving dinner for 20. I did. It was horrible, but I did because there was no other choice. And what happened in that house was that when she left, the person in our society who was supposed to teach me how to love was gone. So, I didn't know how to love.

Seventeen years of age, I went to college, Catholic University of America, just so you know. And, when I arrived there the first day, I met someone. I met someone who was from Upstate New York. And through time, something amazing happened. I was taught how to love. Someone taught me how to love. And what turned out to be was the person who did that was a man.

The damage from my childhood was such that if I considered for one second that I could fall in love with a man, I would have never let that happen. And so, what happened, I fell in love by accident, and what I learned from him was that I should love myself, too. No one believed in me. No one. No one thought what he always thought of me.

To many people in this room, the perception must be you run out and you find someone, and that's not what happened to me. My story is love found me in the body of a person who was a man, and I struggled with that. And it was with no hyperbole or exaggeration that I say to you today that not only would I not be standing in this room were it not for this man, but, folks, I would not be alive. I could not have survived my late teens and 20s if I didn't have John Banta in my life to make sure that I was okay.

All gay people, when they realize what and who they are, live in fear. Like Ms. Sayward's son, they live in fear of getting beat up. They live in fear of being disclosed. They live in fear, and they feel different. That is the most accurate thing I can tell you. So, here was my problem: Did I feel different from other kids? Yes, I did. But I thought that I was different because I had to go home and wash my own clothes and make my own bed and cook my own dinner; I never equated that feeling of difference with anything that was connected to sexuality or love.

When we had this American revolution, it was not set in stone. It is a perfect revolution because it was also an evolution. People can evolve. Societies can evolve if you have a democracy. Joe Lentol has evolved, okay? There is evolution that takes place. There is. And if there wasn't evolution, we would not be here because our society, our experiment would have failed. If there was no evolution, American citizens would still be slaves. If there was no evolution in our system, women would not be permitted to vote. So, clearly, evolution is built into the American revolution.

I have tried desperately, since introducing this bill, to talk to as many of you as I can, to charm you, to flirt with you, whatever it takes, and some of you have witnessed the flirting in the Members' Lounge, but I'm not giving names up. I have done everything that I can to get you to try to understand what it's like to stand in my shoes. And I was very lucky this week because I got a letter from Mrs. Loving, the African-American, Native-American woman who was arrested in her bedroom in 1958 [sic] for, ironically, loving a man named "Loving" because he was white. And I don't know how old she is, but she can't be that young. She was willing to say, "This is the same issue." And for those of you who are not so sure, let me make this clear. In the 1980s in Georgia, a man, Michael Bowers, was arrested in his bedroom because he was in bed with a man. And for those of us, at that time, who were involved in relationships with people of the same sex, we lived in fear of the knock on the door, of the landlady calling the police and having us arrested for being who we are, but we evolved. No one thinks that so much anymore. We evolved.

In her letter, she said, "I didn't want to be a hero. I didn't set out to be a heroine, I just did what was right." There are heroes here. Deborah Glick is a hero. She paved the way to allow me to stand here and make this case. She is a hero. Governor Spitzer is a hero, chose to send us this bill written in a way that can be palatable across the board to say what's right. Shelly Silver is a hero. He let me have this bill to let me give me my shot at trying to convince each and every one of you that this is simply about fairness and equality.

So, what do I seek? What does this bill seek? Let me address some of the issues that you have raised. This is not about the sanctity of anything. Sanctity means holy. Holy means of or pertaining to religion. That's from Webster's, folks. That's what they mean. I am not seeking anyone's religious agreement. I am not seeking anything from any religious person, whatsoever. I seek a piece of paper, a license from my government to whom I pay taxes and to whom I serve in this body. I do not seek anything from anyone's church. I don't want a seat in your synagogue. I don't want a church pew. I want a license that all of you have, some of you have had two or three times.

The current state of law is the following: You could get on a plane, fly to Las Vegas, where what happens in Las Vegas, stays in Las Vegas, allegedly, get married in front of an Elvis impersonator, drunk, come back to New York and you will be given a piece of paper that will protect that relationship. And, yet, the man who I have loved for 26 years, who I share a home and a dog with, the person who every day I talk to before I go to sleep, he and I can't get that piece of paper. Is that right and fair? Is that justice? Is that equality? The answer is hell no.

I want you to search your heart and think about this. And I am asking you from my heart to do this for me and my family so that I know that he is protected. That's what I am asking of you tonight. People in life fear many things: global warming, nuclear proliferation, heterosexuals in retail. Whatever you fear, you fear and that's okay. I used to fear getting beat up and I used to fear getting exposed and I used to fear people saying bad things about me. I no longer fear those things.

Ladies and gentlemen, I have one fear, that the horrific gene pool that runs through my family line will take my life, that a bus will hit me, that I will have a heart attack, like my grandfather did, and the one thing that I wanted most to do in this life, which is protect John Banta, I was unable to do.

And so, if you have it in you to find a way to take my fear away, I cannot express to you how deeply—the gratitude I will have for you for the rest of my life. And if you can't, I implore you to do this for your own family, because I have learned a lot about your families in the last month, okay? And I know which ones of you have gay kids, I know which ones have gay siblings, I know which ones have gay grandchildren and gay nieces and gay nephews. And you know what, folks? If you don't have that today you're having it tomorrow, okay? And one day, one of those people is going to come to you and say to you, "Where were you? Where were you on the day that my equality was on the line? Where were you?"

This revolution, revolutionary women, revolutionary men had some revolutionary concepts and a Constitution that was flexible and designed to incorporate everyone. So, here's a revolutionary concept: Are you ready? "Our civil liberties have no dependence on religious opinion." Let me repeat that. "Our civil liberties have no dependence on religious opinion." That, my friends, was Thomas Jefferson. So, whatever tradition you have in your life, I stick with the Founding Fathers and what this Constitution was supposed to mean rather than what that tradition is. And, I know that with this vote, with enough green lights on that board, that the dream of America laid out by Thomas Jefferson will be one step closer to reality.

Thank you very much.

The Human Case Against Same-Sex Marriage[*]

Glenn T. Stanton

Director for Family Formation Studies, Focus on the Family, 2006– ; born Arlington, VA, February 21, 1962; B.A., humanities, University of West Florida, 1991; M.A., humanities, University of West Florida, 1992; researcher, Focus on the Family, 1993–97; president and executive director, Palmetto Family Council, Columbia, SC, 1997–2000; editor, Christianity. com, 2000–01; researcher and analyst, Focus on the Family, 2001–06; author, Why Marriage Matters: Reasons to Believe in Marriage in Postmodern Society *(1997),* Marriage on Trial: The Case Against Same-Sex Marriage and Parenting *(2004),* My Crazy Imperfect Christian Family: Living Out Your Faith With Those Who Know You Best *(2004).*

Editor's introduction: In this speech on gay marriage, delivered at Otterbein College, in Columbus, Ohio, Stanton claims that the question of gay marriage "demands us to look at the most obvious essence of humanity in a different way." He asserts that throughout history and in every culture marriage has involved a man and a woman, and thus is the only natural definition of marriage. Because gender is an essential part of who we are, Stanton argues, same-sex marriage is actually anti-human. Because man and woman are unique in their representation of God, he describes same-sex marriage as an attack on "the very image of God." Focus on the Family is a nonprofit evangelical organization that produces the nationally syndicated, vastly popular radio programs of its founder, Dr. James Dobson. The organization is often identified with the conservative Christian movement.

Glenn T. Stanton's speech: I want to start tonight by contrasting two of the— and arguably—most divisive and volatile issues to surface in our national dialogue and debate since slavery and the struggle for the civil rights of Black Americans: abortion and same-sex marriage. These two contrasting issues may seem completely unrelated, connected only in their ability to divide folks, but there is a deeper connection.

Hang with me for that connection.

---

[*] Delivered on February 5, 2008, at Columbus, OH. Reprinted with permission.

Focus on the Family—where I spend my days as a researcher, writer and speaker on family-formation dynamics—regularly fields a flood of calls from reporters asking questions about family issues and the culture war. I am one of the many employees who respond to these calls. A journalistic staple is, "Will same-sex marriage continue to be a big issue in the '08 election?" And these people are supposed to be insightful. Of course it will be! And it will be long beyond that, and the reason is this: When questions that were once inconceivable are raised and take hold, it is nearly impossible to put the genie back in the bottle. The same-sex marriage question, which at bottom is really a question about the necessity of male and female for the family, will take a long time to die.

These reporters remind me of many pundits who rejoiced at the news of *Roe v. Wade* 35 years ago by symbolically brushing the dust off their hands with a sigh of relief and the short-lived comfort of, "I'm glad we got THAT little issue settled!" Of course, it was anything but settled! The abortion issue became exponentially more volatile and divisive. It has stayed with us for so long and reached such a fevered pitch in the culture war because it questions the once unquestionable: What does it mean to be a person?

In the same way, the same-sex marriage issue will be with us for decades to come because it too questions the previously unquestionable: What does it matter that we are gendered persons?

Same-sex marriage is not primarily about sexual orientation, individual rights or equality. The same-sex proposal is more about the nature and public purpose of marriage or family, but this is not its deepest point. At bottom, it is a different way of understanding the fundamental essence of humanity. Let me say that again: Just as abortion demanded that we look at the unborn child in different way—with a fundamentally different value—same-sex marriage demands us to look at the most obvious essence of humanity in a different way.

At its core, same-sex marriage questions our historic and collective understanding that humanity is one nature embodied in two mysteriously diverse and distinct forms: male and female. This is the first human universal.

Consider at least what *National Geographic* magazine has taught us about the remarkable and starkly different cultures of the world. For all their diversity, for all the amazing and distinct ways they structure their personal and community lives, they share a few immutable commonalities. All cultures have rituals for collecting, preparing and eating food. Of course they do, for this is essential to human thriving. But just as essential, all cultures have a system of marriage and family, some form of socially encouraged and approved permanent pair-bonding. And there is something specific about marriage and family in every human culture. It always links the two streams of humanity: male and female. Marriage everywhere and always is about heterosexuality. There were no exceptions to this until the Netherlands embraced genderless marriage in 2001 and a few other countries have followed since. Prior to this, marriage always serves heterosexuality in every culture at every time. This is true, even though homosexual behavior appears in most cultures to varying degrees.

So why this unbending universality of this "narrow" view of marriage? Who enforced this terribly exclusive way of viewing marriage? My senior position at Focus on the Family affords me insights that few have access to, so I will tell who enforced this narrow view. Is it because the leaders of the religious conservative movement went everywhere at every time and forced this limited view of family upon all these helpless cultures?

No, of course that is not the case. I tell you, there *is* a vast-right wing conspiracy, but it is not *that* vast! There is a larger force at work here on marriage and family.

Marriage and family requires male and female because nature demands it. Marriage as an exclusively heterosexual union is the statement from nature that the family needs both parts of humanity, not just for procreation, but for all of life. And as such, marriage transcends the movements and motions of culture, politics, economics, religion and law. Marriage, as the glue that creates new families and links kin together, is the primary human institution; both anthropologists and theologians hold this as true.

Marriage is humanly fundamental because it is the way we solve the primary paradox of humanity; that men are not women and women are not men, but both are fully human. It is the way we bring these two parts of humanity together in the most intimate and cooperative way. No other social union bridges as marriage does what Bono and U2 call "the mysterious distance between a man and a woman." Because every society consists of these similar but different beings, every society finds it must have marriage. Marriage—and particularly its monogamous form—performs a number of essential tasks for every community. It socializes men. It protects women from unattached, opportunistic males. Marriage regulates sexuality. And it ensures that the people who create the babies that every culture requires are the ones who provide for and raise those babies. For cultures have long found that these two people—who we call "parents"—are typically the best ones to raise these children: best for the culture, best for the two parents and best for the children themselves. The stronger a marriage is practiced and esteemed in performing these four tasks, the fewer social problems that culture will face and the healthier its participants will be, physically, psychologically, intellectually and materially. Social science over the past 50 years consistently and persuasively shows us this is true for both men and women, boys and girls.

But the same-sex marriage experiment (for that is exactly what it is, an experiment!) says we can ignore all this, and the mighty river of human experience can be diverted in a genderless direction in the present age without a hint of harmful consequences. In fact, we are told by many same-sex proponents that preventing this new direction itself is harmful, as if we have been getting by on blind luck 'til now.

To the contrary, we should understand it as a short-sighted and arrogant proposition driven by the adult, nouveau wishes of a few, eclipsing child and societal needs and ignoring the pan-cultural wisdom of the ages. This experiment's biggest stumbling block is that male and female are not mere social constructs, regardless of how much we are told they are by the terribly hip folks over in the gender-studies department. A tragic, but dramatic refutation of this silly idea is found in the very real-life story of David Reimer, a boy whose parents were advised by professionals to raise him as a girl because of a medical complication. The utter tragedy of the theory behind this dangerous advice is eloquently told in the book, *Just as Nature Made Him: The Story of Boy Who was Raised as a Girl* [sic]. Every human life is a beautiful declaration that gender matters profoundly, an advertisement of the boundless wonders of what it means to be made masculine and feminine. This advertisement expresses itself in two ways: existence and embodiment.

First, our own existence is an endorsement of the wonder of male and female. Every human person is inconceivable without a significant contribution from both streams of humanity. Every breathing wriggling human baby that makes a debut upon the earth is a flesh-packaged message from Creation that man and woman as a functioning unit are about the coolest thing going. Together they create new beings. Apart they do not. One is essential to the other. Nature sends no such endorsement of genderless unions. Every one of us gained access to our existence by passing through the door of heterosexuality, whether that is by either the mechanical or intimate union of sperm and egg. There are no other options. Biology is a rigid and very close-minded gate-keeper.

Second, there are two complementary models of embodied persons. We find these models in all male and female persons. Sylviane Agacinski, a leader in the French feminist parité movement, points out in her important book *The Parity of the Sexes* what was obvious to our grandparents:

> "One is born a girl or boy, one becomes woman or man. . . . This division, which includes all human beings without exception, is thus a dichotomy. In other words, every individual who is not a man is a woman. There is no third possibility."

(Only 0.018 percent of the human population can be termed truly intersexed.)

The miracle of my existence as a male person is not only an important value statement about the significance of male, but also about female. For every male proclaims the virtue, wonder and necessity of female simply by contrasting her in his "otherness." Of course, female does this for male as well. We could not conceive of straight unless we relate them to curves. Cold is meaningless if warm is unknown. We would not be able to understand "old" without a value called "youth." This is why same-sex unions are fundamentally genderless. The yin holds its full essence in contrast with the yang and is unknown for what it really is in a yang-less community.

And the legalization of same-sex marriage, and the resulting same-sex family, brings all these basic human realities into question. The infamous Massachusetts Goodridge decision demonstrates this when it declared the procreation argument brought by the State in defense of natural marriage inadequate because the "argument singles out the one unbridgeable difference between same-sex and opposite-sex couples." The court then said that current marriage law "identifies persons by a single trait and then denies them protection across the board."

What is this one unbridgeable difference, this single trait?

It is the norm of male and female being able to procreate—to make new people—without the need to import genetic material from an outside source. But are we to believe, as this Court said, that male and female are specialized only (ONLY!) in their reproductive material and beyond that, everything else is bridgeable?

That is exactly what this court said, and it is why they imposed the new form of marriage on the citizen of Massachusetts, as well as all the rest of us. The same-sex marriage proposal does reduce the beautifully complex and profound nature of male and female to mere sperm and egg. It says your masculine nature, your female nature, is located only in your gonads. How does that make you feel as a man or woman? Do you feel kind of reduced? I think it is terribly reductionist and humanly scandalous, for we are much more profound as male and female. Our gender touches every part of our being, every piece of our DNA. It touches our very heart, mind and soul. This is exactly why gender is such an important and explosive topic today, it is so humanly profound.

Consider this. If two men or two women can be the functional equivalent of a male and female family (for this is what the same-sex family proposition asserts!), the only thing that the first couple needs from the former to start a family is their respective gametes. In order to make the next human generation, the male same-sex couple must go next door and borrow an egg from heterosexuality. The men say, "Thank you. This is the only part of your female-ness we want or need." Women say the same thing to men they allow to be merely sperm donors, whether homo- or heterosexual. This reduction of gender to reproductive material is dramatically evidenced in a lesbian mothers' website which sells little t-shirts and bibs for their babies that inform the world "My daddy's name is donor." I always get a little chuckle like this from the audience, but it is no laughing matter. It is the objectification of man, just like pornography is the objectification of women.

This gender reductionism amounts to a radical deconstruction of humanity. This genderless rationale is why marriage licenses in Massachusetts now read "Party A" and Party B" rather than the antiquated "bride" and "groom" or "male" or "female." It is also why birth certificates in Spain, after accepting same-sex marriage, now ask for the name of "Progenitor A" and "Progenitor B." This is what we have come to. "Party A, you may now kiss Party B." How many little girls do you know that take their greatest comfort in their identity as "Progenitor A's Little Girl"?

If this does not offend you as a man or woman, I mourn the shallowness of your understanding of how your own humanity is expressed in the wonder of your gendered body, mind and soul. It is much deeper than your genitalia, your sperm or egg. If same-sex marriage is socially valid, then male and female are no longer essential for the family and therefore, humanity. They are simply preferential, like vanilla, chocolate or rocky road ice cream. "Mother" and "father" become meaningless, merely sentimental words. It is the individual adult choice that matters, not the selection or the result. But is this true?

If you are married, think about your relationship with your spouse. There is so much more happening in the female/male dance of human difference than procreation. To understand how the value of male and female exists beyond being able to create new human beings, think about how different your workplace would be if it consisted only of males or females. I ask this of the journalists I talk to: "I can hear a great deal of activity through the phone of your newsroom. How different would your newsroom be if it were male- or female-exclusive? Would that change have no effect?" They get the point and it is not just because the women in the office get maternity leave. There are much more values both male and female bring to life, marriage, the family and the workplace. Consider as well how Goldling's novel *Lord of the Flies* would have turned out if there were a few girls cast away on the island with the boys. Only one girl would have changed the dynamic and ending of the story. It is through the profound value—and mystery—of our embodiment and essence as male and female that we understand and experience much of the power of our collective humanity. This cannot be erased.

Think of the gender of your parents. Did their gender-specific roles as parents end at fertilization? Could any loving adult have successfully taken over the parenting job from that point of donation or birth? We know that mothers and fathers are different in the ways they play, speak, discipline, protect and prepare their children for the world. To believe that parental distinctions make no difference in children's development flies in the face of a large and impressive body of literature on what mothers and fathers uniquely contribute to healthy child development.

Consider the playground. Close your eyes there and listen to the parents. Who is saying, "Swing higher, run faster, throw farther"? Who is saying, "Be careful, not so high, watch out for others?" Children gain a healthy balance of both confidence and caution from these "mixed" messages. A recent lifestyle profile of a lesbian family in a national newspaper unwittingly illustrated this dynamic. This family consisted of two lesbians as the primary couple, their male sperm-donor friend and his gay partner, a young boy and another on the way. The reporter asked this parental foursome if there were any problems in raising the child in such an unconventional setting. The biological father said he was concerned the boy gets "pampered too much," explaining, "When Alec falls down, she wants to rush over and make sure he is OK. I know he will be fine." The father said he stays quiet with such concerns, deferring to the women because they are the legal parents. As a result, this child was deprived of the essential "be patient and figure it out for yourself" manner of most fathers and his security and confidence will suffer. Mothers teach comfort and fathers teach independence, but only if the father is not intentionally neutered in the family. Healthy child development demands the push of father and the caution and comfort of mother.

We hear that love makes a family, but can an abundance of love from two men turn one of them into a mother? Can any amount of love make a father out of a woman? I often tell my twelve-year-old daughter as I drop her at school that she looks lovely today. Would these same words from her mother's lesbian lover have the same effect, as genuinely as it might be expressed? Any daughter knows the power of a father's affirmation . . . or the pain of its absence.

This is why same-sex families are not just anti-human, but actually cruel. They intentionally deny every child they touch either their biological mother or father. And they do so, not in the best interest of the child, but in order to fulfill adult desire. A loving and compassionate society always comes to the aid of motherless and fatherless children; it never intentionally creates them.

Family configuration has always been intricately bound up with the structure and health of the larger community, and we cannot change it without significantly changing society. Look at what has happened in our inner-cities as the family has changed there, particularly as the welfare check replaced the father in the home. When we no longer have mores concerning the structure of marriage and family but settle for a buffet model—just pick what suits you because one choice is as valid as another—society loses a shared norm without which it cannot function cohesively. This is why the male/female norm of marriage is humanly universal. And embracing this relativism in an effort to serve "fairness" cannot soften the consequences. And this deconstruction of who we are will not be without profound and deeply painful consequences.

And allow to me to close tonight with a thought from a belief system that is very important to me and many Americans. Christians must recognize that this attack on humanity is an attack on something greater. At the dawn of humanity, God's enemy provoked us to question the Word of God, saying: "Indeed, has God said . . . ?"

But this current attack challenges us to question something deeper, the very image of God, because male and female are both unique in their iconic representation of the Trinitarian God in the physical world.

"Let us make man in Our image, according to Our likeness.

". . . And in the image of God He created them, male and female He created them."

The effort to defend natural marriage is so much more than the next skirmish in the culture war or the next political topic to come along. It is an effort to defend the essence of humanity and the very image of God.

In Opposition to Senate Bill 689-Domestic Partnerships[*]

Peter Sprigg

Vice President for Policy, Family Research Council, 2005– ; B.A., political science and economics, Drew University; M.Div., Gordon-Conwell Theological Seminary; Government & nonprofit sectors, including economic development assistant to Congressman Robert F. Drinan of Massachusetts; actor and unit leader, Covenant Players; pastor, Clifton Park Center Baptist Church, Clifton Park, NY. Senior Director of Culture Studies, Family Research Council, 2001–05; author, Outrage: How Gay Activists and Liberal Judges Are Trashing Democracy to Redefine Marriage *(2004); co-editor,* Getting It Straight: What the Research Shows about Homosexuality *(2004).*

Editor's introduction: In this speech, delivered in opposition to a Maryland State Senate bill that aimed to provide some limited domestic-partnership rights to same-sex couples, Sprigg testifies that the measure aimed to abolish civil marriage between a man and a woman, which he argues is the only natural form of marriage. The bill was passed by the General Assembly and went into effect on July 1, 2008. The Family Research Council (FRC) was founded in 1983 to "promote marriage and family and the sanctity of human life in national policy." The decision to found the organization came from a night of discussion and prayer among Christian leaders, including Dr. James Dobson, founder of Focus on the Family, with which FRC merged in 1988.

Peter Spriggs's speech: Senators, I come before you today in opposition to Senate Bill 689.

There come moments in the debate over controversial issues when the true agenda of one side is laid bare. I believe that the introduction of this bill in this body represents such a moment in the contemporary debate over the definition of marriage.

A few years ago, one of my colleagues in the pro-family movement, the distinguished marriage scholar Maggie Gallagher, wrote a book called *The Abolition of Marriage*. At the time, the title seemed extreme—an exaggerated way of describing

---

* Delivered on February 14, 2008, at Annapolis, MD.

what many claim is merely an ongoing "evolution" of the institution. Yet now you have before you, so far as I know for the first time in any state legislature in the country, a bill that would, quite literally, abolish the institution of civil marriage. This proposal is shocking, it is extreme, it is outrageous, and it should be rejected by this body.

I understand, however, the rationale behind this legislation. Some who support so-called same-sex "marriage" believe that the resistance to this idea rests largely on the fear that it would interfere with the right and power of religions to define marriage as they see fit. If religions are given a monopoly on defining the word "marriage," while the legal and financial benefits of civil marriage are "divorced" from that word and distributed under another name, then opposition to government affirmation of same-sex sexual relationships will simply fade away. Or so the sponsors hope.

But this line of reasoning begins with a false premise. If you remember only one thing from my testimony, please remember this: Marriage is not primarily a religious institution or a civil institution. At its heart, marriage is a natural institution, rooted in the order of nature itself. Marriage existed before civil government and before religion as we know it. Neither religions nor civil government create marriage, they simply recognize and regulate it. Marriage arose because society needs to reproduce itself, and such reproduction takes place primarily through the sexual union of a man and a woman; and because children need the mother and father who produce them to cooperate in raising them. These are facts of anthropology under every religion and every form of civil government. Society gives benefits to marriage because of these benefits which marriage gives to society. Therefore, separating the legal benefits of marriage from the word "marriage" accomplishes nothing of value.

Although I do not believe marriage is something uniquely religious, I will close by mentioning one story in the Bible—not as an argument, but as a metaphor. You may recall that King Solomon gained his reputation for wisdom in part because of a famous story of two women who were fighting over the custody of a baby (1 Kings 3:16–28). The sponsors of this bill remind me of the woman who was prepared to see the baby cut in half, rather than concede custody to the baby's real mother. In this case, the baby is the institution of civil marriage, which the sponsors would rather kill than reserve for the union of one man and one woman. I hope that in this case, you will display the wisdom of Solomon by continuing to recognize only the natural institution of marriage.

5

The Obesity Epidemic

Address to the Obesity Society[*]

Bill Richardson

Governor (D), New Mexico, 2002– ; born Pasadena, CA, November 15, 1947; B.A., French and political science, Tufts University, 1970; U.S. Congressman, New Mexico, 1982–1996; chairman, Congressional Hispanic Caucus, 1983–85; chairman, House Natural Resources Subcommittee on Native American Affairs, 1993–94; U.S. Ambassador to the United Nations, 1997–98; U.S. Secretary of Energy, 1998–2000; adjunct professor at Harvard University, Kennedy School of Government, 2001; lecturer, Armand Hammer United World College of the American West, 2001–02; Senior Fellow, United States Institute of Peace 2000–01; senior managing director, Kissinger McLarty Associates, 2001–02.

Editor's introduction: In his address to the conference "The Obesity Challenge: What the Next President Should Do," hosted by the Obesity Society in Washington, D.C. on September 19, 2007, New Mexico Governor and then-contender for the Democratic Party's presidential nomination Bill Richardson calls America's current course on obesity "unconscionable." Arguing that the condition is a disease, not a behavior, he advocates for legal protections for the obese. Richardson outlines the steps he has taken in New Mexico and those he would take as president to address the problem. Since 1982 the Obesity Society has encouraged research on the causes and treatment of obesity; it publishes the journal *Obesity.*

Bill Richardson's speech: Thank you for that kind introduction, President Eric Ravussin. It's all true.

First and foremost, I wanted to take this opportunity to thank Mr. Morgan Downey and the membership of the Obesity Society for inviting me to this conference. It's a pleasure to be with all of you today.

I'd also like to thank Ms. Christine Ferguson and the other faculty members of the George Washington University School of Public Health and Health Services, and the STOP Obesity Alliance for helping to organize this conference.

And I would like to thank *you*, the conference attendees, for the hard work you are doing to solve this critical public health problem that affects so many lives.

---

[*] Delivered on September 19, 2007, at Washington, D.C.

I noticed that none of the other presidential candidates are here today. I know they may not weigh as much as I do, but I still think you should have invited them.

But, in all seriousness, it's a shame they couldn't join us. No matter their weight, every American is affected by this quiet epidemic.

As we all know, the prevalence of obesity in this country has skyrocketed in recent years. Nearly 200 million Americans—two-thirds of our population—are now considered overweight or obese.

The effects of this disease are not cosmetic. Millions of Americans are suffering from the effects of obesity-related illnesses. We spend at least $97 billion per year on health care needs to combat obesity. Our current course is unhealthy, it is unsustainable, and, frankly, it is unconscionable.

Make no mistake about it—this is a critical problem that has the potential to become a nationwide crisis. We must deal with this problem before it is too late. We as a country need to have some long-term vision. We can't afford to continue to put our communities and society at risk.

And I pledge to you that when I am president, we will fight obesity every day.

Our first step must be making sure that every American has access to affordable, quality health coverage. My health care plan provides a common-sense path to achieve that.

It focuses on the three critical issues of coverage, cost, and care. We build on proven programs that already work for millions of Americans, instead of building new bureaucracy. With my plan, working families and small businesses will be able to purchase the same coverage that members of Congress and the president have, and those aged 55 to 64 will be able to purchase coverage through Medicare.

All Americans will be required to have health care coverage, and employers will pay their fair share of employee health care costs. We'll make sure that proven preventive services are covered under every health plan, and we'll support quality initiatives—like medical homes—that treat the patient as a whole person and emphasize continuity of care—critical to improving clinical care for conditions like obesity.

I encourage all of you to visit my website and review my health care plan in more detail at www.richardsonforpresident.com.

But helping all Americans obtain health coverage is only one part of a multi-prong strategy to beat obesity.

Our next president must take a prominent and public role, joining all of you in your efforts, to increase the public's understanding of obesity and remove the stigma. We must help people understand that it is a disease, not a behavior. And that those of us who are overweight or obese are *not* lazy or undisciplined. We cannot allow Americans to be taken in by the easy comfort of stereotypes.

We must also eliminate discrimination of those who are overweight. This is an issue of basic civil rights. There are no federal laws that protect obese Americans from discrimination in the workplace, school, or anywhere else. This must change.

As president, I will work with Congress to include federal protections for the obese in the Americans with Disabilities Act and by the Equal Employment Opportunity Commission.

We need to dramatically boost our research efforts associated with obesity and we need to involve the NIH, CDC, FDA, USDA, and others. The more we know about obesity, the more we know how to prevent and treat it. It is imperative that we better understand what works to help overweight and obese people improve their health.

Perhaps the most critical part of what our next president must do, however, is to drastically shift our focus from the endgame to the pre-game. That means a serious investment in prevention. A wise man once said that "an ounce of prevention is worth a pound of the cure." Apparently, this age-old wisdom has not yet made its way to Washington.

Take diabetes for example. Obesity is one of its greatest contributing risk factors. Our federal government spends $80 billion per year to treat diabetes, but only $4 billion to prevent and manage the disease. There are already many proven strategies for preventing and managing diabetes and other obesity-related illnesses, but unfortunately these are not reaching enough Americans. We've got to change that.

Research shows that prevention is what can help young Americans the most. You know, many health care experts are telling us that our own children could be the first generation of Americans who do not outlive their parents. That is an ugly and awful break with America's historic promise of a better tomorrow, and it is unacceptable.

Much of this is due to the fact that an astonishing 17 percent of our children are overweight and therefore, more of them are developing what have been considered "adult diseases"—high blood pressure, type II diabetes, heart disease, and asthma.

As Governor of New Mexico, I've attacked this problem head-on. In my state, we've regulated vending machines in schools and we've worked to ensure that children have access to a healthy breakfast. We've taken the junk food out of our schools, and we're putting physical education back in. And it's working.

Last year, the Center for Science and the Public Interest ranked New Mexico second for food availability and fourth nationally for its strong nutrition policy.

It is essential that we address obesity throughout the lives of our citizens—especially at key moments when weight gain is most likely.

Another generation of students is starting college right about now, and it's about time we made the "Freshman 15" a thing of the past—through healthier cafeteria food, more opportunities for exercise, and better educational programs.

We also need to ask adults to consider what they can do within their own lives to reduce obesity and its effects.

Obesity is not a behavior, but we can adopt lifestyle choices—such as exercising and eating right—that can mitigate obesity and obesity-related diseases.

Of course, many Americans do care about their weight and their health—this is not just about willpower.

Americans and their doctors need the right tools, information, and incentives to make healthy choices and treatment decisions—and that means that the food and fitness industries, the insurance companies, the schools and government, the individuals and families, all have to do their part. If we work together, we can end this epidemic.

I'm proud of my record as Governor in fighting obesity in New Mexico, particularly in helping my state's children.

We need to take solid, bold steps to address this problem at the national level, and I look forward to working with all of you to make it happen.

Thank you very much.

Address at the AAAS Town Hall Meeting on Childhood Obesity[*]

Thomas M. Menino

Mayor (D) of Boston 1993– ; born Boston, MA, December 27, 1942; A.A., business management and advertising and sales, Chamberlayne Junior College, 1963; B.A., community planning, University of Massachusetts, 1988; District City Councilor, 1984–1993.

Editor's introduction: At a town hall meeting on childhood obesity organized by the American Association for the Advancement of Science (AAAS) in February 2008, Boston Mayor Thomas M. Menino discusses the challenge of obesity in the context of government subsidies that promote processed foods, along with children's habits of eating more junk food and exercising less. He goes on to describe a number of initiatives in Boston that encourage healthier eating, especially in schools. Founded in 1848, AAAS is an international nonprofit that publishes the journal *Science*, the world's most widely circulated peer-reviewed general science journal.

Thomas M. Menino's speech: Thank you, Sally [Squires], for the introduction. And thank you, Alan Leshner and Dr. David Baltimore and the organizers of the AAAS Town Hall, for inviting me here today.

Nothing is more important than the health and well being of our children. So I'm truly honored to have this opportunity to talk about the challenges we are up against when it comes to childhood obesity and how we are working to combat this epidemic.

As many of you know, childhood obesity has been increasing nationally for about 20 years. While all children are affected, we know that the impact is disproportionately high in Boston and in other communities with high concentrations of low-income families.

Nearly half of Boston schoolchildren are at unhealthy weights. This worries me. Childhood is a critical time when young people are establishing the habits they

---

* Delivered on February 17, 2008, at Boston, MA.

will carry into adulthood. And I want every child to be healthy so they can reach their full potential.

Kids today are exercising less and eating more junk food, creating a kind of "perfect storm" for childhood obesity.

On top of that, we have national policies that subsidize agricultural products like corn and soy, creating a marketplace in which many processed foods and sodas are cheap, readily available, and heavily marketed, especially to kids.

In contrast, fresh fruits and vegetables and whole grains are much more expensive. And it's actually difficult to find these products in many inner city neighborhoods, because merchants don't make the same profit margin on them as they do on junk foods, and because healthier foods are more perishable.

For low income families, the affordability of food is a major concern.

If you look at the per-calorie cost of purchasing processed foods vs. healthier foods, the difference is astonishing. The cost of a 200 calorie donut or 200 calories of pasta is about 20 cents.

The cost of 200 calories worth of grapes or baby carrots is about $2.50—almost twelve times as much! So a parent trying to stretch the family dollar will get the most calories for the least cost by purchasing food that is less nutritious.

And with most parents working, the time to prepare meals from scratch is limited. We spend almost half our food dollars away from home, where the portions tend to be bigger and higher in calories.

So those are some of the challenges we're up against. They can be daunting, but here in Boston, we're committed to fighting this epidemic.

In 2004, the Boston School Committee banned soda from school vending machines and adopted a policy that all beverages and snacks sold to students in schools meet nutritional guidelines developed by the Boston Public Schools Food and Nutrition Services staff.

Two years ago, the School Committee adopted an overall Wellness Policy to increase physical activity and nutrition education in our schools.

The outline of the policy includes a 5-2-1-0 message, which translates to at least 5 fruits and vegetables a day, no more than 2 hours of TV, 1 hour of exercise, and zero tobacco use.

We need to make sure that our students learn the specifics of these healthy behaviors. I'm pleased that later in today's program, there will be a discussion about two great pieces of curriculum we're using in 29 Boston Public Schools.

Planet Health and Eat Well Keep Moving were developed by the Harvard Prevention Research Center to teach kids about healthy eating and physical activity in the context of their regular academic subjects, like math and science. Dr. Steve Gortmaker from Harvard will be talking more about this later today. And we've got the best possible person to help us implement this curriculum, because the principal author of Planet Health, Jill Carter—who you'll also be hearing from later—is now the Wellness Coordinator for the Boston Public Schools.

Last year, we hired a gourmet chef to upgrade the quality and nutrition of meals at two of our middle schools. The chef is creating meals that are healthier but also more appealing to kids.

So far, the program's been a great success among teachers, principals and the kids. Project Bread has been our funding partner in this, for which we're very grateful. With their help, we plan to expand this initiative to additional schools next year.

The success of that program has lead to a cooking show on Boston City TV called Cooking with Kirk, in which the chef, Kirk Conrad, teaches parents how to prepare healthier meals at home.

The Boston Public Health Commission's Steps program also sponsors workshops for parents and community health educators to help families make healthy food choices at home. The curriculum for the workshops comes from the NIH We Can program, and we're proud of this successful partnership.

Institutions also have a role to play in combating childhood obesity. Tufts University is one of five local colleges who have teamed up to provide targeted Boston Public Schools with $10 million in additional resources and support services.

Through this collaboration, called Step Up, Tufts is providing a nutrition and physical activity curriculum to several after-school programs. This curriculum was developed by Professor Christina Economos as part of the Shape Up Somerville research study. It aims to improve eating habits and increase physical activity among children ages 5 through 10.

Last month, we launched another program called the Boston Corner Store initiative, a pilot program to encourage Boston middle-school students to make healthier beverage choices when they go to convenience stores before and after school.

We're also working aggressively with youth advocacy groups to curb the marketing of tobacco products, sodas and junk food at convenience stores.

It is critical that we as a city work together to limit access to foods with low nutritional value, advocate for more affordable fresh produce in the neighborhoods, and support safe and affordable physical activity and exercise opportunities.

Helping community organizations that serve children and families develop healthy policies and practices is an important part of what we are trying to do.

And we must engage all of these stakeholders in advocating for better state and federal policies that will support healthier communities, and give our children the kind of future that they deserve.

Children are our city's greatest asset. They are our future. And I want all our children to grow up healthy and happy so that they can reach their full potential. Together, we're moving towards that goal.

Once again I want to thank you for inviting me to speak with you today. Let's keep working together to build a brighter future for our young people. Thank you.

Prevention of Childhood Overweight and Obesity[*]

Steven K. Galson

Acting Surgeon General of the US, October 2007– ; baccalaureate degree, Stony Brook University, 1978; M.D., Mt. Sinai School of Medicine, 1983; MPH, Harvard School of Public Health, 1990; epidemiological investigator, Centers for Disease Control; director of the Office of Science Coordination and Policy, Office of Prevention, Pesticides and Toxic Substances, Environmental Protection Agency; Chief Medical Officer, Department of Energy and Department of Health and Human Services; deputy center director, Center for Drug Evaluation and Research, Food and Drug Administration (FDA), 2001–05; director, Center for Drug Evaluation and Research, FDA, 2005.

Editor's introduction: In remarks to the National Congress on Childhood Obesity, organized by the National Initiative for Children's Healthcare Quality (NICHQ), Galson details the alarming statistics regarding childhood overweight and obesity in America and describes his own efforts to promote locally initiated programs that are effective in combating the problem. Founded in 1999, NICHQ is a national organization, based in Cambridge, Massachusetts, and lists prevention of childhood obesity as one piece of its four-part agenda to improve children's health care.

Steven K. Galson's speech: Good morning.

Thank you, Charlie (Dr. Charlie Homer, Chief Executive Officer, National Initiative for Children's Health Quality (NICHQ)) for that gracious introduction.

I want to also thank Dr. Ana Viamonte Ross, Florida's Surgeon General, for joining us.

My boss, Department of Health and Human Services (HHS) Secretary Michael Leavitt, and I extend our greetings and best wishes to everyone.

It's a special treat to be here with you today. My activities in your state will include not only my speech here; I'll also be visiting the Miami-Dade County and State of Florida Health Departments as well to talk about prevention.

---

[*] Delivered on March 18, 2008, at Miami, FL.

At the outset of my remarks, I want you to know how much I appreciate the opportunity to share my thoughts with you at this important conference.

Protecting and maintaining kids' good health is what NICHQ is about.

So, talking to you is like preaching to the choir. And I like that.

I appreciate your singleness of purpose: for those of you who are practitioners, that purpose is to ensure the best possible health status in the children and adolescents you see for those of you who are here on behalf of constituency or community organizations, it means improving the quality of care and quality of life enjoyed by those you represent.

In those pursuits, my sense is that NICHQ successfully combines vision—to eliminate the gap between what IS and what CAN BE for all children—with the recognition that collaborations are essential to timely progress in bettering children's health.

And your compilation of resources for clinicians is a model for other public health organizations.

I salute NICHQ's pro-activity, your ongoing advocacy, your visibility and your support of this conference and others.

I want to recognize in particular the 1,500 members of NICHQ's Childhood Obesity Action Network (COAN). You demonstrate a keen awareness of the serious economic consequences of childhood overweight and obesity.

You are on the front lines of the fight against America's obesity epidemic. Thank you.

You are on the front lines of the cultural change we must make to prevent pediatric overweight and obesity.

I know how well most of you appreciate that prevention should be our number one priority in health care.

Yet, you also recognize how much work we have left in moving from a treatment-based system of care to one which emphasizes preventive medicine.

I want to talk to you today about my role and quickly run through my priorities as the Acting Surgeon General before I get into the heart of this talk.

FIRST: MY PRIORITIES

As Acting Surgeon General, I serve as our nation's chief "health educator"—responsible for giving Americans the best scientific information available on how to improve their health and reduce the risk of illness and injury.

My top priorities are:

First, disease prevention—we spend the vast proportion of our health care dollars in this country treating preventable diseases. Yet, a modest increase in investment in preventing these diseases will save lives and precious health dollars.

My next priority is public health preparedness—we must be prepared to meet and overcome challenges to our health and safety, whether caused by nature or humans.

Preparedness must involve planning by every level of society, including every family.

One important area that we continue to work on—even as the media buzz has died down—is pandemic flu preparedness.

Frankly, we must prepare as if the pandemic strikes tomorrow. This way, we do everything we can, everyday, to be ready. And, our job is never done; we can always do more.

For pandemic flu, we have preparedness checklists on our website. These include checklists for individuals, families, schools, businesses, hospitals, long-term care and child care providers, and community organizations.

I encourage you to check them out, and check them off your to-do list.

ELIMINATING HEALTH DISPARITIES

While, over the last few decades, our nation's health has improved, not all populations have benefited equally—and too many Americans in minority groups still suffer from illnesses at a disproportionate rate.

That's why eliminating health disparities is also on the top of my priority list.

You know that:

African Americans are 1.5 times as likely as non-Hispanic whites to have high blood pressure.

Cancer is the second leading cause of death for most racial and ethnic minorities in the United States. For Asians and Pacific Islanders, it is the number one killer.

Hispanic women were 2.2 times as likely as non-Hispanic white women to be diagnosed with cervical cancer.

And the statistics, unfortunately, go on and on.

It is imperative that things change, and we need to work collaboratively to improve health care access.

The last priority I want to share with you is improving health literacy.

We won't make improvements in health care and prevention without our messages being understood through language and education barriers that exist in this country.

We need to steadily improve the ability of an individual to access, understand, and use information and services to make appropriate health decisions.

All of us, everyone—indeed, any public health professional—can be an ambassador for health literacy.

THE CHALLENGE OF OVERWEIGHT

The primary reason I am here today, and the reason you are attending this particular conference session, is to discuss a pressing public health challenge that cuts
across state boundaries, geographic areas, age groups and socioeconomic status.

Childhood overweight is among the foremost health challenges of our time.

Back in 2001, the Office of the Surgeon General released a "Call To Action to
Prevent Overweight and Obesity."

The CTA strongly urged all sectors of society to take action to prevent and
decrease overweight and obesity.

The challenges which prompted the "Call to Action" are the same ones that
led NICHQ in 2006 to designate "assessing, preventing and treating childhood
obesity" a priority.

The factors which brought about the CTA, and which led NICHQ to act, still
exist; some would save they are even *more* pressing today.

In addition to the social burden on our kids, overweight children are at far
greater risk for numerous health consequences, including cardiovascular disease,
type 2 diabetes and other chronic diseases.

I am visiting communities across the country to encourage discussions and
implementation of best practices to address this alarming crisis.

During this "Healthy Youth for a Healthy Future" tour, I am working to identify and bring attention to communities with effective prevention programs to
help motivate organizations and families to combat this problem by:

- Helping kids be more active
- Encouraging healthy eating habits in young people
- And promoting availability and selection of healthy choices

I know it seems easy to say and much more difficult to do.

For, as you are well aware, our society has become more and more inactive and
is seeing a rise in obesity rates.

Chronic diseases linked to obesity have become a catastrophe—and its going
to become worse.

Chronic diseases cause seven out of 10 deaths every year—and the costs are
staggering.

Food is abundant, portion sizes have increased, and society has become increasingly sedentary.

Our efforts to reduce overweight among our nation's children are critical—and
pediatric and family physicians are among our "first responders."

Childhood overweight prevalence has nearly tripled for children ages 6 to 11
years since 1980. Today, approximately 9 million children over the age of 6 are
considered overweight in this country.

Imagine . . . the population of New York City is 8.6 million people.

And physical activity rates among our youth are also declining: just a quarter of high school students are moderately physically active for 30 minutes a day, five days a week—half the time needed for youth.

Florida, the host state for this conference, offers an illustration of what we are facing:

Approximately 11 percent of high school students were reported overweight in 2005 (Youth Risk Behavior Survey, 2005), and about 30 percent of high school students met currently recommended levels of physical activity in 2005.

Because the factors contributing to overweight and obesity are complex, reversing the epidemic will take concerted action, by parents, educators, and youth—indeed by all sectors of society.

That's why I am especially eager to move forward now in leading the Surgeon General's coordinating council to prevent childhood obesity.

Our "Healthy Youth for a Healthy Future" initiative seeks to change children's eating and activity habits.

The initiative concentrates on many of the people who influence our children including parents, caregivers, schools, public health leaders, the food industry and local community leaders.

We want to spread the word about creative ideas—and the communities and organizations that support them.

The primary focus of "Healthy Youth for a Healthy Future" will be programs and campaigns through which local communities address the problem of overweight and obesity.

I am also interested in sharing information about useful products and how to access them.

And one of the best illustrations of a product tailored to improve children's health and fitness is close to home.

I am referring to the "Implementation Guide" accessible through the NICHQ website.

As a web-based resource, it is easy to access.

And again its focus on "sharing knowledge, successful practices and innovation to address the obesity challenge, closely tracks our own interest.

I find this clinician's guide notable for its emphasis on "well care visits," prevention counseling and the recommended "staged approach" to addressing overweight and obesity in patients.

Just as your Childhood Obesity Action Network, through the Implementation Guide and other means, is successfully reaching out to the wider community of practitioners with important information. So too must we must broadly recruit parents, families, community organizations, teachers, mentors and kids themselves if we are to make progress against the national overweight epidemic.

Our approach must be multi-faceted—clinical, educational (and ultimately transformational).

The approach must always be one which appeals to those who will benefit most.

One example is a new national fitness challenge initiated by the President's Council on Physical Fitness. The Council was going strong when I was in grade school and it's going strong today.

This "National President's Challenge" is a six-week physical activity challenge to get America moving—30 minutes a day, five days a week. It's designed to help people live healthier by finding activities they really like to do.

Anyone here can sign up on the web through April 3.

We are going to be announcing this new President's Challenge tomorrow at the National Press Club in Washington with football star Eli Manning.

As exciting as this may be, I know the federal government cannot be alone in the fight against overweight and obesity—and need not be, as the NICHQ and other partners have demonstrated.

As I'm traveling around the country, I'm collecting examples of locally-initiated programs that work.

The food, sports, beverage and entertainment industries must step up to the plate and do their part.

The American Beverage Association has worked with educational administrators in public schools to establish guidelines which limit those beverages available in public school vending machines during the school day.

Local communities are doing likewise.

The Austin, Texas school district has prohibited the sale or distribution of "Foods of Minimal Nutritional Value," during the school day, at all grade levels.

These items include carbonated beverages and particularly sweet products like hard candy and candy-coated popcorn.

These foods cannot be sold or distributed to students during the school day.

Another good example is the National Football League, Ad Council and HHS collaboration to produce a public service announcement designed to motivate young people to get the recommended 60 minutes of daily exercise into practice.

Few organizations have the visibility, resources or cultural stature of the National Football League, but anyone can get on board and join our effort.

Commitments like this—and I expect to see more of them—*can* make a difference.

However, the process starts in communities across America. It starts with the promotion of healthy lifestyle activities in local settings, in communities like the one in which you live.

One way to jump start this locally is to become a WE CAN community or participant organization, like 555 others in the United States. This is an NIH/NHLBI program to motivate people on the local level to 'get up and move.'

Participation can take the form, for example, of creating a walking path. Or constructing an all-weather track for runners. Or sustained, community-wide promotion of healthy eating habits.

We in HHS are helping on the physical activity front by issuing later this year inaugural Physical Activity Guidelines for Americans.

The guidelines will provide a consistent message for the American public about physical activity, one which will be flexible enough for use by children as well as other specific population groups.

The guidelines will send the messages that wellness is a hard-won habit, physical activity is important, and the adoption of a healthy lifestyle begins with simple, but important steps.

I have met with the committee working on these guidelines, and they're really interested in making the key link between activity and overall health.

Their work will be enormously helpful.

CLOSING AND CHARGE

In closing, we will not achieve results against childhood overweight and obesity overnight.

But, we will make progress, thanks to commitments like that which NICHQ membership has made.

We will make progress as you and others of like mind remain steadfast in your commitment to make prevention the highest priority of the patients you see, the individuals to whom you provide information and guidance or the organizations you represent.

I look forward to working [with] NICHQ on our fight against overweight and obesity and my other priorities.

The end result of this work will need to be a population of physically active Americans centered on prevention, routinely conscious of diet and nutrition whose healthy choices add years and quality to their daily lives.

This outcome is one which can best be achieved through day-to-day efforts, collaborations all across this country—among practitioners, scientists, government at every level, parents, teachers and kids themselves.

As I close—a final web address for your reference. One that I hope will be easy to remember. You can find more information on the Surgeon General's website: www.surgeongeneral.gov.

Thank you.

Remarks to the Food Update Foundation 2008 Annual Meeting[*]

Heather Hippsley

Assistant Director, Division of Advertising Practices, Bureau of Consumer Protection, Federal Trade Commission (FTC); B.S., Georgetown University, School of Foreign Service, 1979; J.D., Northwestern School of Law of Lewis and Clark College, Portland, Oregon, 1984.

Editor's introduction: In this address before the "Obesity and Marketing to Kids: A Moving Target" panel at the Food Update Foundation's 2008 Annual Meeting, Heather Hippsley discusses the role food advertising, particularly on television, has played in childhood obesity and what the FTC is doing to better understand and counteract the negative consequences. She states that, "Although kids' exposure to food advertising on TV has remained fairly constant over the past 30 years, marketing to kids certainly has become more omnipresent because of the Internet and other new electronic media." The Food Update Foundation Annual Meeting is billed as "the premier gathering for food industry executives, regulatory officials and academics," according to its Web site.

Heather Hippsley's speech:

I. INTRODUCTION

I am pleased to be here today, and I would like to thank the Food Update Foundation for inviting me to be part of this panel. The title of this panel is "Obesity and Marketing to Kids: A Moving Target." As this title suggests, the policy landscape on this issue has really evolved over the last 30 years or so. According to the CDC, the prevalence of overweight kids has increased about three-fold over the last 25 or 30 years.[2] Marketing and advertising to kids has also evolved with technology—30 years ago, we didn't contemplate the existence of the Internet, let alone behavioral advertising, text message advertising, and word of mouth mar-

* Delivered on April 14, 2008, at Ponte Vedra Beach, FL.

keting on blogs and social networking sites. And on the legal front, First Amendment jurisprudence on advertising regulation has changed over the last decades.

Despite these changes, some things have remained constant. The FTC has continued to be involved in advertising and marketing to children. For those of you who are not familiar with the Federal Trade Commission and its mission, let me give you a brief introduction. The FTC is an independent agency with five Commissioners at the helm and a staff of approximately 1,100 employees, primarily lawyers and economists. The agency has two essential missions—to protect consumers and promote competition. It carries out these missions through its two primary bureaus, the Bureau of Consumer Protection and the Bureau of Competition. The agency accomplishes its missions primarily through law enforcement, but it also engages in rulemaking, research, policy development, and consumer and business education. The authority of the Commission stems from Section 5 of the FTC Act, which—elegant in its simplicity—prohibits unfair or deceptive practices in commerce. That is a broad mandate and, indeed, a very large task in this technological age.

Although the Commission has been looking at advertising and marketing to kids for many years, its focus is constantly being reshaped by the dynamics of the marketplace and by the needs of consumers. Health care and health issues are an important and growing part of this landscape. Therefore, with the alarming rise in childhood overweight and obesity rates, the Commission made it a priority to find new ways to address the problem.

The statistics from the CDC are startling: nearly 20 percent of children between the ages of 6 and 11 are overweight.[3] The long-term health consequences—with increased risk for cardiovascular disease and increased prevalence of type 2 diabetes—are obviously very serious.

The causes of the problem are complex, with numerous contributing factors in the way kids live today—inadequate physical activity; too much time spent before television, computer, and video-game screens; and over-reliance on food choices that are quick and easy, but not necessarily healthy for daily consumption. In confronting new and growing problems such as this one, there is always the temptation to search for a target to blame and an easy "fix" to the problem. But that approach rarely works, and in this case, the solutions are as complex and multi-faceted as the sources of the problem. Finding meaningful ways to address the issue demands creativity from all of us—the food and entertainment industries, government agencies, and consumer advocacy groups. For the FTC, there is a bit of *déja vu* in tackling this issue. So before I tell you what we are doing now—and what we are asking you to do—let me relate to you an episode from the archives of FTC history.

II. THE "KIDVID" EXPERIENCE

In the 1970s, the Commission embarked upon a well-intentioned, but ultimately ill-fated, effort to regulate television advertising directed toward children. That proceeding—which came to be known as "kidvid"—had long-range negative consequences for the agency, as well as its consumer protection mission. The health issue during that time was not obesity, but dental cavities. Nevertheless, the concern about marketing efforts to persuade young children to ask for and consume sugary foods that may be harmful to them was similar to the concern we hear today.

In April 1978, the Commission published in the *Federal Register* a Notice of Proposed Rulemaking that invited comment on a proposed rule to do the following:

1. Ban all television advertising for any product, which is directed to, or seen by, audiences with a significant proportion of children too young to understand the selling purpose of advertising;

2. Ban television advertising for food products posing the most serious dental health risks, which is directed to, or seen by, audiences with a significant proportion of older children; and

3. Require that television advertising for sugared food products not included in the ban, but directed to, or seen by, audiences with a significant proportion of older children, be balanced by nutritional or health disclosures funded by advertisers.[4]

In response to that very ambitious proposal, hundreds of written comments were submitted by consumers and consumer organizations; individuals with academic, scientific, and technical expertise; broadcasters; product manufacturers; and advertising agencies and associations. Hearings were held in two cities. And three years later the proceeding was terminated, with none of the recommendations adopted. The evidence—contained in thousands of pages of comments and testimony—showed cause for concern, but no clear way to craft workable rules restricting the advertising of food to kids.

Howard Beales, former Director of the Bureau of Consumer Protection, published a law review article in which he described the children's advertising proceeding as "toxic" to the Commission.[5] That statement is not an exaggeration. Congress allowed the FTC's funding to lapse, and the agency was even shut down for a brief time. Congress passed a law prohibiting the FTC from adopting any rule with regard to children's advertising based on the theory that such advertising was unfair under the FTC Act.[6] And it was more than a decade later before Congress was willing to re-authorize the agency. Even *The Washington Post* excoriated the FTC for trying to become "a great national nanny."

What we learned from that experience is the great difficulty of designing rules to restrict advertising to children. The data gathered by our staff in 1978 showed that if an advertising ban were to apply when young children (six and under) comprised 50 percent, or even 30 percent, of the TV audience, only one network program—the popular and highly acclaimed *Captain Kangaroo*—would have been affected. The situation is even more complex today, as children are exposed to advertising in many kinds of media that did not exist 30 years ago.

In addition, as I alluded to earlier, First Amendment protection of commercial speech is much broader today than it was 30 years ago. Any government-imposed limitation on advertising that is not deceptive or misleading would have to be based on a showing that the restriction would *directly* advance a substantial state interest and that the interest could not be served as well by a more limited restriction on commercial speech.[7] That would be a very high hurdle to clear. Clearly, there is a substantial interest in improving children's diets and health. Crafting restrictions on advertising that could be shown directly to advance that interest, on the other hand, would be a daunting—perhaps insurmountable—task. For that reason, the Commission has made it a priority to identify and promote actions that the food industry, the entertainment industry, and others can take to address the problem.

III. CHILDHOOD OBESITY INITIATIVES

In 2005, the FTC, together with the Department of Health and Human Services, convened a workshop on Marketing, Self-Regulation, and Childhood Obesity. This event brought together some of the largest food manufacturers and entertainment companies, as well as academics, consumer advocates, pediatricians, and government officials. Out of that workshop came a series of recommendations:

- enhanced self-regulation to change the nutritional profile of products marketed to children;
- reformulation of products, particularly those marketed to children, to make them lower in calories and more nutritious;
- use of packaging to make nutritious, lower calorie products more appealing to children and to help consumers with portion control;
- labeling initiatives, such as nutrition icons or seal programs, to help consumers easily identify more nutritious, lower calorie choices;
- revision of policies and practices for marketing in the schools;
- use of TV and movie characters popular with children to promote nutritious foods; and
- development of public education programs, targeted to both kids and adults, that address both nutrition and fitness.[8]

In July 2007, the FTC and HHS conducted a follow-up forum to review progress in implementing self-regulatory and educational initiatives, and we were happy to showcase a number of significant developments in the two-year intervening period.[9] We were especially pleased to hear that our joint workshop and report had provided a stimulus for many of those industry initiatives. The most dramatic of these efforts was announced in 2006 by the Council of Better Business Bureaus and the BBB's National Advertising Review Council. The Children's Food and Beverage Advertising Initiative is a bold effort to change the profile of food advertising directed to children under 12 and to encourage healthier eating choices. To date, 13 major food companies have joined the Initiative making concrete pledges that when fully implemented will significantly alter the landscape of food marketing to kids. Lee Peeler will provide more details about the program, but I find it very encouraging that many of these companies have committed either not to advertise directly to children under 12 or to limit such advertising—including TV, radio, print, and Internet—to foods that qualify as "better for you" by meeting specified nutritional standards, such as limitations on calories, fat, sugar, and sodium and/or providing certain nutritional benefits to children. In addition, the companies have pledged to limit use of licensed characters to promote "better-for-you" products or healthy lifestyles, not to seek product placements in child-directed media, not to advertise food or beverages in elementary schools, and to use only their "better-for-you" products in interactive games directed to kids. These CBBB pledges are a major step forward, and we expect they will bring about a significant change in children's food marketing.

At the same time, media and entertainment companies are using their considerable talent to reach young audiences with positive health messages. Disney, Nickelodeon, and Cartoon Network have adopted policies to limit the licensing of their characters to foods meeting certain nutritional guidelines. As a result, Nickelodeon's SpongeBob and Dora the Explorer now appear on packages of carrots and spinach. Disney has formed a partnership with Imagination Farms to license favorite Disney characters to promote fresh fruits and vegetables. Ion Media Networks—which through a partner produces children's weekend programming on NBC and Telemundo—made a commitment not to air advertising for less healthy foods and beverages on children's programs and to create story lines that promote good eating habits and physical activity.

In another important initiative, the Alliance for a Healthier Generation—a partnership of the American Heart Association and the William J. Clinton Foundation—has set standards for changing the nutritional profile and limiting the container size of beverages and snacks sold to kids in school, from elementary through high school. A number of food and beverage companies have joined this effort. As of September 2007, the Alliance reported a 41 percent reduction in the total number of calories contained in beverages shipped to the schools between 2004 and the 2006–07 school year. It also reported a 45 percent reduction in the number of full-calorie drinks shipped to schools and a 23 percent increase in shipments of water. The industry is committed to 100 percent compliance by the 2009-10 school year. In addition, the beverage industry is supporting proposed legislation that would set limits even exceeding those of the voluntary guidelines for beverages sold in schools.

We welcome all of these industry initiatives, but at the same time we want to urge more:

1. We want to see more companies join the CBBB initiative so that it grows to cover the universe of food companies that engage in marketing to kids.

2. We want to encourage companies to expand their definitions of "advertising directed to children." We don't want to see marketing efforts simply shifted to other venues, such as new digital technologies.

3. We want to see stepped-up efforts directed to product reformulation. The nutritional criteria adopted for "better for you" products should not be set in stone, but can be improved upon as companies find ways to lower the sugar, fat, and sodium without sacrificing taste and appeal.

4. We want to see the media and entertainment companies expand their participation in this effort, so that cross-promotions with popular kids' movies and TV characters will favor the more rather than the less nutritious foods and drinks.

Other countries are also adopting the self regulatory model. The Canadian Children's Food and Beverage Advertising Initiative, announced in April 2007, is a voluntary effort undertaken by 16 of Canada's leading food and beverage companies. Advertising Standards Canada, an independent self-regulatory body, administers the program, which is similar in structure and scope to the CBBB program in the U.S. In December 2007, 11 food and beverage companies announced their participation in a European Union Pledge Programme to be implemented by the end of 2008. Thus, the idea of a pledge program initiative seems to be catching on. Because many food marketers are multi-national companies, there is a great deal of overlap in program participation. Eight of the EU participants and 11 of the Canadian participants are members of the CBBB initiative.

IV. THE FOOD MARKETING REPORT

As many of you are aware—and some all too well aware, I'm sure—our Division of Advertising Practices is working very diligently on a study of food marketing directed to kids. Initiated at the request of Congress, this is a comprehensive study of promotional expenditures and activities targeted toward both children and adolescents. The Commission report will explore what is happening not only in the traditional measured media—TV, radio, and print—but also in the many non-traditional, and generally unmeasured, promotional activities targeted to kids. The Internet, for example, has opened up a whole new venue for reaching kids, with websites offering online games that incorporate branded food products right into the game. Digital devices, such as cell phones—now in the hands of most teenagers and even many younger children—afford other kinds of marketing opportunities, such as text messaging. These new electronic media are far less costly for advertisers than the traditional broadcast media, and our children, of course, are far more adept at using them than many of us will ever be. We are also collecting information about forms of marketing that may not be new, but have not heretofore been measured, such as product packaging, in-store promotions, premium distribution, character licensing, athletic sponsorship, event sponsorship, movie theater advertising, and celebrity endorsements. In addition, we are looking at product placement in movies, on TV programs, and in video games; marketing in the schools; marketing in connection with philanthropic activities, and—in a kind of "back to the future" phenomenon—even word-of-mouth marketing. One might have thought that went out with the 19th century, but apparently it's back with the 21st.

We are finding that everything is connected—one advertising campaign will incorporate many of these venues at the same time. Premiums or prizes often are tied to a licensed character or sponsored team or athlete and promoted on the Internet, in stores, and on packaging, as well as in broadcast or print media. To collect the prize, you find a code on the product, in the package, or under a bottle cap, and you enter the code on the company's website to see if or what you have "won." The prize itself frequently will display a food or beverage brand name or logo. Moreover, products are no longer just advertised adjacent to a TV program or a film—the products may also be embedded within the story itself.

We are also finding that the media and entertainment companies are spreading their promotions of children's movies or popular TV characters across many food products and companies. A hit children's movie of 2006, for example, was promoted in connection with most of the food categories covered in our data request—beverages, a fast-food restaurant, candy, cereals, snacks, baked goods, prepared foods, dairy products, and—we are happy to report—fresh fruit. The promotions made use of TV, packaging, point of sale materials, movie theater ads, websites, prizes and premiums, as well as stickers on fruit.

This is a significant study, because we are measuring something that has not been measured before. Other researchers have not had access to this data, and in many cases the companies themselves had not previously compiled such data. This report will provide the first comprehensive look at the entire landscape of how foods are marketed to children and adolescents.

We appreciate the fact that those of you who were called upon to participate in this endeavor, *albeit* involuntarily, have had to dig deep into your records and even re-structure your accounting to come up with the data we requested. Our compulsory process orders were sent to 44 food, beverage, and quick-serve restaurant companies in August of last year, seeking data for 2006. Our selection of target companies was based on extensive staff research into the foods and drinks most heavily marketed to kids. In addition, we included some fresh produce companies that are now beginning to promote fruits and vegetables to children—an activity we certainly want to encourage.

The responses to the orders arrived in November and December, and our staff has spent the winter working with the companies to resolve any problems and inconsistencies in the submissions. In general, I can say that the companies were thorough and conscientious in preparing their responses, and we are grateful for that. Now we are engaged in data analysis and writing—or number and word crunching. We expect the report to be submitted to Congress—and released to the public—sometime this summer. Expenditures will be reported by food and marketing categories, but always in aggregated form so that the confidentiality of individual company data will be protected.

This study has been a massive undertaking—both for us and for the companies that were "asked" to participate in the research. However, it will provide an important benchmark—activities and expenditures for food marketing to children and teens in 2006. Thus, the data will provide a "before" photo, as it pre-dates implementation of the CBBB initiative and reflects a time early in the implementation of the Alliance guidelines for in-school marketing. If the FTC study is repeated at some point down the road—and I should warn you that studies of this nature often are repeated in order to document change in the marketplace—the 2008 report will be the baseline for measuring the impact of self-regulatory initiatives.

Another important piece of research was published by the Commission last year. Economists in the FTC's Bureau of Economics compared children's exposure to TV advertising in 1977, based on data gathered for the "Kidvid" rulemaking proceeding, with their exposure in 2004.[10] What they found is that children's exposure to food ads on TV has not risen and may have fallen modestly. Children ages 2–11 saw approximately 5,500 food ads in 2004, which constituted 22 percent of their total TV ad exposure. This is about 9 percent less than the number of food ads they were estimated to have seen in 1977. The leading categories of food ads seen by kids in 2004 included fast-food restaurants, sugared cereals, sweets, snacks, and sweetened drinks. The same categories were present in 1977, but were dominated by cereals and sweets.

V. CONCLUSION

The food marketing report will complement the Bureau of Economics study—with its focus on expenditures and activities in the many newer media that did not exist in 1977. Although kids' exposure to food advertising on TV has remained fairly constant over the past 30 years, marketing to kids certainly has become more omnipresent because of the Internet and other new electronic media.

Few people would disagree with the notion that childhood obesity is an extremely complex problem, or that there are many social and economic factors that have contributed to rising obesity rates. At the FTC, we're not interested in assigning blame. The simple fact is that all segments of society—parents, schools, government, health care professionals, food companies, and the media—have an obligation to fight this public health crisis, regardless of how we got here. Industry self-restraint from promoting high-fat, high-calorie, low-nutrition products to children is one arrow in the quiver against childhood obesity. We have seen a good start down the road of self-regulation. However, it is only a start. More needs to happen, and the pace needs to accelerate. Thank you, and I would be happy to take any questions.

FOOTNOTES

1. The views expressed herin are my own and do not necessarily represent the views of the Federal Trade Commission or any Commissioner.

2. Centers for Disease Control and Prevention, "Obesity and Overweight: Childhood Overweight," available at http://ww.cdc.gov/nccdphp/dnpa/obesity/trend/index.htm.

3. Centers for Disease Control and Prevention, "Obesity and Overweight: Childhood Overweight," available at http://ww.cdc.gov/nccdphp/dnpa/obesity/trend/index.htm.

4. 43 Fed. Reg. 17967, 17969 (Apr. 27, 1978).

5. J. Howard Beales, III, "Advertising to Kids and the FTC: A Regulatory Retrospective that Advises the Present," 12 Geo. Mason L. Rev. 873, 879 (2004).

6. FTC Improvements Act of 1980, Pub. L. No. 96-252, Sections 11(a)(1), 11(a)(3), 94 Stat. 374 (1980) (current version in 15 U.S.C. § 57a(h) (1980)).
7. *Cent. Hudson Gas & Elec. Corp. v. Pub. Serv. Comm'n*, 447 U.S. 557 (1980).

8. FTC, *Perspectives on Marketing, Self-Regulation, & Childhood Obesity: A Report on a Joint Workshop of the Federal Trade Commission and the Department of Health and Human Services* (Apr. 2006) at 50-54, *available at* http://www.ftc.gov/os/2006/05/PerspectivesOnMarketingSelf

9. Regulation&ChildhoodObesityFTCandHHSReportonJointWorkshop.pdf.
See http://www.ftc.gov/bcp/workshops/childobesity/index.shtml.

10. *Children's Exposure to TV Advertising in 1977 and 2004: Information for the Obesity Debate*, FTC Bureau of Economics Staff Report (June 2007), *available at* http://www.ftc.gov/os/2007/06/cabecolor.pdf.

Testimony to the House Committee on Education and Labor*

Richard Simmons

Fitness guru; born New Orleans, LA, July 12, 1948; owner, exercise studio, Los Angeles, 1973; actor on General Hospital, *1979; talk show host,* The Richard Simmons Show, *1980–83; author,* Richard Simmons' Never-Say-Diet Book *(1982),* Richard Simmons' Never Give Up: Inspirations, Reflections, Stories of Hope *(1994),* Sweetie Pie: The Richard Simmons Private Collection of Dazzling Desserts *(1997),* The Richard Simmons Farewell to Fat Cookbook: Homemade in the U.S.A. *(1999),* Still Hungry After All These Years: My Story *(1999).*

Editor's introduction: In an impassioned appearance before the House Committee on Education and Labor, fitness guru Richard Simmons recalls how obesity resulted in his own unhappy childhood. In his remarks, he describes the ill effects of budget cuts that led to the elimination of fitness training in U.S. schools, including increased health problems among America's youth. Simmons goes on to volunteer to work with fitness instructors in American schools. As reported by Dana Milbank in the *Washington Post*, the occasion at times resembled a support group. "I'm still waiting to get picked for the congressional basketball team," announced George Miller (D-Calif.), the chairman. When a witness mentioned having lost 30 pounds, Representative Phil Hare (D-Ill.) added "I've lost 42. Hopefully, in another six months I can get off these pills."

Richard Simmons's speech: Good morning, ladies and gentlemen. My name is Richard Simmons and I never took a P.E. class in my life. I was overweight, a little lethargic, a little short. At St. Louis Cathedral School in New Orleans it was all sports and I was not a jock. I spent my elementary school, my high school and my college sitting on the benches watching everyone play sports. And to get back at them, while they were playing sports, I ate their lunch.

I was 268 pounds. I tried a lot of ways to lose weight, including taking laxatives, throwing up, starving, because I never took P.E. I was 23 years old when I took my first exercise class. I was bitten by the sweat bug. Thirty-six years ago I opened

---

* Delivered on July 24, 2008, at Washington, D.C.

my exercise studio up in Los Angeles, and there I began my pilgrimage to help people. Overweight, out of shape, 200 pounds, 400 pounds, 800 pounds, and I've dedicated all these years to giving them some support and some self-esteem.

Five years ago my mail shifted dramatically. I get thousands of emails a day, but when the No Child Left Behind Act came about I got lots of letters from parents and children saying "My kid is overweight. My kid is going to the doctor's. My kid has high cholesterol." So what I did was, I went on shows like the *Today Show*, *Ellen*, David Letterman, Howard Stern, and I put a four-page questionnaire on richardsimmons.com and 60,000 people filled out that questionnaire. And I learned what was happening in the schools in the United States of America.

I took a trip to Washington to meet Congressman Wamp and Congressman Kind. I told them my ideas. I began another campaign on my website asking people to write their Congressmen and presidential candidates in order to let everyone know how important this is.

And here I stand with a vision today. Everyone is not a jock! Everyone cannot play sports! Everyone cannot run! But everyone can be fit. It's not important if you're a jock! It's important that you have your health! And our children right now do not have it.

I have a vision. I know a very economical way to bring fitness to every child in every school in the United States of America. There are hundreds of thousands of certified fitness instructors who travel around and teach classes. I want to head and be part of this Committee to train teachers to go into the school systems and teach the three things that we all need: we all need cardio, we all need strength training, and we all need stretching. Every school that I've been in, I put the kids' music on, I get them going, they feel great, and as Congressmen Wamp and Kind said, when you're feeling great about yourself, when you have self-esteem and self-respect for yourself, there isn't nothing you can do.

I'm not 268 pounds anymore. And I'm still not a jock. But I am fit and I've dedicated my life to this. And I'm hoping that the Committee today will know there is no other way to do this. Or our children will get more sick. And there's a statistic that says our children today will not live as long as their parents.

What have we done? What have we done to the kids of the United States of America? This is wrong. And I will dedicate the rest of my life—and, Chairperson George Miller—I just may run for office to help this really get through and not have one kid feel lousy about himself because he can't throw a ball. One kid who cannot run a mile, he cannot be made fun of. We have to support him and what he can do. Every child can dance! Every child can dance! I've seen it. I travel 200 days a year, and I see what happens when the music goes on—their music, not mine! When the music goes on, they feel so good about themself, they go back in that schoolroom, and they learn.

I do not want any child in America to have my childhood! Because it was taken away from me because I just wasn't good enough. Well, I'm good enough now. And I've devoted—I'm 60 years old now—and I've devoted my life to this. And I will devote my life to this to the day I die! And I hope that one day, every kid gets to feel the self-esteem and the self-respect that I have. God bless you all and God bless the children of America. Thank you very much.

Cumulative Speaker Index: 2000–2008

A cumulative speaker index to the volumes of Representative American Speeches for the years 1937–1938 through 1959–1960 appears in the 1959–1960 volume; for the years 1960–1961 through 1969–1970, see the 1969–1970 volume; for the years 1970–1971 through 1979–1980, see the 1979–1980 volume; for the years 1980–1981 through 1989–1990, see the 1989–1990 volume; and for the years 1990–1991 through 1999–2000, see the 1999–2000 volume.

Index